After Marx

AFTER MARX

Edited by

TERENCE BALL

University of Minnesota

and

JAMES FARR

University of Wisconsin – Madison

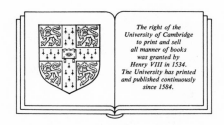

The right of the
University of Cambridge
to print and sell
all manner of books
was granted by
Henry VIII in 1534.
The University has printed
and published continuously
since 1584.

CAMBRIDGE UNIVERSITY PRESS

CAMBRIDGE

LONDON   NEW YORK   NEW ROCHELLE

MELBOURNE   SYDNEY

Published by the Press Syndicate of the University of Cambridge
The Pitt Building, Trumpington Street, Cambridge CB2 1RP
32 East 57th Street, New York, NY 10022, USA
296 Beaconsfield Parade, Middle Park, Melbourne 3206, Australia

First published 1984

Printed in the United States of America

Library of Congress Cataloging in Publication Data
Main entry under title:
After Marx.
Includes index.
1. Marx, Karl, 1818–1883 – Addresses, essays, lectures.
I. Ball, Terence.   II. Farr, James.
HX39.5.A546   1984   335.4   83-25237
ISBN 0 521 25702 6 hard covers
ISBN 0 521 27661 6 paperback

Contents

v

CONTENTS

Preface

The twelve essays presented here were written to mark the centenary of Marx's death in 1883. But instead of appearing in 1983 they appear, alas, in 1984 – a year forever freighted with its own symbolic significance. Ironists and numerologists may make of this what they will. That our volume ever appeared at all is due to the dedication, patience, and good humor of our contributors. We are in their debt. We are also indebted to Mr. Frank Smith for his able editorial advice and assistance, and to the Syndics and staff of Cambridge University Press. To two anonymous referees we owe a special debt for the courtesy, care, and thoroughness with which they reviewed the original manuscript. Finally, each of the editors wishes to thank the other for the pleasure of the collaboration.

TERENCE BALL
JAMES FARR

Contributors

Terence Ball, coeditor of this volume, received his Ph.D. in political science from the University of California, Berkeley, in 1973 and is now Professor of Political Science at the University of Minnesota. In 1978–9 he was Visiting Fellow of Nuffield College, Oxford. He is the author of *Civil Disobedience and Civil Deviance* (1973), editor of *Political Theory and Praxis* (1977), and a frequent contributor to professional journals. He is currently completing two studies, *Reappraisals in Political Theory* and *Positivism, Politics, and Social Science.*

Terrell Carver has degrees from Columbia University and Balliol College, Oxford. After five years as Lecturer in Politics at the University of Liverpool, he moved recently to a similar post at Bristol. His books include *Marx's Social Theory* (1982), *Engels* (1981), and *Karl Marx: Texts on Method* (1975). He has also translated *The Logic of Marx* (1980) by Jindřich Zelený and is at present working on a study of the Marx-Engels intellectual relationship.

Jon Elster holds advanced degrees from the University of Oslo and the University of Paris. He has published widely on a number of topics, from Marx and Leibniz to rationality, logic, and society. His main publications include *Logic and Society* (1978), *Ulysses and the Sirens* (1979), *Explaining Technical Change: A Case Study in the Philosophy of Science* (1983), and *Leibniz et la Formation de l'Esprit Capitaliste* (1975). He is currently Associate Professor of History, University of Oslo, and Director of the Working Group on Rationality, Maison des Sciences de l'Homme, Paris.

James Farr, coeditor of this volume, is Assistant Professor of Political Science at the University of Wisconsin. He received his Ph.D. in 1979 from the University of Minnesota. He is interested in the history and philosophy of social science in general, and in Marx's method in particular. His articles on Marx, Hume, and Popper have appeared in *Inquiry, Philosophy of the Social Sciences,* and *History and Theory.* He is currently writing a book about the history of the science of politics.

Alan Gilbert is an Associate Professor at the Graduate School of International Studies of the University of Denver. His book, *Marx's Politics: Communists and Citizens,* was published in 1981. His articles on ethics and on Marx's historical theory and revolutionary activity have appeared in *Philosophy and Public Affairs, Political Theory, The American Political Science Review,* and *The Occasional Review.* He is currently writing a book defending the objectivity of morality.

C. B. Macpherson is Professor of Political Science at the University of Toronto. He is the author of *The Political Theory of Possessive Individualism* (1962), *The Real World of Democracy* (1966), *Democratic Theory: Essays in Retrieval* (1973), *The Life and Times of Liberal Democracy* (1977), *Burke* (1980), and numerous articles on the history of political thought and democratic theory and practice.

Richard W. Miller is Associate Professor of Philosophy at Cornell. In addition to work in epistemology, aesthetics, and the philosophy of mind, he has published articles on ethics and the philosophy of science, discussing Marx's writings or developing Marxist themes. They have appeared in *Philosophy and Public Affairs, Philosophy of Science, The Canadian Journal of Philosophy,* and in a volume edited by Norman Daniels, *Reading Rawls.* His *Analyzing Marx* will soon be published by Princeton University Press. He is currently working on a book on the philosophy of science.

James Noble received his Ph.D. in political science from the University of Rochester. He has written on a number of topics in Marxism and the philosophy of science and has published on Chinese Marxism and the Cultural Revolution in *World Politics.* After having taught for several years at Ohio State University, he has turned his attention to the law.

John E. Roemer is Professor of Economics at the University of California at Davis. He received his Ph.D. in economics from the University of California at Berkeley in 1974. He taught secondary school in San Francisco for five years. He is the author of *Analytical Foundations of Marxian Economic Theory* (1981) and *A General Theory of Exploitation and Class* (1982) and articles on Marxian economic theory.

CONTRIBUTORS

William H. Shaw holds a Ph.D. from the London School of Economics and Political Science. Currently he is Associate Professor of Philosophy at Tennessee State University. He is the author of *Marx's Theory of History* (1978) and coeditor of *Justice and Economic Distribution* (1978), and has published articles in *The American Philosophical Quarterly, History and Theory, the Canadian Journal of Philosophy,* and other journals, as well as in various anthologies. He is currently coediting a volume entitled *Rationality in Belief and Action.*

Paul Thomas is Associate Professor of Political Science at the University of California at Berkeley. He specializes in political theory and Marxism, and also writes about film. He is the author of *Karl Marx and the Anarchists* (1980) and has written articles on Marx, Mao, and Habermas for *Political Studies, Politics and Society,* and *Discourse.* He received his Ph.D. from Harvard University. He has also been a Junior Research Fellow at Wolfson College, Oxford, and a Lecturer at the University of California at Davis and at the University of Liverpool.

Philippe Van Parijs received his Ph.D. in sociology from the University of Louvain and his D.Phil. in philosophy from Oxford University. He is now a Permanent Research Fellow at the Belgian National Fund for Scientific Research. He is the author of *Evolutionary Explanation in the Social Sciences: An Emerging Paradigm* (1981) and has published a number of essays in *New Left Review, Philosophy of the Social Sciences, European Journal of Sociology,* and the *Review of Radical Political Economics.* He is currently engaged in research toward a book, *Justice, Injustice, and Crisis.*

Editors' introduction

TERENCE BALL AND JAMES FARR

Several years ago *Time* magazine carried on its cover a picture of Marx's massive tombstone in London's Highgate Cemetery. "Marx is Dead," it proclaimed with an almost audible sigh of relief. In its most literal sense, this assertion has been true for just over one hundred years. Marx slumped quietly in his armchair and ceased to think on the afternoon of 14 March 1883. But if the man is long dead, the ideas of the thinker continue to live on, a source of inspiration to some and of moral and mortal peril to others.

Why have Marx's ideas proved so durable? How might we account for their longevity? Various explanations have been offered. Lenin's, characteristically, was the simplest: They endure because they are true (1968: 20). Others have been rather less sanguine in their assessments. Marx's modern critics see his ideas' appeal as lying less in their truth than in their false claim to "scientific" status, their too-simple explanations of complex social pheonomena and historical processes, and their ideologically heady mixture of moralism and Manichaeanism. These critics can find no other way of accounting for "the continuing success of a failed theory" (Wesson 1976). Other observers, more sympathetic but by no means uncritical, suggest that the longevity of Marx's ideas is due neither to their being true *simpliciter* nor to their catechistic character, but to their continuing relevance. Sartre, for example, remarked that Marxism "remains the philosophy of our time. We cannot go beyond it because we have not yet gone beyond the circumstances which engendered it" (1967: 30).

But whatever the explanation, the fact remains that Marx's ideas are still a potent political and intellectual force a century after his death. Yet to speak of "a" force here is already misleading in one crucial way. For Marx's ideas were not passed on from generation to generation, in anything like a fixed and frozen form. They were refined, extended, amended, supplemented, and sometimes supplanted by later Marxists. The process began with Engels and continued through several long lines of Marxist theoreticians, including Kautsky, Plekhanov, Lenin, Trotsky, Bukharin, Lukács, Luxemburg, Korsch, Gramsci, Horkheimer, Adorno, Habermas, Milliband, Mandel, Anderson, Althusser, and Poulantzas, among many others. Indeed, so thoroughgoing and wide-ranging have been many of the changes wrought by these and other Marxists that we invite confusion if we speak of Marx*ism* as a single tradition. If anything, the century after Marx has been the century of Marx*isms*. An unsuspecting undergraduate might well be forgiven for supposing that there were a dozen different thinkers named Marx.

In retrospect we can see why this proliferation of Marxist traditions was perhaps inevitable. The tale begins with Marx himself. At the time of his death Marx's ideas were far from complete, and several of his subsequently influential texts remained unpublished. Of the theoretical and political works, only *The Communist Manifesto, Wage Labor and Capital, A Contribution to the Critique of Political Economy*, and the first volume of *Capital* were published. Aside from some earlier works of philosophical criticism, like *The Holy Family* and *The Poverty of Philosophy*, the only other works to take ink were commentaries on current political events, like *The Eighteenth Brumaire of Louis Bonaparte* and *The Civil War in France*.

The rest lay in shambles or had long since been abandoned, like *The German Ideology*, to "the gnawing criticism of the mice." Marx's quarter-century-old intention to "examine the system of bourgeois economics" in its totality as "capital, landed property, wage labor, state, foreign trade, and world market" went with him to the grave, for he had barely begun to scratch the surface in his first installment. Engels rightly complained of the mess that he had inherited from Marx, but at least his herculean editorial labors succeeded in completing the trinity of volumes of *Capital*. Later efforts were required by numerous other sorters and sifters to locate, order, and edit Marx's seemingly inexhaustible supply of sketches, notebooks, and drafts. Their subsequent publication bore scant resemblance to their original order of composition. The *Critique of Hegel's "Philosophy of Right," The Economic and Philosophical Manuscripts, The German Ideology*, the three volumes of *Theories of Surplus Value, The Ethnological*

Notebooks, and perhaps most important, the *Grundrisse,* emerged haltingly and haphazardly. The new light shed by successive volumes meant that later generations worked with, and on, a decidedly different corpus. Quite simply, the published Marx of the 1870s and 1880s and the published Marx of the 1970s and the 1980s have made and continue to make for different Marxes – and hence for diverse and divergent Marxists and Marxisms.

Even if all of Marx's works had been published during his lifetime, Marxisms would have multiplied nonetheless. For besides the proliferation of interpretations that inevitably attend so monumental and ambitious an undertaking, Marx himself often seemed to speak with several different voices. There are ambiguities and tensions, not to say contradictions, in many of his most important ideas. For example, on the practical political plane he repeatedly changed his mind about which strategies the working-class movement should pursue, just as he left very different assessments of the possibilities of a socialist revolution in Russia. On a more theoretical level, the materialist interpretation of history frequently pits the growth of human productive power against class struggle as the prime mover in history. And then there is, of course, the tension between abstract theoretical generalizations and their application to concrete historical circumstance, as found for example in *The Eighteenth Brumaire* or the historical chapters of *Capital.* These tensions can neither be brushed aside nor explained away – for example, by drawing a neat biographical distinction between early and mature periods – for they appear in works of the same period and often, indeed, in the same work.

We would be well advised to apply reflexively Marx's own ideas to their subsequent development. For one of his central insights was that as knowledge grows it changes because of changes in social and economic conditions. New conditions bring about changes in knowledge, if not causally, then at least by bringing to the fore new objects or processes, which themselves then require explanation. This is a feature of all scientific, political, and philosophical theories, and Marxian theory is no exception. Needless to say, the century after Marx's death has been a tumultuous one indeed. As Trotsky remarked with uncharacteristic understatement, "Anyone desiring a quiet life has done badly to be born in the twentieth century" (quoted in Berlin 1969: 1). Two world wars, revolutions in Russia and China, new movements and nations in the Third World, and the remarkable resilience of capitalism have wrought conceptual and theoretical changes of considerable magnitude. Marxism-Leninism, Maoism, peasant communism, and continental Marxisms – Eurocommunism, existential Marxism, Althusserian structuralism, the Critical Theory of the Frankfurt School – represent the application and adaptation of Marxian concepts and categories to radically different contexts.

The English-speaking countries have until very recently been distant if not entirely disinterested witnesses to these intellectual and political developments. With our revolutions completed two and three hundred years ago, and our own intellectual traditions more or less intact, Marx's ideas have found fairly infertile soil in the United Kingdom and in North America. As late as 1966 Charles Taylor complained that the character of British and American writing on Marx and Marxism "represents a study of Marxism from the outside. At its worst, it so to speak takes the measure of an ideological enemy, and can even degenerate into Cold War polemics, but at its best, it can only approach the sympathetic and detached study normally accorded Oriental religions. Marxism may be of burning interest for all sorts of reasons, but never because it might be true" (1966: 229). Although such bemused detachment continues to characterize much contemporary writing on Marx, at least some things have shown signs of changing since these words were written.

The serious interest with which Marx's work is now widely regarded can be seen, for example, in the number of first-rate works on Marx or developing Marxist theory that have been published in the last fifteen years.[1] Moreover, the *Collected Works of Marx and Engels* are emerging volume by volume, and individual works of Marx's have been made more generally available in ever more popular editions. New translations – and even previously unpublished works, especially the *Grundrisse* – have appeared. In short, there is a veritable (and dare we say profitable?) Marx industry in the making. Whether this turn of events is attributable to the political climate of the late 1960s and 1970s, or to the economic and cultural crises characteristic of late capitalism, or to the belated appreciation of the sheer scope and force of Marx's ideas is hard to say with any cer-

[1] We have in mind the work of – inter alia – David McLellan, particularly his magisterial biography (1973), Leszek Kolakowski's monumental history of Marxian theory (1978), Ollman (1971), Avineri (1970), Cohen (1978), and – not least – the several studies written by contributors to the present volume.

4

tainty. But for whatever reason, and happily for the intellectual pluralism so often boasted of in the English-speaking countries, the iron curtain around Marx's ideas has largely been lifted.

In this more congenial climate, a collection of original essays commemorating the centenary of Marx's death requires neither excuse nor explanation. *After Marx* is "after" Marx in several senses. The first and most obvious of these is the purely chronological sense: We are after Marx in time. We are therefore able to see what he did not or could not see and to see more clearly that which he foresaw only dimly. The second sense in which we are after Marx is political: We write in the aftermath of Marx and in his shadow. In this century virtually all revolutionaries call themselves Marxists and purport to apply Marx's precepts to political practice. Armed with their different interpretations of a nineteenth-century theory, they have altered – and continue to radically reshape – the political landscape of the twentieth century. Finally, *After Marx* is after Marx interpretatively, critically, and theoretically. In different ways and with different emphases, these twelve essays are in quest of the meaning of Marx's texts; they pursue Marx's fallacies, overstatements, or omissions in order to overcome them; and in the critical spirit, if not always the letter of Marx's theory, they develop themes that his theorizing made possible, but that he himself did not pursue.

As befits a volume marking the centenary of the passing of so prodigious a polymath, our essays are diverse in their aims, approaches, and concerns. We do scant justice to Marx's many interests and manifold influences. We say nothing, for example, of his interest in, or influence on, historiography, literature and literary criticism, aesthetics, feminist theory, anthropology, geography, and a dozen other disciplines. We are also virtually silent on the multiplicity of Marxisms in our century.[2] Yet there is some measure of unity within this diversity, disagreement, and silence. We are agreed that the central problems with which Marx wrestled are still with us. And in spite of his having been so often misrepresented as a dogmatist, Marx raised more questions than he, or anyone else, could ever reasonably hope to answer. To raise anew some of these questions, and to approach them in the critical spirit of Marx's own thinking, is the common theme – or the red thread, if you prefer – running through these twelve essays.

[2] See Howard and Klare (1972), Kolakowski (1978), vol. 3, McLellan (1979), and Parkinson (1982).

REFERENCES

Avineri, Shlomo (1970). *The Social and Political Thought of Karl Marx*. Cambridge: Cambridge University Press.

Berlin, Isaiah (1969). *Four Essays on Liberty*. Oxford: Oxford University Press.

Cohen, G. A. (1978). *Karl Marx's Theory of History: A Defence*. Princeton, N.J.: Princeton University Press.

Howard, Dick, and Karl E., Klare, eds. (1972). *The Unknown Dimension: European Marxism Since Lenin*. New York: Basic Books.

Kolakowski, Leszek (1978). *Main Currents of Marxism*. 3 vols. Oxford: Oxford University Press (Clarendon Press).

Lenin, V. I. (1968). "The Three Sources and Three Component Parts of Marxism." In Lenin, *Selected Works*. Moscow: Progress Publishers.

McLellan, David (1973). *Karl Marx: His Life and Work*. London: Macmillan Press.

  (1979). *Marxism After Marx*. Boston: Houghton Mifflin.

Ollman, Bertell (1971). *Alienation: Marx's Conception of Man in Capitalist Society*. Cambridge: Cambridge University Press.

Parkinson, G. H. R., ed. (1982). *Marx and Marxisms*. Cambridge: Cambridge University Press.

Sartre, Jean-Paul (1967). *Search for a Method*. Translated by Hazel Barnes. New York: Knopf.

Taylor, Charles (1966). "Marxism and Empiricism." In B. Williams and A. Montefiore (eds.), *British Analytical Philosophy*. London: Routledge & Kegan Paul.

Wesson, Robert G. (1976). *Why Marxism? The Continuing Success of a Failed Theory*. New York: Basic Books.

History and revolution

The belief not merely in the possibility of change but in the inevitability of progress is central to the thought of the Enlightenment; so too is a marked aversion to religion, conjoined with the conviction that reason and science can save us from this and other ostensibly benighted beliefs. The stage-by-stage progression from ignorance to enlightenment and emancipation is, moreover, encapsulated in and explained by what we are apt, after Voltaire, to call a philosophy of history. In all these respects, it is commonly observed, Marx's thinking is thoroughly imbued with the concepts and categories of the Enlightenment. What this common observation obscures, however, is the extent to which Marx was a most uncommon thinker. To old concepts he persistently gave new meanings and to old categories he almost always added new content. Thus, for example, although he set great store by "science," Marx meant by it something different than did Diderot, say, or Comte. A consideration of Marx's novel understanding of science we shall save for Part III. The essays in Part I are all concerned, in their different ways, with what we might with due caution call Marx's philosophy of history.

True, Marx denied that he had a philosophy of history, by which he meant that he never sought to construct an all-encompassing speculative system after the fashion of Hegel and Comte. For these imaginary air castles he had the greatest contempt. But Marx readily acknowledged having a "guiding principle" or "leading thread" for tying together, understanding—and altering—otherwise disparate and disconnected phenomena. This he called the materialist conception of history, or more simply, "our conception" (1970b: 22).

Despite the considerable theoretical load he placed on it, however,

Marx never elaborated a consistent and detailed statement of the materialist interpretation of history. The principal texts (*The German Ideology, The Communist Manifesto,* the 1859 Preface to the *Critique of Political Economy,* and the historical sections of *Capital*) sometimes seem to give very different answers to fundamental and troubling questions. Three particularly troublesome questions command the attention of our first five essays.

Consider first the question of revolution. According to the materialist interpretation, history is the story of the development of human productive powers and of class struggles, punctuated periodically by revolutions resulting in the victory of one class over another. This now-familiar story line is, alas, more dramatic than clear. What is it, for example, that motivates one class to take up arms against another? Is the development of revolutionary class consciousness more or less automatic and inevitable, or is it an objective historical possibility to be actualized through agitation, argument, and persuasion? Marx's failure to provide a concise answer to this question left a hermeneutical vacuum that later interpreters were not slow to fill. Although confident that a socialist revolution would be in the interest of the proletariat – and eventually of all people – Marx was less sure about what the optimal revolutionary conditions would be, where they would first appear, and whether the workers would in fact seize their chance. In his middle years he anticipated the outbreak of proletarian revolution in the advanced capitalist societies. Later in life, however, the possibility that a revolution in Russia might trigger a belated revolution in the West loomed larger in Marx's mind. His later intuitions became Lenin's intentions and, by 1917, historical fact. Whether the Russian Revolution was genuinely proletarian or a premature and ill-fated simulacrum of socialist revolution is still a matter of some dispute among Marxists. Doctrinal disputes aside, one central fact remains beyond dispute: Despite Marx's expectations, the firebird of socialist revolution has so far failed to come home to the capitalist roost.

Why was Marx mistaken? Was it because technological and revolutionary change were, after all, less intimately intertwined than the materialist interpretation of history suggests? Or was it because it is simply irrational for the proletariat to undertake revolutionary action? An argument along the latter lines has been advanced by several modern economists and game theorists. Using a variant of the free-rider problem for public goods, they contend that it is irrational for an individual proletarian, or for the entire proletariat, to turn to revolutionary action.

8

In the opening essay, William Shaw offers a spirited internal critique of several recent efforts to demonstrate the irrationality of proletarian revolution. Turning game theory and the theory of rationality back on its partisans, Shaw argues that there are conditions under which rational proletarians would have good reasons for turning toward revolution. He concludes, less critically and more constructively, by considering some of the genuine problems facing proletarian revolution.

The problem of revolution is also addressed by Jon Elster, albeit in the broader context of economic backwardness and historical materialism generally. Elster begins by recognizing the paradox that, contrary to Marx's theoretical expectations, socialist revolutions have occurred, not in advanced, but in economically backward countries. Attempting to rethink and refine Marxist theory, Elster starts afresh with the general notion of backwardness, which he ties to a theory of change and to criteria of progress. By these means he brings to the fore a crucial dilemma for Marxist theory: The conditions for economic and technological change and the conditions for revolution need not go together, and the historical record shows that they have not in fact gone together. This poses a special and persistent problem for uniting historical materialist theory with revolutionary practice.

At least two other troubling questions arise in connection with Marx's theory of history. The first of these concerns the alleged centrality, primacy, and progressiveness of technological change in Marx's vision of history. In the 1859 Preface to the *Critique of Political Economy*, which Hobsbawm terms the "most pregnant" statement of the materialist interpretation of history (1964: 10), Marx seems to suggest that historical development is directly attributable to changes in the material forces of production, around which revolve the social relations of production, which are in turn legitimated by the institutions and ideologies of the legal and political superstructure. Thinkers as different as Plekhanov, Bober, Acton, and, more recently, G. A. Cohen and William Shaw, have advanced versions of this "technological determinist" interpretation. Theirs is, however, not the only possible reading of the materialist interpretation, or even of the 1859 Preface, particularly in light of some of Marx's other oft-expressed views and, indeed, his own historiographical practice. Oddly, the 1859 Preface makes no mention whatsoever of classes or class struggle. The omission is all the more striking since Marx on other occasions appears to accord explanatory primacy to class struggle.

The second question concerns the nature of the "dialectical connection" between the forces and the relations of production (Marx

9

1973: 109). Marx clearly rejects the simplistic view that the productive forces are the contingent Humean causes of the relations of production since he allows the latter to have considerable influence over the former. What sort of connection, then, did he envision? A coherent answer to this question would surely solve one of Marxism's primary puzzles. In his recent reconstruction and defense of Marx's theory of history, G. A. Cohen (1978) claims that the connection is a functional one. The social relations are as they are, he argues, because they function to develop the productive forces. Cohen's account, if correct, has the virtue of preserving the primacy of forces over relations, while at the same time allowing the relations to exercise considerable influence over the forces.

The next three essays challenge Cohen's provocative claims. Richard Miller begins by contesting the technological determinist interpretation itself. In his own practice as an economic historian, Marx did not treat technological change as the basic source of historical development. Miller outlines two alternative reconstructions of Marx's theory of history. The first accepts the explanatory primacy of the productive forces, but only by including work relations and forms of cooperation within the very constitution of the productive forces themselves. Change then comes about largely through alterations in the forms of cooperation. The second and more fundamental alternative, which Miller calls "the mode-of-production" interpretation, contends that economic change arises out of a self-transforming tendency of the mode of production as a whole, and this includes the totality of relations of production, forms of cooperation, and technology. Sometimes technology, but more often the relations of production, is accorded the primary causal role. This latter interpretation, Miller concludes, best fits Marx's own practice.

The central puzzle of Marx's theory of history, Philippe Van Parijs contends, is how Marx can claim, at one and the same time, that the productive forces are primary over, but causally dependent on the form taken by, the relations of production. Cohen, as we have seen, favors a functionalist solution to this puzzle. Van Parijs, by contrast, contends that there is a fundamental ambiguity in the way Cohen sets up the question of explaining relations by way of forces. At best, Cohen's functional account offers only one possible solution to the central puzzle. Van Parijs sketches a more general account of the two-way causal relationship between forces and relations that depends on the rates at which the two affect each other's levels. A functional explanation, he concludes, corresponds to only one possible combination of the dynamics involved.

James Noble also takes up the problem of functional explanation in historical materialism. After criticizing Cohen's particular elaboration of functional explanation, he delineates the adequacy conditions that must be met for a functional explanation to be accepted. Using Marx's historical account of the rise and functional maintenance of a surplus laboring population in capitalism, Noble shows how a functional explanation, if it is to be persuasive, requires a backup genetic theory as well. He concludes by criticizing any positivist interpretation of Marxian functionalism and so anticipates the themes treated at some length in Part III.

REFERENCES

Cohen, G. A. (1978). *Karl Marx's Theory of History: A Defence.* Princeton, N.J.: Princeton University Press.
Hobsbawm, E. J., ed. (1964). Introduction to *Pre-Capitalist Economic Formations.* London: Lawrence & Wishart.
Marx, Karl (1970a). *The German Ideology.* New York: International Publishers.
(1970b). *Critique of Political Economy.* New York: International Publishers.
(1973). *Grundrisse.* (Translated by Martin Nicolaus.) Random House (Vintage Books).

CHAPTER 1

Marxism, revolution, and rationality

WILLIAM H. SHAW

What induces the proletariat to make the socialist revolution? Although a full, Marxist reply to this question rests on the historical-materialist view of history coupled with a detailed analysis of the nature and evolutionary trajectory of the capitalist mode of production, the short answer is simply that it is in the working class's self-interest to bring the reign of capital to a close. As capitalism matures, Marx thought, its internal economic difficulties intensify, and it becomes obvious that the system is increasingly dysfunctional. The well-being of the vast bulk of the population continues to be sacrificed, with less and less historical justification, for the benefit of a dwindling number of industrial magnates. The capitalist system is unable to satisfy the interests of the majority of society in anything like the manner that the productive capacity it has developed makes possible. Since the system cannot resolve its own problems and since the capitalist class has no interest in altering fundamentally existing arrangements, simple rationality leads the working class to conquer political power in order to emancipate itself by reshaping the socio-economic organization of production.

Marx thought socialism was inevitable, not because preordained by any theory, but because the mass of the citizenry would soon cease to tolerate an increasingly burdensome social order. Socialist revolution would simply be "the expropriation of a few usurpers by the mass of the people" (Marx 1970: 764), a straightforward result of "the self-conscious, independent movement of the immense majority, in the

Parts of this paper appeared in abridged form in Shaw (1982). I thank John Arthur, G. A. Cohen, and David C. Paris for their helpful comments on earlier versions of this essay.

interest of the immense majority" (Marx and Engels, vol. 6: 495; cf. Marx 1972: 315). The self-interest of the working class (which in this instance coincides with the interests of the broad majority of the population) and not any altruism on its part is what makes revolution erupt. Material conditions – the travail of the working class's present lot and the historical feasibility of a more humane social order – goad it into action and underwrite its eventual victory. Rationality in the pursuit of its self-interest precipitates the proletariat's push for socialism.

Marx's account of socialist revolution as the natural result of the workers' rationally pursuing their interests fits well into his material-ist perspective of history, but the rationality of revolutionary action by the proletariat, even granting the facts as Marx saw them, has been challenged by Mancur Olson (1965) and more recently by Al-len Buchanan. Buchanan puts the charge this way:

> Even if revolution is in the best interest of the proletariat, and even if every member of the proletariat realizes that this is so, so far as its members act rationally, this class will *not* achieve concerted revolutionary action.

> Concerted revolutionary action is a public good for the proletariat as a group. Yet each proletarian, whether he seeks to maximize his own interests or those of his class, will refrain from revolutionary action . . . The point is not that inaction is *compatible* with rationality. Rationality *requires* inaction. (1979: 63, 65–6)

The radicalness of this thesis is hard to exaggerate. Critics of Marx have long argued that socialism is not really to the advantage of the working class or that even if it is, the conditions of capitalist society (ideological mystification and the like) will prevent workers from appreciating where their real interests lie. And there is the old charge that Marx cannot account for the allegiance of nonworkers – like Engels and himself – to the proletarian cause. The Olson-Bucha-nan thesis, however, is a much more fundamental objection: Ra-tional proletarians will not join the revolution even if they know socialism to be in their interest and know that its advantages to them will outweigh the costs of joining.

Section I of this essay presents the reasoning that undergirds their contention, and the next two sections rebut it, Section II with regard to utility-maximizing agents and Section III with reference to self-interested proletarians. The final section continues the discussion of revolution and rationality and elaborates on the genuine problems of revolutionary motivation, comparing the predicament of the capi-talist class with that of the proletariat.

WILLIAM H. SHAW

I. THE IRRATIONALITY-OF-REVOLUTION ARGUMENT

The argument against the rationality of revolution is a variation of the familiar free-rider problem for public goods. The distinguishing features of a public good are indivisibility (or jointness of supply) and nonexcludability. If a public good is made available to some members of a given group, it is more or less automatically available to every other member of that group. Unlike private goods, the quantity produced cannot be divided and purchased by individuals, and it is practically impossible or financially infeasible to exclude any member of the relevant group from the good in question (and indeed those who do not want it frequently cannot exclude themselves). Clean air, police protection, public parks, energy conservation, and population control are standard examples. National defense is a public good that is indivisible over a whole society, but there can be various kinds and degrees of public goods, depending on the size and nature of the relevant public and the degree of indivisibility and nonexcludability of the good in question.

The availability of such goods does not, however, usually require that all of the relevant public contribute to their production. When coupled with this fact, the indivisibility and nonexcludability of a public good entail that the benefits in question will be available even to those members of the group who have not shared in the costs of producing that good. This circumstance is the relevant one in the present context. Wherever action by some, but not all, members of a group suffices to produce a public good, the problem of free riders arises. As Rawls put it:

Where the public is large and includes many individuals, there is a temptation for each person to try to avoid doing his share. This is because whatever one man does his action will not significantly affect the amount produced. He regards the collective action of others as already given one way or the other. If the public good is produced his enjoyment of it is not decreased by his not making a contribution. If it is not produced his action would not have changed the situation anyway. (1971: 267)

If others in the community refrain from polluting the air by burning fires, we all benefit equally from more breathable air regardless of whether I cooperate or not. Since my burning or not burning has at most a negligible effect on the quality of the environment, I can treat the production of clean air as independent of my action. Accordingly, even though the value of clean air to me outweighs the cost of pulling my share, rational self-interest requires that I not join

14

the collective effort. Since cooperating in refraining from burning is a cost to me, the relevant decision matrix looks like this:

		Others	
		Cooperate	Don't cooperate (burn)
Me	Cooperate	Clean air 2 Cost to me	Air stays dirty 4 Cost to me
	Don't cooperate (burn)	Clean air 1 No cost to me	Air stays dirty 3 No cost to me

My ordinal preferences are ranked 1 through 4. The rational thing for me to do is to refuse to cooperate since whatever the others do, that will put me in the best position: If they refrain from burning, I get a free ride (1); if they do not, then my effort will not have been wasted (3). The same reasoning transfers to the case of revolutionary action. The revolution is a public good for proletarians like me, but contributing to it is a cost. The noncooperative posture maximizes my expected gain. It is the rational and strategically dominant policy. As Mancur Olson puts it, "There are *no* individual economic *incentives* for class action" (1965: 108).

Allen Buchanan pushes this reasoning further and argues (1979: 65; cf. Olson: 64) that the free-rider problem arises not just for rational egoists, but also for maximizers of overall utility (or, in the Marxist case, total class utility). Individual utility maximizers will reason that regardless of what they do, either enough others will contribute to the revolution or they will not. In the first case, not only is my effort superfluous, but it also lowers total group utility. In the second case, my effort would be wasted and, again, group utility diminished. With regard to possible revolutionary action, then, Buchanan contends that rationality requires that I refrain from enlisting in the collective effort, whether I seek to maximize my own interests or those of my class. Marx's theory that elementary rationality, when linked to an accurate assessment of the workers' interests, would lead them to revolt is mistaken.

The obstacle for Marx has been presented so far as a free-rider

15

problem, but this label is a little misleading. For the root problem is not that there will be free riders during the revolution, but that "class-oriented revolutionary action will not occur if the individuals that make up a class act rationally" (Olson: 105). Within an established institution, the existence of free riders can often be ignored and a certain level of noncooperation simply tolerated, or parasitism can be discouraged by incentives and subsidies for cooperation or by penalties for noncooperation. The problem of free riders is not what to do about them, but that free-rider reasoning will thwart the voluntary production of public goods. Thus, with regard to Marx's theory of revolution, the Olson-Buchanan thesis is that if the workers are rational, then there will be no free riders because there will be no collective, revolutionary action in the first place.

II. MORALITY AND THE MAXIMIZATION OF UTILITY

In this section I address the argument that those who seek to maximize overall utility (or overall class utility, which is what matters here) are in the same boat as the rational egoist. If sound, Buchanan's reasoning would strengthen greatly the case against the rationality of revolutionary action. But, as I shall show, his argument fails.

Presumably, our maximizer of utility is so motivated for moral reasons. If he acts on the basis of moral conviction, this will be either because he is a convinced utilitarian or because the principle of utility looms large in his deontological system. In the latter case, there is good reason to suppose that the agent will not choose the noncontribution position because other claims – fairness, for example, or universalizability – may very well enter into his moral deliberation alongside his commitment to utility. Specifying the exact nature and extent of these other moral claims is not a simple task (Simmons 1979; Strang 1968), and I ignore the issue of whether a plausible moral code must incorporate nonutilitarian principles. But it does seem clear that, from a perspective that admits deontological claims, those who adopt the free rider's reasoning will quite frequently be shirking their moral responsibility.

If the others cooperate in keeping the air clean by refraining from burning their fires, I take advantage of them by burning mine while enjoying the benefits of a better environment that they have made possible. I cannot universalize my action; indeed, I prefer that no one burn than that all burn. We can thus appeal to a number of related moral considerations, it seems, to support our intuitive judgment that the free rider acts wrongly. Suppose, though, that I do not know that the others will cooperate in producing some public good, or even that I know that they will not. I may still be required, by a number of principles of ordinary morality, to do my share by not adding my empty beer cans to those already in the public park or by recycling my cans and bottles, even though my individual action is of negligible effect. Perhaps I need not make as large a sacrifice as I would if all were cooperating, but I may well be obliged to make some public effort, signaling my willingness to cooperate and encouraging others to do likewise.

That deontological principles may underwrite a policy of cooperation is not surprising, but one may wonder if it is otherwise when our agent is committed only to the maximization of total utility. Will it be irrational for a utilitarian to cooperate? The answer is no, not necessarily, because a maximizer of total utility must take into consideration the effect his action or inaction will have on others. Buchanan suggests that this effect is relevant only if it occurs at the "threshold point" that must be crossed if the public good is to be produced or the revolution won (1979: 65n). But from the utilitarian's perspective, the situation is more complicated than this and his reasoning, accordingly, more subtle.

First, the decision environment is not parametric; an actor's choices will influence the choices and behavior of others, and a utilitarian must take this into account. On the one hand, the utility of his public cooperation in terms of promoting the good in question may very likely outweigh its disutility to him since it will set an example and stimulate others to cooperate; on the other hand, his failure to cooperate may have extensive negative repercussions, especially if he has earlier given support to the production of the public good in issue. Second, even if it is unlikely that our utilitarian's contribution will be the crucial one without which the public good would not be realized, contributing may still be the action with the highest expected utility. A small chance of producing a very large benefit – of being the threhold contribution – may be the best option open to a utilitarian (Parfit 1981). Third, even if his action is not the decisive one at the threshold of the public good, it may not be without benefit. The contribution of each is not literally imperceptible. If it were, as Brian Barry argues, how could all the contributions add up to something?[1] My refraining from burning helps preserve the qual-

---

[1] Barry (1978: 32), but see Sartorius (1982: 212–14). Richard Tuck (1979) illuminates the connection between the free-rider problem and the ancient Sorites paradox in logic.

ity of the air, and my burning adds measurably, if only slightly, to total air pollution. Public goods are rarely all-or-nothing affairs, such that no benefit is gained by any effort below the supposed threshold (e.g., victory of the revolution); nor is it likely that every contribution beyond the threshold is wasted. Fourth and relatedly, a small contribution, especially where it affects many others, may be the most a utilitarian can hope to contribute to general welfare. My burning or littering, or refraining therefrom, affects no one person's welfare more than slightly, but it slightly affects the welfare of numerous parties and, thus, cannot be ignored by a utilitarian. Finally, there may be good utilitarian reasons for supporting publicly, internalizing in oneself, and inculcating in others norms that lead individuals to cooperate in the production of public goods without basing that cooperation on a direct appeal to utility.

Let us elaborate on these points, beginning with an example. Suppose that forming a union in a certain factory is a public good, and we display the situation on our earlier decision matrix. Union representation will not only maximize total welfare, it is *ex hypothesi* in the interests of each individual. Each will prefer unionization to non-unionization, and the costs of joining are outweighed for each individual by the advantages of a unionized factory, though it is only necessary for 75 percent of the work force to enlist for these benefits to accrue to all. Prior to the day on which the workers are invited to step forward and pay their dues, our utilitarian will clearly support joining the union. When he talks to friends, he will point out the advantages of union representation, he may cajole some of his more conservative workmates to join and even put up posters and distribute union literature. Enlistment day now arrives. If he thinks it unclear whether a sufficient number will join, our utilitarian will sign up, make this fact known, and engage in some last-minute recruitment. If he thinks too few will join, he will still enlist and prepare to win the battle on some future occasion. He will not disillusion the others by failing at this crucial moment to back the cause he has endorsed. He would only consider deserting the union if he were convinced of the impossibility of 75 percent of the work force ever being persuaded to sign up, and this does not seem likely given the stipulated facts.

Even in that circumstance, though, the overall utility of the utilitarian's forsaking the cause in order to cut the losses of the union side is far from obvious. For one thing, this sort of behavior is difficult to sustain psychologically. Acting contrary to one's professed goals and commitments – and our utilitarian continues to think unionization good – can engender cognitive dissonance. It also lowers one's credibility in the eyes of others. Of course, one may argue that a clear-thinking act utilitarian would not be troubled, for his ultimate principle has not been compromised, and a society of philosophers would not deem him insincere. But his work place is not likely to be such a society and he himself, for reasons given later, will not find it easy psychologically to shed his union commitment.

If on the other hand the utilitarian sees that the union will score a clear victory, these last sorts of considerations also give him reason not to abandon a seaworthy ship. A long-term view of utility may also suggest that the union's receiving the minimal enrollment necessary for representation, and no more, is not the optimal outcome. Considerations of future solidarity and strength at the bargaining table may lead a utility maximizer to contribute to the cause, even when from the point of view of the initial victory this contribution is superfluous. Similar reasoning may lead the maximizer of class utility to add his body to the already sufficiently large group storming the Winter Palace. This is not to contend that total (class) utility is not ultimately a function of aggregate individual utility, but rather that there may be a more complicated connection between the two than the Olson-Buchanan argument suggests. Contributing to the collective cause can bring benefits even after the threshold has been crossed.

The course of action counseled by utilitarianism in any given circumstance depends on the specific consequences of rival courses of action. In discussing utility-maximizing behavior in a potentially revolutionary context one is obliged to transcend the artificial confines of the matrix for, obviously, a revolution is not a one-shot, all-or-nothing event. Very likely, neither eventual success nor failure is guaranteed. Those who are committed to its triumph on utilitarian grounds will do what they can to support it; what exactly this will be – writing an anticapitalist letter to the newspaper, discussing socialists ideas with friends, or joining the guerrilla forces – depends on the particular situation and the utilitarian's estimate of the extent of the good in question and of the likelihood of its achievement. Even if a utilitarian can reasonably expect to have only a modest effect himself – by making the revolution a little more likely, by speeding it up a tiny bit, or by lessening very slightly the birth pangs – supporting the revolutionary cause may still have more expected utility than any alternative course of action open to him. A small contribution to the general welfare may be the most good an individual utilitarian can hope to produce.

Where the revolution's success is uncertain, as it usually is, utilitarians will take some pains to champion it, but they can also have reasons for supporting both lost causes and winning ones, as we have seen in the union example. It will be utility maximizing, for instance, to support the sentiments that underlie the call for revolutionary change, since these sentiments can lead to good consequences in other areas. It will also be utility maximizing to support those social feelings that incline people to cooperate with one another, as Rolf Sartorius has noted:

Rational act-utilitarians . . . would be willing to support social norms which would provide them with individual incentives to share in the cost of providing public goods; norms backed by social sanctions of sufficient strength so that most individuals would not view acting as a "free rider" as likely to maximize utility (1975: 77).

Utilitarians would wish to cultivate sentiments, convictions, and instincts in themselves and others that would dispose them to participate in the production of public goods even in those circumstances where an individual's direct appeal to utility might not warrant such cooperation. (If a utilitarian opts for an indirect theory of the right, for instance, some version of rule utilitarianism, this point will be even stronger.) This explains why our factory organizer will not be in a position to shed readily his allegiance to the union, even when the prospects for victory are slim. One can, of course, jerry-build hypothetical situations in which the weight of utilitarian considerations, notwithstanding all of the preceding, goes against one's participating in the revolutionary process, but this poses no problem. The point here is not that utilitarians will join collective efforts in any circumstance whatsoever, but that in general utilitarianism is far from thwarting cooperation in the production of public goods.

Thus, moral agents, whether utilitarians or not, will not as a rule attempt to ride for free. A policy of noncooperation will not be strategically dominant for them. Such an agent can find it rational to collaborate in revolutionary action since it can be rational to follow one's moral principles even when they conflict with one's self-interest. Moral behavior may or may not be in one's self-interest, but it can nonetheless, given the desires and sentiments of the agent, be perfectly rational behavior.

Marxism, revolution, and rationality

III. PRISONERS AND PROLETARIANS

So far I have argued that cooperation in revolutionary action need not be irrational for a maximizer of total class utility or for a moral agent of a nonutilitarian sort. The public-goods objection to Marx's theory of revolutionary motivation still remains for the case of proletarians who rationally pursue only their self-interests. One might simply swallow this objection and concede that individual members of the working class will be motivated to join the revolution only insofar as they are swayed by moral considerations. But obviously the Marxist position will be stronger to the extent that it makes weaker assumptions about proletarian motivation. I do not suppose that Marx thought the workers to be rational egoists; no evidence suggests he thought that they are impelled only by selfish concerns or that they are perfectly rational in the pursuit of their interests. The theoretical plausibility and practical feasibility of proletarian revolution are, however, enhanced if it can be shown that self-interested proletarians would enlist in the collective cause (remember that it is being assumed that the revolution is, and is known to be, a good for the working class, both individually and collectively). Can this be shown?

The situation of the proletariat as depicted by Olson and Buchanan is an instance of what A. K. Sen (1967) calls the "isolation paradox," which is charcterized by two features. First, regardless of what other persons do, each is better off doing A than B. Second, each prefers everyone doing B to everyone doing A. The outcome in this situation is that individual strategy dominates, with each doing A, and a Pareto-inferior outcome results. Sen's paradox is just the generalization to n-person of the notorious Prisoner's Dilemma. Focusing on that dilemma, which has been extensively studied, will help us with the issue of the rationality of revolutionary action.

Two criminals, Alfred and Bob, are arrested for a joint crime, kept in separate rooms, and brought before the prosecuting attorney individually. If either turns state's evidence and squeals, while the other does not, he will go free and his partner be jailed for ten years. If neither talks, they both will be found guilty of a lesser charge and sentenced to one year. If they both talk, five years in prison awaits them. Since Alfred does not know what Bob will do, the rational strategy for him is to confess: If Bob does not talk, Alfred will walk, and if Bob does, Alfred will have saved himself from an additional five years of incarceration. Letting D stand for deserting his partner and C for cooperating with him by remaining silent, Alfred's preference ranking is as follows: (D_a, C_b), (C_a, C_b), (D_a, D_b), and (C_a, D_b). Since Bob's situation is symmetrical, his preference ranking is the same as Alfred's only with the subscripts reversed. The inevitable consequence of their individual pursuit of self-interest is (D_a, D_b), an outcome that is obviously suboptimal.

Within game-theoretic parameters, a consensus holds that (D_a, D_b) is the equilibrium outcome, even though inferior to the cooperative option (C_a, C_b). For each individual, strategy D is dominant; it is the rational maximin choice. (For a discussion of attempts to show that strategy C is rational, see Shaw 1982: 103–6.) Each prisoner will reason, correctly, that he is best off by deserting, regardless of what the other does. But the combined result of the individually unimpeachable rationality of the two prisoners is mutual disaster. Nor does knowing this inevitable result give either prisoner a reason to elect C instead of D; doing so would only make him worse off. The paradoxical features of the Prisoner's Dilemma have thus led some writers to contend that there is an incoherence in attempting to limit rationality to the principle of maximizing one's interests (Lucas 1980: 52; cf. Gauthier 1975), that collective rationality is distinct from individual rationality (Rapoport 1966: 130–1; but see Harsanyi 1977: 277), or that here the idea of rationality simply breaks down (Watkins 1970: 205)[2]

Inveighing against the model of rationality employed in game theory, however, seems misguided; there are good reasons within its conceptual framework for its specific assumptions, however counterintuitive the results of the Prisoner's Dilemma may be. In any case, nothing hangs on a word. Withdrawing the honorific of "rational" from strategy D in the case of the Prisoner's Dilemma establishes nothing, since a natural and attractive line of reasoning will still lead the prisoners to (D_a, D_b). It is better to concede that some games are truly noncooperative and that, as Mill observed long ago, the antisocial structure of some situations can militate against optimal results.[3]

---

[2] By contrast with Watkins, Lawrence H. Davis (1977) writes that "rationality has never been supposed to be a *guarantee* of the best possible outcome" (p. 320). Davis's comments suggest a parallel between the concepts of "rational choice" and "best possible outcome," on the one hand, and "justified belief" and "true belief," on the other.

[3] Mill (1970: Book V, Part XI, section 12). In the case of real criminals facing the Prisoner's Dilemma, the optimal outcome from society's perspective would seem to be (D_a, D_b). Mill and a long line of writers have

And why should this be surprising? That there are limits to atomistic reasoning or that individual rationality can fail to provide collective goods should come as no shock to socialists. After all, it is one reason for their repudiation of a market system. But, of course, the issue remains whether participation in the socialist revolution is best viewed as an instance of the isolation paradox, whether it really is irrational for proletarians to join the socialist movement, despite the fact that one's gains from socialism would outweigh one's fair share of the costs of bringing it about.

Although Sen calls the paradox "isolation," it is worth noting that communication and negotiation leave the situation unaltered. Consider the problem of Hobbesian individuals trying to contract their way out of the state of nature. Promises can be made and hands shaken – just as the prisoners can give each other a wink before they are called to the prosecutor's office – but then each must decide whether to stick to the bargain or not. The paradox is simply pushed up a level. Nor is trust really the issue (pace Bartos 1967: 230). Whether one knows that others will adhere to the agreement, knows that they will not, or does not know what they will do, rational self-interest dictates that one renege. Similar reasoning on the part of the others will ensure that all remain trapped in the state of nature.

At this point, though, one will want to protest that the Hobbesian predicament, and by extension the Olson-Buchanan portrayal of the working class, involves (1) a very unrealistic situation, and (2) an implausible conception of human motivation. Let us examine these points in turn.

1. Game-theoretic constructions are abstractions from the real situations that face persons, and as such they are useful only insofar as they capture the crucial features of the decision environment. One important facet of the real world (and in particular of the proletariat's situation) is that the isolation paradox may well be recurrent. But if a Prisoner's Dilemma situation is repeated over and over again, then my failure to cooperate can bring retaliation and injure my long-run interests. Nor am I likely to get away with lying or double-crossing. I may best the other player initially by playing D to his C, but this cannot last. As we settle down to repeated outcomes of

defended the social benefits of state action to help individuals and groups out of Prisoner's Dilemmas, while Gordon Tullock (1967) has noted the social benefits of state action, e.g., antitrust legislation, that puts certain persons into a Prisoner's Dilemma.

(D_a, D_b), the absurdity of noncooperation is manifest. Thus it seems clear to many that the rational strategy is to play C, at least initially, and so signal one's willingness to cooperate in avoiding mutual ruin (Davis 1970: 96–7). If the commitment to cooperation is divided into small steps rather than one big contribution, each can monitor the other's actions, risking little. Empirical evidence in fact suggests that even when the players start noncooperatively, on repeated trials it is possible for mutual trust to develop and for players to break out of the prisoner's trap (Brams 1976: 84–5; Lave 1962; Mueller 1976: 398). And this is what one finds in the real world where, for example, price collusion among would-be competitors frequently occurs. Even arch game theorists Luce and Raiffa contend that (C_a, C_b) can emerge in repeated play as "a sort of quasi-equilibrium" since it is not to the advantage of either player to initiate the chaos that will result from not cooperating (1957: 98, 101).

The Prisoner's Dilemma also assumes that agreements are unenforceable. If they were enforceable, simple negotiation would guarantee the cooperative outcome; similarly, a binding referendum would dissolve the isolation paradox. The cooperative outcome is collectively rational or optimal in the sense that it would clearly result from bargaining or (unanimous) voting. In the Hobbesian state of nature, no such agreements are possible, but in the real world contracts are, to varying degrees, enforceable as a result of formal and informal sanctions and internal constraints on the actors. For instance, honor among thieves, peer pressure, or the threat of gang revenge against stool pigeons could cause Alfred and Bob to keep mum. These factors succeed by changing the payoffs from the game and thus altering the preferences of our prisoners (more on this in [2], later). Keeping the initial payoffs as specified, though, Alfred and Bob would find it rational to arrange for retaliation (perhaps by the Mafia) against whoever breaks the agreement, thus insuring that neither of them will. Knowledge that the situation will be repeated can also make it rational to keep one's word, at the cost of one's immediate gain, in order to reap long-term advantages. In addition, it would be rational for one to internalize the criminal code of silence, thereby encumbering one's future actions, provided one's criminal colleagues did the same (Mackie 1977: 115–18).

The complaint of the last two paragraphs is not that the real world is more complex than the games studied by the decision theorist. No student of game theory is so deluded as to think otherwise. Nor is simplification itself a problem. Science, whether natural or social, frequently proceeds by building idealizing models that attempt to capture the essential and ignore the contingent. And, indeed, game theoretic analyses can be revealing; certain games can distill the crucial features of real situations. The complaint, rather, is that the classic, one-shot Prisoner's Dilemma or the simple isolation paradox does not do justice to the circumstances of the working class. Oversimplification has become distortion; essential features have been omitted. In particular, repetition of the game and the possibility of more or less binding agreements change the logic of the situation. The problem is not with the assumption of rationality nor, so far anyway, with the assumption of egoism, but with a woefully inadequate model of the proletariat's situation.

2. Game theory can be illuminating, I have said, only if it does not ignore important features of the actual decision situation. The same holds true for the motivations of the actual deciders; these can be simplified, but they must not be mischaracterized. To discuss the rationality of proletarian revolution on the assumption that the workers are ruthless egoists is, to say the least, misleading. Much of bourgeois economic theory makes egoism a presupposition (Sen 1977), but nothing in the notion of rationality employed by game theory, welfare economics, or the literature on public choice requires that egoism be seen as anything other than a special case of rational choice. The postulate that agents act to maximize their interests or satisfy their preferences does not entail that their only interest is self-interest, their only preferences and concerns selfish ones. Nor are there any theoretical reasons in the present case for making an assumption (that of egoism) that is not only inaccurate but fundamentally mistaken. As suggested earlier, Marx's theory of revolution would be significantly weakened if it has to make overly strong assumptions about moral behavior on the part of the workers, but there is a continuum of points between complete egoism and totally other-regarding motivation. If one is to have anything useful to say, the object must surely be to find the most appropriate, model-building premise. If Alfred and Bob are incorrigible Hobbesians, then they are doomed to the (D_a, D_b) outcome. If there is not only honor among thieves but charity and their motivations are entirely altruistic, a cooperative outcome is dictated. But there are other possibilities.

Consider, for instance, what Sen (1967; 1974) calls the "assurance game." In this situation, the premises of the isolation paradox are modified only in that where everyone else pitches in, the individual prefers to cooperate. By contrast with the Prisoner's Dilemma, the preference ranking for Alfred would be: (C_a, C_b), (D_a, C_b), (D_a, D_b), (C_a, D_b). Alfred would rather spend a year behind bars with Bob than be free while Bob is in jail for ten. (Note that this differs from the other-regarding, moralistic preference ordering of: $[C_a, C_b]$, $[C_a, D_b]$, $[D_a, C_b]$, $[D_a, D_b]$.) In the assurance game, an individual's dominant strategy is no longer noncooperation. If we assume perfect information for the players, then they will all choose C in the safe expectation that others will too, since it will be in everyone's interest to do so.[4] Compulsory enforcement will not be necessary, and the optimal situation will be individually stable. What is being weakened here is not the assumption of rationality, but of a totally self-seeking egocentric preference set.

A preference structure like that supposed in the assurance game is not psychologically unrealistic. Such a model would make proletarian revolution individually rational since despite the personal cost of cooperation, solidarity with others could bring about the required effort. If we are certain that others will do their share, we may actually prefer doing ours rather than being free riders. Solidarity, as Jon Elster puts it, "is *conditional altruism*, as distinct from the unconditional altruism of the categorical imperative and the unconditional egoism of capitalist society" (1979: 21–2). The possibility of conditional or limited altruism would seem a more plausible assumption, and one more relevant to the actual circumstances of the proletariat, than either egoism or pure altruism. This would mean that even if, contrary to our earlier comments, an egoistic proletarian would not cooperate with his mates, on a more realistic model of the average proletarian's preferences – presumably reflecting a mixture of self-interested concerns, desires for solidarity, and moral commitments, along with some willingness to trust others – revolutionary action might well be rational. Since there is no reason to think such non-self-interested desires as those hypothesized are irrational, and no theoretical or methodological reason for insisting on the less realistic assumption of complete egoism, then the possibility of rational revolutionary behavior does not succumb to the Olson-Buchanan argument.

Proving that even selfish proletarians would always find it rational to join the cause (and thus help to produce the greater good) would bring a kind of Mandevillean pleasure to many of us. Unfortunately,

---

[4] Where he lacks assurance, a rational agent will use a maximin criterion and choose strategy D, which gives him the highest minimum payoff.

this cannot be shown, though egoists will quite frequently be induced to cooperate in collective actions. In addition to such considerations as situation repetition and the possibility of negotiation and agreement, mentioned earlier, an egoist would obviously collaborate if his personal benefit from so doing were positive regardless of the outcome or if he knew that only his effort would guarantee that the threshold to successful collective action was crossed (since his share of the public good outweighs his contribution). More interestingly, egoists can have good reason in general to behave morally and cooperatively, since such behavior – and other persons' knowledge of it – can pay off in the long run, thus diminishing their incentive to be (and certainly to appear to be) free riders. Indeed, egoists can have good reason not only to act morally, but actually to become moral persons or persons with more than selfish desires, since the pretense of moral or cooperative behavior (with continual calculation of the possible advantages of cutting the corner in each particular instance) may be insufficient for reaping the advantages of a good reputation, the trust of others, and friendship. It may be in one's interest to discard one's egoism and inculcate in oneself genuine concerns for others, cooperative instincts, and moral desires. If this sort of reasoning is tenable (and it is a staple of moral philosphers), then it not only supports the contention that selfish proletarians might be strongly motivated to cooperate, but also indicates that narrow egoistic calculation can itself be self-defeating and thus less than purely rational.

Olson and Buchanan claim to have shown that collective action by the workers is irrational, but the logic of their argument presupposes, incorrectly, that the simple Prisoner's Dilemma captures fully the circumstances and preferences of the working class. When this presupposition is amended, however, the possibility of rational collective action by the proletariat in defense of its interests cannot be ruled out. On the one hand, once the original dilemma is modified to mirror the proletariat's situation more accurately, then even totally self-regarding proletarians may find a way to realize their common interests. Enlightened egoists can be brought into collusion because of their knowledge that the situation will be repeated and that reprisals are possible; they can have self-interested reasons to stand by their agreements. Only the most benighted self-seeker would rest content with repeated outcomes of (D_a, D_b). On the other hand, once the preferences of the workers are modeled more realistically, then the possibility of rational revolutionary action is further enhanced.

Conditional altruism is a plausible motivational assumption that envisions the workers as neither self-sacrificing or moralistic on the one hand, nor egoistic on the other: One is willing (and would like) to cooperate but only if others join in. Self-interest can still be seen as the impetus to revolution. In both the Prisoner's Dilemma and the assurance game, the workers prefer socialism to the present order, or (C_a, C_b) to (D_a, D_b). The only change is that in the latter game they are assumed to prefer socialism to backstabbing (that is, to $[D_a, C_b]$). The benefits of fraternity, solidarity, and cooperation – which will be fully harvested in the socialist future, but whose early fruits can be tasted today in the socialist movement – and their superiority to the pleasures afforded by capitalistic individualism are familiar themes of Marxist and radical literature. But even if today's workers have Prisoner's Dilemma preferences, they will be better off, in terms of those preferences, if they act as if they had the preferences associated with the assurance game. Thus, class consciousness for a worker might simply be defined as his understanding the isolation paradox facing his class and the necessity of solidarity overcoming free-rider reasoning.

IV. GAME THEORY AND CLASS STRUGGLE

The previous section's critique of Olson and Buchanan is also relevant to the work of public-choice theorists like Gordon Tullock who have offered an economic model, expressed in various quasi-mathematical equations, of the rationality of one's participating in revolutionary action (Coleman 1978; Mueller 1976; Silver 1974; Tullock 1971). When simplified (but not overly so), their main equation looks like this:

$$R = PB + D - C$$

where R stands for the potential revolutionary's reaction, B for the new government's public-goods benefits, P for the probability that the individual's participation brings success, and D and C for the private gains and costs, respectively, of participation. If R is positive, the agent should participate; if negative, not. Since P will almost always be negligible, the public-goods aspect in effect drops out of the equation, and rational persons will weigh only their personal gains and costs in deciding whether to participate. This conclusion is then used to buttress such reactionary reflections as the suggestion that revolutionaries are generally motivated by a hope for high office in the new regime.

The argument of the previous section should have established that so much more than narrow self-interest has to be packed into *C* and *D* that Tullock's equations are rendered vacuous. Moreover, individuals who understand the isolation paradox will not let *P* eliminate the weight of *B* in their calculations. The inane algebra and reactionary ruminations of theorists like Tullock make it easy to dismiss their work as pseudoscientific ideology, and indeed it is hopelessly naive to believe that such theorems could be at all informative about revolutions, let alone the basis of a scientific approach. Novels, memoirs, and historical narratives tell us more about real individuals in revolutionary circumstances, and Marx should have taught us that a scientific account of revolution requires that one come to grips with the deeper structures and processes involved.

But it would be wrong to eschew altogether the "economic" approach to social science, which sees human action as intentional, rational, and motivated by future rewards. Despite its difficulties, it may be more promising than the rival "sociological" approach, in which action is viewed simply as the product of such casual antecedents as tradition, roles, and norms (Barry 1978; Elster 1979: 112–17; cf. Boudin 1981, Hollis 1979, and Popkin 1978). This is too big an issue to resolve here, and Marxists clearly wish to stress the extent to which the preferences of actors and the situations in which they act are structured by more fundamental social and historical forces. Indeed the central theses of historical materialism concerning productive forces, relations of production, base, and superstructure are functionalist in character (Cohen 1978).[5] But although the economic approach or the theory of rational choice is not at the very core of Marxism, it nonetheless can be used to illuminate other topics of importance to the Marxist view of history and society, for example, the dynamics of capitalism and the vicissitudes of class struggle.

In particular, viewing revolutionary activity as rational action provides a more useful heuristic, for Marxists and non-Marxists alike, than seeing it, say, as a problem of mass psychology or a nonrational response to subjectively experienced frustration like rising expectations, relative deprivation, or status inconsistency. Marxists, certainly, have a theoretical and practical interest in representing socialism as to the advantage of the workers, both collectively and individually, and

[5] By contrast, Jon Elster (1982) argues that Marxists should abandon functional explanation for game theory. He illustrates well how game theory can serve as a tool for Marxist analysis, but his commitment to it goes much further than anything envisioned by this discussion.

the overthrow of capitalism as a rational response to their objective circumstances. Furthermore, since Marxists view classes as corporate actors locked in combat, they can only benefit from a study of the dynamics of the class struggle in strategic terms and thus from game theory, that branch of rational-choice theory devoted to strategic thinking.

Although some Marxists may think that decision theory and kindred "economic" subjects rest on alien, even ideological assumptions, this is simply not so. We have seen that the theory of rational choice involves no commitment to egoism, nor need it depict individuals as isolated atoms. Game theory in particular brings out the interdependent character of decision situations for it makes the choices and rewards of each player depend on those of others. "What is society, whatever its form may be? The product of men's reciprocal action" (Marx to Annenkov, 28 December 1846). Furthermore, the Prisoner's Dilemma and related puzzles highlight actual obstructions in the social world. This discussion has defended the possibility of rational collective action by the working class, but although the Olson-Buchanan objection can be met in principle, the isolation paradox remains a real-life obstacle, which socialists must overcome not just in theory but also in practice.

Marx recognized that egoism, competitiveness, and individualism—the factors that prevent a cooperative (C_a, C_b) solution from emerging—are not only rampant under capitalism, but fostered by that economic system. "Competition separates individuals from one another, not only the bourgeois but still more the workers . . . who live in conditions daily reproducing this isolation" (Marx and Engels vol. 5: 75).[6] Union organizers, for example, often have trouble even when union affiliation is known by the workers in a given plant to be in their interests and the cost of affiliation is not large. The problem of fashioning an effective and responsive organizational vehicle that is at the same time capable of mobilizing the overthrow of capitalism is similar. No doubt this endeavor is hampered by theoretical underdevelopment, and there are genuine difficulties with fetishism, ideological mystification, and plain ignorance to be overcome. But even when the working class has seen through the ideological facade and into the heart of capitalism, as Marx perhaps overoptimistically

[6] See also p. 247: "The communists . . . are very well aware that egoism . . . *is* in definite circumstances a necessary form of the self-assertion of individuals."

thought they inevitably would, barriers to coordinated, collective action remain.

The Prisoner's Dilemma shows not only how atomistic reasoning can stymie collective rationality, but also how the structure of certain situations can guarantee suboptimal, antisocial results. Consider, for example, universal suffrage and the institutions of representative democracy. Contemporary Marxists rightly emphasize that bourgeois democracy is the "ideological lynchpin" of Western capitalism (Anderson 1976–7; Geras 1975), but more than ideology is at stake. The very structure of national elections (take the quadrennial media carnival that passes for democracy in the United States) can generate apathy and impotence, as Hegel realized long before it was confirmed by contemporary studies of voting behavior:

> As for popular suffrage . . . it leads inevitably to electoral indifference, since the casting of a single vote is of no significance where there is a multitude of electors . . . Thus, the result of an institution of this kind is more likely to be the opposite of what was intended; election actually falls into the power of a few, of a caucus, and so of the particular and contingent interest which is precisely what was to have been neutralized. (1967: 202–3)

This sort of alienation is just one manifestation of the isolation paradox facing the workers. The collective action and group solidarity necessary for achieving socialism have to be forged from the individualistic behavior of uncoordinated monads, from the atomism produced by the present system. This is not theoretically impossible where the agents are rational, as Olson and Buchanan suppose, but it is far from automatic.

Within the narrow confines and presuppositions of the classic Prisoner's Dilemma, the only "solution" is to change the game – either by altering the environment within which the players act, for example, by allowing repetition of the game, or by restructuring their preferences. Socialists cannot do much to modify the preference structure of workers. To a large extent they must work with people as they find them under capitalism, although they can try to encourage, and to create organizational forms that nurture, people's non-egoistic, collective instincts. In addition, through painstaking organizing they can help overcome the small, daily Prisoner's Dilemmas facing the working class and aid in developing relations of trust and solidarity. Theorists generally concede that the isolation paradox is most amenable to resolution in relatively small groups, and this is precisely where socialists organize – in the neighborhood and on the factory floor. Socialists do not preach altruism or moralize, but they do seek to raise class consciousness and demonstrate the benefits of collective action. "The Communists are distinguished from other working-class parties by this only: . . . they point out and bring to the front the common interests of the entire proletariat . . . they always and everywhere represent the interests of the movement as a whole" (Marx and Engels, vol. 6: 497).

Understanding the isolation paradox, socialists can avail themselves of organizations that will provide them and others with incentives that will make it in their interest to participate in groups that act to provide public goods. There is a simple truth to be learned from the literature on this issue, namely, that any group seeking to procure a public good should strive to make membership a boon instead of a cost to individuals, and one generally recommended way to do this is for the organization to supply collateral goods to those who support it (Riker and Ordeshook 1973: 74; Sartorius 1975: 76–7). Left-wing organizations are often perceived even by those sympathetic to their aims as taking a high personal toll; membership in them is a definite, and frequently inordinate, cost to be borne for the cause. Yet successful mass organizations are precisely those that manage to integrate themselves into the day-to-day existence of the working class in such a way that cooperative behavior is a desired, organic feature of people's lives – not an alien burden that self-interest counsels one not to bear. Socialist organizations can offer activities, services, and programs – not to mention group ties and fraternal relations (Marx and Engels, vol. 3: 313) – that by catering to people's needs make it in their interest to support an organization capable of furnishing them with a public good.

It must be borne in mind that the bourgeoisie, too, has an isolation paradox to overcome. Although classical political theory since Hobbes can plausibly be interpreted as seeing the state as a cooperative solution to the common Prisoner's Dilemma facing its citizens, Marx "argued that society should be broken down into two or more distinct classes, each of which has its internal Prisoner's Dilemma" (Elster 1979: 97). For the capitalist class the state functions to resolve the failures of atomistic rationality – Marx's favorite example was provided by the English Factory Acts – and to prevent the workers from realizing the cooperative solution to their own isolation paradox.

Each class has internal contradictions to surmount and a struggle to wage with its class opponent. In the case of the proletariat Marx thought that countervailing factors under capitalism would, despite the competition and egoism fostered by that system, facilitate collective action and a class perspective (Marx and Engels, vol. 6: 210–11, 492–3, 496). The capitalist factory, for instance, would organize, centralize, and discipline the workers, schooling them in coordinated group action (Marx 1970: 763, 764n). Perhaps Marx was too sanguine on this point, and Buchanan (1979: 66–8) criticizes him for too readily assuming that class cooperation will be forthcoming for the proletarians, while making the insolubility of the public-goods problem for the bourgeoisie a cornerstone of his theory of revolution.

Marx did allow, though, that the bourgeoisie could display class unity and pursue a cooperative strategy, and he was far from holding that revolution results simply from the proletariat's achieving a collective rationality that eludes the bosses. The deeper dynamics of the capitalist system and the conflicts between the forces and relations of production they embody, the details of which cannot be specified here, set the state of the class struggle and tip the balance in favor of the workers, just as earlier material conditions favored the bourgeoisie against the feudal lords (Shaw 1978: Chap. 3). In this sense Marx thought a kind of historical rationality underwrites the proletariat's effort to find a cooperative solution to the isolation paradox facing it.

REFERENCES

Anderson, Perry (1976–7). "The Antinomies of Antonio Gramsci." *New Left Review* 100: 5–78.
Barry, Brian (1978). *Sociologists, Economists and Democracy.* Chicago: University of Chicago Press.
Bartos, Otomar J. (1967). *Simple Models of Group Behavior.* New York: Columbia University Press.
Boudin, Raymond (1981). *The Logic of Social Action.* London: Routledge & Kegan Paul.
Brams, Steven J. (1976). *Paradoxes in Politics.* New York: Free Press.
Buchanan, Allen (1979). "Revolutionary Motivation and Rationality." *Philosophy and Public Affairs* 9: 59–82.
Cohen, G. A. (1978). *Karl Marx's Theory of History: A Defence.* Princeton, N.J.: Princeton University Press.
Coleman, James (1978). "A Theory of Revolt Within an Authority Structure." *The Papers of the Peace Science Society* 28: 15–25.
Davis, Lawrence H. (1977). "Prisoners, Paradox, and Rationality." *American Philosophical Quarterly* 14: 319–27.
Davis, Morton D. (1970). *Game Theory.* New York: Basic Books.
Elster, Jon (1979). *Ulysses and the Sirens.* Cambridge: Cambridge University Press.

(1982). "Marxism, Functionalism, and Game Theory: The Case for Methodological Individualism." *Theory and Society* 11: 453–82.

Gauthier, David (1975). "Reason and Maximization." *Canadian Journal of Philosophy* 4: 411–33.

Geras, Norman (1975). "Rosa Luxemburg after 1905." *New Left Review* 89: 3–46.

Harsanyi, John C. (1977). *Rational Behavior and Bargaining Equilibrium in Games and Social Situations*. Cambridge: Cambridge University Press.

Hegel, Georg W. F. (1967). *The Philosophy of Right*. Translated and edited by T. M. Knox. Oxford: Oxford University Press.

Hollis, Martin (1979). "Rational Man and Social Science." In Ross Harrison (ed.), *Rational Action*. Cambridge: Cambridge University Press.

Lave, Lester B. (1962). "An Empirical Approach to the Prisoners' Dilemma Game." *The Quarterly Journal of Economics* 76: 424–36.

Lucas, J. R. (1980). *On Justice*. Oxford: Oxford University Press.

Luce, R. Duncan, and Howard Raiffa (1957). *Games and Decisions*. New York: Wiley.

Mackie, J. L. (1977). *Ethics: Inventing Right and Wrong*. Harmondsworth: Penguin Books.

Marx, Karl (1970). *Capital,* vol. 1. London: Lawrence & Wishart.

(1972). *Theories of Surplus Value,* vol. 3. London: Lawrence & Wishart.

Marx, Karl, and Frederick Engels (1975–). *Collected Works*. New York: International Publishers.

Mill, John Stuart [1848] (1970). *Principles of Political Economy*. Reprint. Harmondsworth: Penguin Books.

Mueller, Dennis (1976). "Public Choice: A Survey." *Journal of Economic Literature* 14: 395–433.

Olson, Mancur (1965). *The Logic of Collective Action*. Cambridge, Mass.: Harvard University Press.

Parfit, Derek (1981). "Correspondence." *Philosophy and Public Affairs* 10: 180–1.

Popkin, Samuel (1978). *The Rational Peasant*. Berkeley: University of California Press.

Rapoport, Anatol (1966). *Two-Person Game Theory*. Ann Arbor: University of Michigan Press.

Rawls, John (1971). *A Theory of Justice*. Cambridge, Mass.: Harvard University Press.

Riker, William H., and Peter C. Ordeshook (1973). *An Introduction to Positive Political Theory*. Englewood Cliffs, N.J: Prentice-Hall.

Sartorius, Rolf E. (1975). *Individual Conduct and Social Norms*. Encino, Calif.: Dickenson.

(1982). "Benevolence, Collective Action, and the Provision of Public Goods." In Harlan B. Miller and William H. Williams (eds.), *The Limits of Utilitarianism*. Minneapolis: University of Minnesota Press.

Sen, Amartya K. (1967). "Isolation, Assurance and the Social Rate of Discount." *The Quarterly Journal of Economics* 81: 112–24.

(1974). "Choice, Orderings and Morality." In Stephen Körner (ed.), *Practical Reason*. New Haven, Conn.: Yale University Press.

(1977). "Rational Fools: A Critique of the Behavioral Foundations of Economic Theory." *Philosophy and Public Affairs* 6: 317–44.

Shaw, William H. (1978). *Marx's Theory of History.* Stanford, Calif.: Stanford University Press.

(1982). "Prisoners, Proletarians, and Paradox." In Michael Bradie and Kenneth Sayre (eds.), *Reason and Decision.* Bowling Green, Ohio: Applied Philosophy Program, Bowling Green State University.

Silver, Morris (1974). "Political Revolution and Repression: An Economic Approach." *Public Choice* 17: 63–71.

Simmons, A. John (1979). "The Principle of Fair Play." *Philosophy and Public Affairs* 8: 307–37.

Strang, Colin (1968). "What If Everyone Did That?" In Judith J. Thomson and Gerald Dworkin (eds.), *Ethics.* New York: Harper & Row.

Tuck, Richard (1979). "Is There a Free-Rider Problem?" In Ross Harrison (ed.), *Rational Action.* Cambridge: Cambridge University Press.

Tullock, Gordon (1967). "The Prisoner's Dilemma and Mutual Trust." *Ethics* 77: 229–30.

(1971). "The Paradox of Revolution." *Public Choice* 11: 89–99.

Watkins, John (1970). "Imperfect Rationality." In Robert Borger and Frank Cioffi (eds.), *Explanation in the Behavioral Sciences.* Cambridge: Cambridge University Press.

CHAPTER 2

Historical materialism and economic backwardness

JON ELSTER

The central paradox of Marx's theory of history is that when the communist revolution he said would occur finally did occur, it did so in backward agrarian countries rather than in industrially advanced countries. I discuss here how Marx and some later Marxists have understood the problem of revolution in backward countries. Section I proposes a general account of the notion of economic backwardness, suggesting that it typically involves a theory of change as well as criteria for progress. Section II has an overview of Marx's main periodizations of history, relating them to the framework set out in Section I. Section III raises the issue of revolution in backward countries, with emphasis on 1848 and 1917. The argument is summarized in Section IV.

I. BACKWARDNESS IN HISTORY

The notion of backwardness is ambiguous in that it can be defined either with respect to a *theory of development* or with respect to a *criterion of progress*. I shall be concerned only with accounts that embody both, creating the possibility of a tension between the two perspectives on backwardness.

A theory of economic development involves a series of stages or states through which the process must necessarily, or normally, pass. In addition to Marx's theory, Rostow's "stages of economic growth" or Durkheim's theory of increasing functional differentiation may

I am grateful to G. A. Cohen, Gunner Opeide, John Roemer, and Øyvind Østerud for their comments on an earlier version of this paper.

serve as examples. We may classify such theories according to two different perspectives. We may ask, first, whether the development is in some sense also a progress, that is, if each stage ranks higher than its predecessor on some scale of perfection; and, secondly, whether the theory applies to each exemplar (e.g. nation-state) of the entity undergoing development.

The main answers to the first question can be stated with geometrical metaphors: The successive stages may form a linear, a circular, or a spirallike movement. The spiral for our purpose is a combination of line and circle; it returns toward the origin, but at ever-higher levels. It may also be characterized as a cycle superimposed on an upward trend, or as a progression of the form "One step backward, two steps forward." Vico is often credited with the invention of the spiral theory of history, but the view was stated before him, with unsurpassable precision, by Leibniz.[1] Observe that a given sequence of stages may be linear, circular, or spiral according to the criterion of progress that is chosen. Thus Tocqueville and Schumpeter argued that, respectively, democracy and capitalism were progressive as concerns the creation of resources, but not as concerns the efficient use of given resources (Schumpeter 1961: 83; Cf. also Schumpeter 1939: 496; Tocqueville 1969: 88, 224). John Roemer similarly argues that relations of production that are progressive with respect to the development of the productive forces need not be so with respect to exploitation.[2] Or, more simply, a regular growth in GNP per capita need not go together with a regular growth in consumption per capita.

According to the spiral theory of history, development takes the form of growth, setbacks, and more growth. Since we are dealing here with *theories* of history, not simply with descriptions, the setbacks cannot be mere accidents. They must be necessary, either in the sense of being *indispensable means* to the next step forward, or in the sense of being *inevitable by-products* of the previous step forward.

[1] The relevant passages are quoted and discussed in Elster (1975: Chap. VI).

[2] Roemer (1982); cf. also his contribution to the present volume (chap. 9). One may argue, that is, either that a given set of relations of production is progressive as long as the relations are optimal for the development of the productive forces, or that they are so as long as the exploitation they entail could not be abolished without making the exploited worse off. For a confusion of these two senses, see Ste Croix (1981: 112).

The first idea is graphically expressed as *reculer pour mieux sauter,* and may be exemplified by the case of investment. If the criterion for progressiveness is consumption per capita, then less consumption now may be needed for investment and more consumption later. This, as it were, has the pattern "One step backward, two steps forward." The pattern may also be "Two steps forward, one step backward," as in Kaldor's Schumpeterian theory of the business cycle (Kaldor 1954). He argues that entrepreneurs tend to be over-optimistic and invest more than is rationally warranted, but that the ensuing slump does not do away with all that was gained in the upswing. Observe that if the pattern is of the first kind, there is a temptation to *explain* the setbacks by their beneficial consequences for further progress. Unless one is prepared to see a divine design in history, the temptation should be firmly resisted. There is no nonintentional mechanism that could induce temporary retreats as a means to long-term gains (see also Elster 1979: chap. 1).

The second question can also be answered in three main ways. For the sake of specificity, we now assume that we are dealing with several nations within a wider geographical area, for which some theory of stages has been proposed. Excluding the notion that all nations could move in parallel through the same stages, we may focus on three possibilities. (1) All nations go through the same stages in the same order, although different nations will reach a given stage at different times. This we may call *the model of unique development.* (2) For one country to be in stage n, at least one country, not necessarily the same, must already have passed through stage n-1. We may refer to this as *the model of bloc development.* (3) If one country is the first to arrive at stage n, then it is necessarily another country that is the first to arrive at stage $n+1$. Following Ernest Gellner, we may refer to this as *the torch relay model of development* (Gellner 1980). Of these, the first and the third are polar cases. The second is compatible with both, but it may also assume a form that differs from each.

I shall not go into the tedious detail of crossing the trichotomy of answers to the first question with the trichotomy of answers to the second, but only note the following connections. First, the often-used expression "unilinear development" may plausibly be understood as a form of unique development exhibiting uninterrupted progress. Secondly, a combination of the torch-relay model and a development of the form "One step backward, two steps forward" corresponds to the notion of *sacrifice* in history. Thirdly, there is often a tension between

the model of unique development and the idea of progress inter-
rupted by temporary setbacks. This is related to the second point: If
one nation has gone through purgatory, must others follow in its
step – or can they enjoy the advantages of backwardness?

I shall say that a country is backward relative to another, and with
respect to a given sequence of stages, if at a given time it is at an
earlier stage than that other country. And I shall use "advanced" as
the antonym of "backward." A country is regressive relative to
another country, and with respect to a given criterion of performance, if at a given time it performs less well than that other country. And I shall use "progressive" as the antonym of "regressive." It
follows from what has been said that of two countries at a given
time, one may be both advanced and regressive, if it is engaged in a
necessary step backward that the other has not yet begun taking.
Clearly, this can cause considerable intellectual confusion, creating
simultaneous feelings of superiority and inferiority in the backward
country (see, e.g., Feuerwerker 1968). These terms can also be used
to compare successive states of a given country: It can advance along
the sequence of stages, and it can progress or regress according to
the criterion for performance. It can even move backward in the
sequence of stages, as in the phenomenon of "deindustrialization."[3]

The notion of backwardness may be used to characterize development or, more ambitiously, to explain it. If the advanced and the
backward countries do not interact, the fact that one is backward will
not explain the peculiarities of its development. It is awkward to say,
as does Anthony Tang, that in the pre-modern era Europe enjoyed
advantages of backwardness compared to China, when all he means
is that they were on different trajectories, one of which involved fast
initial growth and a later slowing down, with the other following the
opposite pattern (Tang 1979). The explanatory interest of backwardness arises in the cases in which the development of the backward country would have followed a different course in the absence
of the advanced countries, and for this some interaction between
them must occur. The two main forms of interaction would appear
to be *borrowing* and *learning*. By borrowing I mean the flow of
workers and goods from one country to another, by learning the
flow of (disembodied) information and ideas – including political
ideas. In his comparative study of German and English industrializa-

---

[3] On the deindustrialization of India by the British, see Maddison (1971:
53 ff).

tion, Thorstein Veblen argued that England overcame Germany by borrowing rather than learning, whereas later Germany was able to reverse the situation more rapidly by taking over theoretical knowledge rather than skilled artisans (Veblen 1939: 199, 187–92). Clearly, a crucial factor is whether the backward country has men and women capable of learning or whether these have to be borrowed as well.

How can backwardness make a difference? First, any given stage may be of shorter duration, or longer, or even indefinite. A backward country may be able to skip stages, or on the contrary be unable to leave the stage at which it finds itself. Secondly, backwardness may make for solutions that differ in qualitative rather than in quantitative respects. Thus Alexander Gerschenkron has argued that the banks in Germany and the state in Russia had to perform the task that in Britain was undertaken by private industry, because these countries entered the process of industrialization at a time when England was far ahead (Gerschenkron 1966). More specifically, a country may enjoy *advantages of backwardness,* a term also coined by Veblen. The backward country could use the innovations made by the pioneer in their most rational and general form, whereas the forerunner was irreversibly committed to inferior forms, thereby paying "the penalty for taking the lead."[4] Before Veblen, and probably unknown to him, Herzen and Chernyshevsky had also stated that Russia might enjoy these advantages, although unlike him they did not suggest a mechanism to bring it about (Venturi 1966). Later this was provided by Trotsky, although with respect to a somewhat different problem, as we shall see.

Today, of course, we are more struck by the *disadvantages* of backwardness. This is, however, a phase in need of clarification. It can mean that the backward countries are experiencing a deterioration in absolute terms of their standard of living, because of their interaction with the developed countries; or that they progress more slowly than they would otherwise have done; or finally that the gap that separates them from the developed countries is widening rather than narrowing. Of these, the relevant comparison is with the counterfactual development, not with the earlier state or with that of the advanced countries. It is also, of course, far less amenable to uncontroversial

---

[4] As noted by Rosenberg (1976), knowledge of this fact may act as a deterrent from taking the lead, with the effect that nobody can enjoy the advantages of backwardness either.

assessment than the others. It is nevertheless possible to identify some mechanisms that work in the disfavor of the contemporary backward nations. First, in the race between innovators and imitators the prizes increasingly go to the former. When the imitators catch up, the innovators have moved on. Second, to imitate one must have reached a certain level of development at which one is able to put the techniques taken over to good use. What the backward country would most need, and could best use, is often knowledge or technology corresponding to a stage that the advanced countries have left behind themselves. It is in the nature of the case, however, that such outdated knowledge may no longer exist in suitable form, and in any case the pride of the backward country may prevent adoption of any but the most modern techniques. Third, there are political factors at work that create impatience in the developing countries. It is, in fact, much easier to assimilate the Western revolutionary ideologies than to absorb Western techniques. Hence it may not be politically possible to create the conditions under which the techniques could be mastered.

II. MARX'S PERIODIZATIONS OF HISTORY

Marx had a philosophy of history in which were embedded several theories of history. By a philosophy of history I mean a speculative scheme, asserted on a priori grounds and with deterministic implications for the future. By a theory of history I mean a causal account of how societies in the past have developed and changed, with at most probabilistic implications for the future. True, in Marx the speculative and the causal accounts are so intertwined that the distinction has mainly heuristic value, but to some extent it also corresponds to distinct and in fact opposed strands in his thought.

The overriding speculative scheme is that of a negation of the negation, most clearly stated in the following passage:

The original unity between the worker and the conditions of production (abstracting from slavery, where the labourer himself belongs to the objective conditions) has two main forms: the Asiatic communal system (primitive communism) and small-scale agriculture based on the family (and linked with domestic industry) in one form or another. Both are embryonic forms and both are equally unfitted to develop labour as *social* labour and the productive power of social labour. Hence the necessity for the separation, for the rupture, for the antithesis of labour and property (by which property in the conditions of production is understood). The most extreme form of this rupture, and the one in which the productive forces of social labour are also most powerfully developed, is capital. The original unity can be reestablished only on the material foundations which capital creates and by means of the revolutions which, in the process of this creation, the working class and the whole society undergoes. (Marx 1969, vol. 3: 422–3)

In some respects this development represents progress mediated by temporary setbacks, viz., as regards social integration and the all-sided development of the individual. Primitive communism is characterized by mechanical solidarity: People are held together by similarity rather than by a conscious feeling of community; each individual can do everything that others can, but they can all do very few things. The splitting asunder of this undifferentiated unity, and the one-sided specialization of the individual, constitutes a necessary stage on the road to the higher communist society, in which the unity is reasserted on a more solid basis and the all-sidedness developed on a much larger scale. In another respect the development shows uninterrupted progress, viz., as regards the productivity of labor. Whereas the development of individual *men* suffers a setback during the middle passage, that of *man* is constantly progressing with the increasing mastery over nature.[5] The rupture introduced by class society is a condition for increased productivity of labor, and the abolition of the rupture a condition for the further increase that will occur under communism.

The productive forces progress not only in the transition from pre-class society and in that from class to post-class society, but also in the transition from one form of class society to another. Moreover, it can be argued that one mode of production replaces another when and because the earlier mode ceases to be the best vehicle for the development of the productive forces: The criterion for progress is also the explanatory factor in the theory of development. Such at least is the interpretation proposed by G. A. Cohen (1978: chap. VI and passim), which I accept subject to three provisos. First, there is a need to distinguish much more clearly than he does between the propensity of the relations of production to promote the *development* of the productive forces and their tendency to promote their efficient *use*. Secondly, one must remove the ambiguity between the view that new relations of production emerge when and because the existing ones prevent *any* development of the productive forces, and the view that they prevent their *optimal* development. There is evidence for both views in Marx, but I believe that the latter

---

[5] For this distinction, see Cohen (1974).

is the more plausible reading.[6] This is also the view that provides the framework for the discussion in Part III. Thirdly, Marx appears to say not only that the relations of production change when and because they no longer optimally develop the productive forces, but also that they change because of a change in the latter. Philippe Van Parijs has shown that these views do not contradict one another, since the change in the productive forces may lead to a change in what relations are optimal for the further development of the forces (see chap. 4 of this volume).

Marx, then, held a linear theory of the modes of production, judged by the criterion of productivity. Did he also hold a unilinear theory? The evidence is ambiguous. On the one hand some very early and very late texts appear to suggest the possibility for some nations of skipping the stage of capitalism, but on the other hand there are passages in *The German Ideology* and *Capital*, vol. I that point to a different view. In the early commentary on Friedrich List the model of unique development is denied in the most explicit terms one could wish for. Having observed that "industry can be regarded as the great workshop in which man first takes possession of his own forces and the forces of nature," Marx goes on to issue a warning against unilinear conceptions:

To hold that every nation goes through this development internally would be as absurd as the idea that every nation is bound to go through the political development of France or the philosophical development of Germany. What the nations have done as nations, they have done for human society; their whole value consists only in the fact that each single nation has accomplished for the benefit of other nations one of the main historical aspects (one of the main determinations) in the framework of which mankind has accomplished its development, and thereafter industry in England, politics in France and philosophy in Germany have been developed, they have been developed for the world, and their world-historic significance, as also that of these nations, has thereby come to an end. (Marx 1975: 281)

Against this we may set the Preface to *Capital*, vol. I in which the model of unique development is asserted just as unambiguously:

In this work I have to examine the capitalist mode of production, and the conditions of production and exchange corresponding to that mode. Up to the present time, their classic ground is England. That is the reason why England is used as the chief illustration in the development of my theoretical ideas. If however, the German reader shrugs his shoulders at the condi-

---

[6] Contra Richard Miller's contribution to this volume (see chap. 3). The arguments for my interpretation are set out in chap. 5 of my *Karl Marx: A Critical Examination* forthcoming from Cambridge University Press.

tion of the English industrial and agricultural labourers, or in optimist fashion comforts himself with the thought that in Germany things are not nearly so bad, I must plainly tell him, "De te fabula narratur!" Intrinsically, it is not a question of the higher or lower degree of development of the social antagonisms that result from the natural laws of capitalism. It is a question of these laws themselves, of these tendencies working with iron necessity towards inevitable results. The country that is the more advanced industrially only shows, to the less developed, the image of its own future . . . One nation can and should learn from others. And even when a society has got upon the right track for the discovery of the natural laws of its movement—and it is the ultimate aim of this work, to lay bare the economic laws of motion of modern society—it can neither clear by bold leaps, nor remove by legal enactments, the obstacles offered by the successive phases of its normal development. But it can shorten and lessen the birth-pangs. (Marx 1967, vol. I: 8)

This passage combines a certain kind of scientism with the model of unique development, modified only by the possibility that the latecomers may spend less time in the successive stages than did the pioneers. In his reflections on Russian socialism toward the end of his life Marx abandoned this view and embraced explicitly Chernyshevsky's idea that Russia could "appropriate all the fruits of [the capitalist regime] without going through all its tortures" (Marx 1962). The drafts of a letter to Vera Zasulich show him pondering the pros and the cons of this idea (Marx 1971). He admits that if Russia were isolated in the world, it would have to undergo all the stages of capitalist development, with the subsequent disappearance of the commune on which the Russian socialists based their hope. He also admits that there are strong forces in Russia that conspire toward the elimination of the commune, notably the alliance between the state and a capitalist class that is supported by the state at the expense of the peasantry. Yet the existence of capitalism also holds out a hope for the commune, which can take over the advanced methods developed in Western Europe: "It can obtain the fruits with which capitalist production has enriched humanity without passing through the capitalist regime." He raises and tries to answer various objections to this proposal. To those who point to the universal elimination of all earlier communes, he holds out that the Russian commune is more flexible because liberated from the bonds of kinship, and more individualistic because containing an element of private property. Concerning the isolation of the communes from one another, he says that this could be suppressed by the simple administrative measure of creating a peasant assembly.

To an implied objection concerning the lack of capital for the transformation of the commune, he answers by asserting that the Russian society "owes" it to the commune at whose expense it has been living.

These are not powerful arguments. They are, in fact, so weak that they underline the essential correctness of the position from the Preface (or at least part of that position). The main objection is that set out in Section I, namely, that the ability to learn already presupposes a fairly advanced stage of development that can only be reached endogenously. There is strong parallel here to the notion of appropriation by conquest, which can succeed only if the conquering country is adapted to the conditions in the conquered country. True, the conqueror may begin by living off the riches of the conquered, but

there is very soon an end to taking, and when there is nothing more to take, you have to set about producing. From this necessity of producing, which very soon asserts itself, it follows that the form of community adopted by the settling conquerors must correspond to the stage of development of the productive forces they find in existence. (Marx 1976: 85)

When I stated that this argument vindicates only *part* of the argument for unilinearity, I had in mind the following. Marx was concerned about the conditions for a transition to communism and argued that these had in the main to be created within each individual country. Their creation might be accelerated by learning, but they could not just be taken over wholesale from more advanced countries. This argument is valid as a statement about necessary conditions, but not as a statement about causal necessity. Nations might well be so wrong-headed as to try to take a shortcut to communism and hence block the process that could have brought it about. With his teleological philosophy of history Marx tended to neglect this possibility. What I called his scientism derives ultimately from his firm belief in the necessary advent of communism, combined with his sound insight into some of its necessary conditions.

I shall pursue some of these issues later. First, however, I want to conclude the present section with a few remarks about an alternative periodization of history that is found in Marx's mature economic writings, where it does in fact play a more important role than the periodization in terms of modes of production. This is a quasi-dialectical, quasi-historical chain of stages that occurs twice in the history of mankind. It can be broken down in five main steps.[7] In the *first stage* production occurs only for the subsistence needs of the producers. Production and consumption may be organized more or less communally, more or less individually, but the immediate purpose always is satisfaction of the immediate needs of the producers. There may be private property, but neither trade nor investment nor extraction of surplus labor takes place. The *second stage* is marked by the emergence of trade between such primitive communities, when their members meet accidentally and exchange their surpluses with one another. The *third stage* is reached when trade, from being accidental, becomes regular, so that the goods exchanged become *commodities*. Part of the production has now become production of exchange value, so that the purpose of production has changed. The ultimate goal is still the satisfaction of individual needs, but this is mediated by production for exchange as the proximate purpose. In the *fourth stage* commodity production is generalized. The exchange between communities reacts back on the communities themselves and gives rise to intracommunity exchange. Finally, the *fifth stage* is the emergence of production for surplus value, largely dissociated from the goal of wants satisfaction.

This sequence occurs twice in the history of mankind. The first time it begins in the oriental commune, with the second, third, and fourth stages corresponding to various stages in early Greco-Roman history and the fifth stage being commercial slavery production. The second time it begins with the subsistence production of isolated peasant communities attached to a manor. Long-distance trade emerges and, as in the first case, reacts back on the internal production, leading to the creation of independent peasants and artisans producing for the market. The inherent instability and vulnerability of such "simple commodity production" lead to its breakdown and the subsequent rise of capitalism. Broadly speaking, the first occurrence of the sequence corresponds to the Asiatic and the ancient modes of production, the second to the feudal and capitalist modes. This is not a circular theory of history, since the second occurrence of the sequence differs from the first, because of the increase in the productivity of labor that has taken place. We are dealing with a cycle superimposed on a linear trend, combining to form a spirallike progression. Presumably the rise of surplus value in each occurrence of

---

[7] The textual evidence for imputing this periodization to Marx is given in the work cited in note 6.

the sequence is to be explained by the impetus on the productive forces, although Marx at times appears to suggest that it has an autonomous, "dialectical" explanation.[8]

From the present point of view, the interest of this periodization is that it suggests how nations may skip a stage in the sequence of modes of production. Since, for instance, the Asiatic mode of production represents an embryonic form of feudalism, the direct transition from the former to capitalism becomes more easily understandable. This, for instance, is what Marx predicted would take place as a result of the British rule in India (Marx 1979). For more substantive, nonexegetical purposes the value of the periodization consists in the priority it accords to long-distance trade over local or national trade. Karl Polanyi, who made this thesis into a cornerstone of his theories, attributed it to Max Weber, apparently ignoring its centrality in Marx (Polanyi 1977: 78).

III. BACKWARDNESS AND THE COMMUNIST REVOLUTION

According to the canonical Preface to *A Critique of Political Economy* and various passages in *The German Ideology,* the communist revolution will occur *when and because* there arises a contradiction between the productive forces and the relations of production. As I understand this view, it means that the revolution will occur when and because the capitalist relations of production become less good at developing the productive forces than communist relations would be. I shall first consider this view, in the form just stated and in a modified version that relaxes the temporal clause, by allowing communism to be set up before it is actually superior to capitalism. In either version the view is quite implausible. Next, a more drastic modification is suggested, by weakening the causal force of "because" to a mere correlation between the development of the productive forces and the revolution. This version also turns out to be implausible, because one basic premise has not been verified by history. Nor, finally, does Marx make it more plausible by introducing a scenario in which the revolution occurs through interaction between the advanced and the backward capitalist countries.

[8] In Marx (1973: 270) or in Marx (1967, vol. I: 151–2) he tries to deduce the notion of capital from that of money, by arguing that money inherently is in need of self-expansion. Elsewhere (e.g., Marx 1967, vol. III 599) he offers the more reasonable argument that an economy based on market exchange without wage labor is inherently unstable.

The discussion will be conducted within a formal model of the transition to communism, more fully presented eleswhere (Elster 1983: App. 2). It assumes that the following time trajectories of the productive forces can be defined. First, we need to know the level of the productive forces under capitalism as a function of time. This function, $f(t)$, must be defined both for the actual capitalist past and for a – possibly hypothetical – capitalist future. If the communist revolution occurs because capitalism has become suboptimal for the development of the forces, we must be able to say something about how the forces would have developed under a continued capitalist regime. Next, assuming that a communist revolution occurs at time s, $f_s(t)$ denotes the level of productivity that would obtain at time t ($t > s$). Again, if communism is to be preferred because it is better for the development of the productive forces, it must be possible to trace out some trajectory of this kind.

In addition to various continuity and consistency requirements, the model rests on two substantive assumptions: the initial indispensability of capitalism and the ultimate superiority of communism. The first says that there exists a time s and a number A such that for all t, $f_s(t) < A$. The second states that there exists a time s such that for all $t > s$, $f_s(t) > f(t)$. To say that the revolution will occur when and because the capitalist relations become suboptimal is to say that it will occur at the earliest time s satisfying the last condition. Let us call this time T_1. It is not obvious that transition at time T is a very attractive ideal, quite independently of the capacity of the suboptimality to motivate workers to action. If this transition time is advocated, it must be because the rapid development of the productive forces is seen as the only argument for communism. This, however, was not Marx's view. Rather, he stressed the free development of the individual – of which the growth of the productive forces is but one aspect – as the main reason for preferring communism. Hence it would seem reasonable to allow the revolution to occur earlier than T_1, if one were certain that the development of the productive forces would ultimately overtake that which would have occurred under capitalism. Formally, we ask whether there is a time $s < T_1$ and a time $s' > s$ such that for all $t > s'$, $f_s(t) > f(t)$, even if by assumption $f_s(s) < f(s)$. If this is the case, we define T_2 as the earliest such s. Clearly, for any s between T_2 and T_1, $f_s(T_1) < f_{T_1}(T_1)$: Preferring an earlier transition time will postpone the time at which communism becomes superior. Hence there is a tradeoff to be considered: Should the material conditions for communism be developed by capitalism, which is the more rapid way, or should one prefer the slower development whereby communism itself creates the conditions for its own future bloom?

If communist conditions are valued for themselves, the second of these options should be taken. Yet one might not want the revolution to occur as early as T_2, if that implies a very long time to catch up with capitalism. It might be better to have a few generations endure the hardships of capitalism than to have many generations live under comparatively poor communist conditions. Needless to say, these considerations have at best a tenuous relevance for political action. Some arguments of this kind may have underlain the debate between Mensheviks and Bolsheviks about the proper communist strategy in a country that had not yet developed capitalism, but I would not expect to find any precise statement of these alternatives. The discussion makes sense mainly from a welfare-theoretical point of view: How would we evaluate the various times between T_2 and T_1 with respect to the maximization of the self-realization of individuals? Communism with undeveloped productive forces may allow somewhat more self-realization than capitalism with more highly developed forces, yet much less than highly developed communism.

I now turn to the issue, already briefly alluded to, of the relevance of suboptimality for political action. I shall assume for that purpose the validity of Marx's basic assumption of the ultimate superiority of communism, in spite of the objections that can be made against this postulate. (Observe, however, that the obvious failure of the actual communist countries to overtake capitalism is not relevant here. In the model this can be interpreted by saying that the revolution in these countries occurred too early – before T_1 and possibly before T_2.) Yet even an objectively valid theory needs subjective acceptance if it is to become a revolutionary force. I submit that it is highly implausible to believe that the workers will accept the assumption to the extent of acting on it. The counterfactual nature of the baseline for evaluating capitalist performance makes the theory too abstract to serve as a basis for action. If one could point to a declining performance over time, this might create an incentive to change the system, but I believe that according to Marx the development of the productive forces under capitalism occurred at an ever-faster rate; hence this cannot provide the necessary motivation. If one could compare the existing capitalist system in one country with an existing communist regime in another, then the proven superiority of the latter might motivate the transition to communism in the former,

49

but of course this argument would not hold for the crucial first country to set up communist relations of production. Internal crises or external examples may suffice to topple a regime, but not the abstract possibility of a superior way of doing things.[9]

Let me, however, pursue a bit further the motivation provided by an external example. The idea is that the superiority of communism would explain its emergence in all countries but the first in which it arose. In that country the explanation must be a different one, to be discussed later. The appearance of communism on the world-historical scene could be more or less accidental, but its subsequent diffusion would be rationally grounded. This, for instance, would provide a support for the functional explanation offered by Cohen, although a different one from the mechanism suggested in his book.[10] A presupposition of this view, however, is that the revolution should not occur too early in the first country. Having dismissed the idea that communism will occur in the pioneer country *because* it is more efficient, it remains essential that it should occur at a moment *when* communism can (immediately or ultimately) overtake capitalism, since otherwise there will be no success to inspire the latecomers. "But societies are not so rational in building that the dates for proletarian dictatorship arrive exactly at that moment when the economic and cultural conditions are ripe for socialism" (Trotsky 1977: 334). In fact, they are so irrational that these dates tend not to coincide, as will be argued later.

I shall now consider the weaker claim that the suboptimality of the capitalist relations of production is causally correlated with the subjective conditions for a communist revolution, both of them being the result of the development of the productive forces to a certain level. In *The German Ideology* Marx states the link between the subjective conditions and the productive forces as follows:

This "estrangement" (to use a term which will be comprehensible to the philosophers) can, of course, only be abolished given two *practical* premises. In order to become an "unendurable" power, i.e. a power against which men make a revolution, it must necessarily have rendered the great mass of humanity "propertyless," and moreover in contradiction to an existing world

9   My colleague Francis Sejersted had provided an anecdotal illustration: The Norwegian Conservative party in 1961 understandably had little success when *in opposition* they adopted the slogan that the British Conservatives and later the Danish Social Democrats successfully used *in power:* "Make good times better!"

10 The mechanism is briefly stated in Cohen (1978: 129–3). See also William Shaw, chap. 1 in this volume.

of wealth and culture; both of these premises presuppose a great increase in productive power, a high degree of its development. (Marx 1976: 48–9)

This argument is, of course, incompatible with the idea that the revolution occurs when *and because* the relations of production become suboptimal for the further development of the productive forces. (It is, however, compatible with another interpretation of the notion of a contradiction between relations and forces, in terms of the suboptimal *use* of the latter. Although there are passages in Marx that suggest this interpretation, it is not supported by the most important theoretical texts.) Yet for many purposes it is sufficient that there should be a correlation between the development of the productive forces to a level at which communism becomes superior for their further development, and the emergence of poverty and alienation that will motivate people to overthrow capitalism. If this correlation could be made to look plausible, we might abandon the general theory without too many qualms. I believe, however, that it is inherently implausible and in fact disproved by the historical evidence. The motivation to abolish capitalism has become weaker, not stronger, with the development of the productive forces, since that development has largely been seen as benefiting the workers. True, one may put one's trust in further capitalist crises, possibly leading to wars between capitalist countries. If these occurred, one would not have to count on increasing misery and alienation to being about communism. This is what socialists have been perversely wanting for a century; I submit that it is time to learn from the historical record that one cannot count on any such events occurring. This is not to say that we can inductively infer that they will not occur, only that socialists should be aware of their own strong tendencies toward wishful thinking in these matters.

Let me state my argument as precisely as I can. First, note that the idea of a successful communist revolution can mean two distinct things. It can refer to success in setting up communist relations of production, and it can also refer to success in generating a technical progress that immediately or ultimately overtakes that of capitalism. We have seen that for success in the second sense the revolution must occur after T_1 if the criterion is instantaneous superiority, and after T_2 if it is ultimate superiority. Similarly we may define a time T_3 in the development of capitalism that represents the earliest time at which the subjective conditions for a communist revolution, that is, for success in the first sense, are present. In particular, the proletariat itself must have achieved a certain size before it can think of taking power. Following the foregoing line of argument, we may also define a time T_4 that represents the latest time at which these subjective conditions are present. The development of capitalism at some stage creates a level of welfare such that the motivation for revolution can no longer be sustained. One might deny that any such time T_4 exists, since it is always possible that a debilitating crisis might occur, but I think that one should ignore this possibility so long as it is not grounded in robust theoretical arguments.

We may now consider various possibilities. If $T_3 < T_1$, the revolution might occur prematurely according to the "immediate superiority" criterion; if $T_3 < T_2$, it might come too early, even according to the weaker criterion of ultimate superiority. It might, but of course it need not. The task of the proletarian leadership would then be to stave off the revolution until the objective conditions have been created. If, however, $T_4 < T_2$, any revolution would necessarily be premature in the strong sense that it could never lead to a superior communist system. In that case societies would indeed be irrational in their building – and I believe that this may very well be the case. With $T_2 < T_1$, the revolution would be premature only with respect to the criterion of immediate success. Even in that case, however, one should ask whether the transition occurs too early according to the welfare-theoretical considerations mentioned previously. Consider the Soviet Union. The October Revolution may well have been premature in the strongest sense, so that the communist world is locked into an ever-lasting inferiority. It may turn out, however, that at some time in the future these countries succeed in overtaking capitalism, and yet one might want to say that the revolution occurred too early since it necessitated the sacrifice of many generations.

Marx was not unaware of this issue. He did not, however, confront it in terms of successive stages of development of the same country, but by considering different countries that at the same time had reached different levels of development, so that in some countries the objective conditions and in others the subjective conditions for revolution were present. Consider first a passage from *The German Ideology:*

Thus all collisions in history have their origin, according to our view, in the contradiction between the productive forces and the form of intercourse. Incidentally, to lead to collisions in a country, the contradiction need not necessarily have reached its extreme limit in that particular country. The competition with industrially more advanced countries brought about by the expansion of international intercourse, is sufficient to produce a similar contradiction in countries with a less advanced industry (e.g. the latent proletariat in Germany brought into more prominence by the competition of English industry). (Marx 1976: 74–5)

Despite some ambiguity, the thrust of the passage is clear enough. In England, the productive forces have developed so far that capitalism is no longer optimal for their further development. In Germany this is not yet the case, and nevertheless its backward situation exposes it to revolution, possibly more so than England. A few years later these tentative propositions have hardened into a general theory:

Just as the period of crisis occurs later on the Continent than in England, so does that of prosperity. The original process always takes place in England, it is the demiurge of the bourgeois cosmos . . . While, therefore, the crises first produce revolutions on the Continent, the foundations for these is, nevertheless, always laid in England. Violent outbreaks must naturally occur rather in the extremities of the bourgeois body than in its heart, since the possibility of adjustment is greater here than there. (Marx, 1978: 134)

In itself this does not solve the problem. The argument is open to two objections. First, even accepting that development of the productive forces in the advanced countries brings about hardships for the backward ones, the synchronization might still not be perfect: It might not be the case that these hardships become "unendurable" only when the development has advanced to the point of making communism superior – immediately or ultimately – for the further development. Secondly, we must ask what difference it would make even were the two processes perfectly synchronized. A viable communism in one country requires a communist revolution in that country. Nothing so far would exclude the conclusion that England in 1850 was too advanced for a successful communist *revolution*, and France or Germany too backward for a successful communist *regime*.

The first objection can be met by simply assuming that it is an empirical fact that the development in one country of the productive forces to the level necessary for a viable communist regime also leads to conditions in other countries that set in motion a process of communist revolution. The suboptimality of the capitalist relations of production in the first country would play no causal role in that revolution, but would be a concomitant feature of the development leading to it. The second objection can be met by arguing that the revolution will spread from the backward countries in which it occurs to the advanced countries in which it can lead to durable achievements. Immediately after the last-quoted passage Marx goes on to say that "the degree to which the Continental revolution reacts back

53

on England is at the same time a thermometer which indicates how far these revolutions really call in question the bourgeois conditions of life, or how far they only hit their political formations." Elsewhere in the same work he prophesies that "the class war within French society turns into a world war, in which the nations confront one another. Accomplishment begins only when, through the world war, the proletariat is pushed to the fore in the nation which dominates the world market, to the forefront in England" (Marx 1978: 117).

This argument does not have the same central place in Marx's work as the view that suboptimality of capitalist relations and poverty will proceed *pari passu* in the same country. His more general theoretical texts suggest that the revolution will come about because of class struggle within the advanced capitalist countries, with no need for an external ignition. Yet if one comes to reject the wholly endogenous theory, on the grounds that $T_4 < T_2$, the diffusion scenario provides an alternative and less vulnerable account. It is, however, beset with difficulties of its own. In particular, the advanced capitalist countries might well resist their historical mission of engaging in counterrevolutionary wars against the communist countries. After all, if Marx and Trotsky could see that this would be the downfall of capitalism, why should not the leaders of these countries also be able to understand it?

I now discuss in more detail the possibility that $T_3 < T_2 < T_4$. I have asserted that this may, but need not, lead to an irreversible and premature commitment to communism. I now want to add some reasons why this might in fact be expected to happen, at least if we are considering a backward country. In such countries the development of working-class organizations will often be in advance of the development of capitalism. The implantation of socialist ideas can proceed more rapidly than the accumulation of capital. Trotsky explained very well why this was so:

In Russia the proletariat did not arise gradually through the ages, carrying with itself the burden of the past as in England, but in leaps involving sharp changes of environment, ties, relations, and a sharp break with the past. It is just this fact – combined with the concentrated oppression of czarism – that made the Russian workers hospitable to the boldest conclusions of revolutionary thought. (Trotsky 1977: 33)

More specifically, Trotsky argued that the political importance of the proletariat depended not only on the proportion it formed of the nation, but also on "the amount of productive forces it sets in motion" – that is, on the size of the individual firm, assuming that size and capital intensity go together. Russia, being a latecomer to industrialization, was free to use the most advanced techniques of large-scale production, requiring huge numbers of workers who, firstly, were not burdened by a reformist past and, secondly, could draw upon the revolutionary ideologies developed in the West (see also Knei-Paz 1977:118).

Under such conditions there will typically be a great deal of impatience, and the workers will take the first occasion to overthrow capitalism. The working-class leaders, assuming them to understand the predicament, will then have the choice of two alternatives. They might try to stave off the revolution to T_2 (or to some acceptable time between T_2 and T_1), or to speed up the economic development to bring T_2 (or that acceptable date) closer to T_3. For easily understood reasons, Marxists have usually chosen the second, less quietist alternative, which has frequently involved helping the bourgeoisie to power in countries where a capitalist revolution has not yet taken place. This was Marx's policy in 1848, that of the Mensheviks before the October Revolution, and of the Chinese Communists up to the Shanghai massacre. As far as I know, it has invariably failed, for two closely related reasons. Once the workers have successfully engaged in a struggle against the feudal-absolutist-colonial regime, it will be difficult to prevent them from turning – prematurely – against their former ally, the bourgeoisie. Moreover, the bourgeoisie will tend to recognize this possibility and therefore be quite circumspect about any alliance with their future enemies. The only scenario that would satisfy the Marxist is one in which the workers successfully help the bourgeoisie to power, and then unsuccessfully try to replace them. This defeat will provide time for capitalist development and will harden the class consciousness of the workers for later struggles.[11] This, however, requires a quite delicate balance: The workers must be strong, yet not too strong; the bourgeoisie must be so weak that they need the help of the workers, yet not so weak that they cannot resist them. In practice it has not worked out.

One might well argue that the October Revolution is better explained in terms of this scenario, $T_3 < T_2 < T_4$, than by assuming that $T_4 < T_2$ or $T_2 < T_4 < T_1$. We would then have an explanation of the premature Russian Revolution in terms of the backwardness of Russian society, its existence as a backward country among more advanced nations. Left to itself, Russian society might not have experi-

---

[11] Compare the argument in Marx (1978: 47).

enced a revolution in the fateful interval between T_3 and T_2. By the foregoing mechanisms, however, the advanced countries may trigger a premature revolution in the backward countries, while being themselves immune to revolution because they have passed beyond T_4.

IV. SUMMARY AND CONCLUSION

My argument has been directed against the idea that the communist revolution will occur "when and because" capitalist relations of production become fetters on the productive forces, and against various weaker versions of the same claim. I have relied heavily on a specific, and contested, interpretation of the idea of fettering: It is a fettering of the development of the productive forces, not of their use; moreover, the fettering is defined in terms of a comparison with a counterfactual development of the forces under a communist system, not with the actual development during the earlier stage of capitalism. Given this interpretation, I have claimed that it is highly implausible to argue that the workers could be motivated by this abstractly defined suboptimality. (True, one might try to rescue the theory, in a way I have not yet mentioned, by suggesting that the suboptimality could cause people to be motivated to action, while not itself providing the motivation. For instance, members of the ruling class might perceive the suboptimality, and to prevent the exploited from perceiving it they might behave in a way that has as an unintended consequence that the exploited are motivated to revolution, although not because they perceive the suboptimality. This is indeed a logical possibility,[12] but in the absence of a more detailed argument it is just as unconvincing as the first version of the theory.)

The theory can be weakened by suggesting that revolution occurs *when* the relations become suboptimal, because this as a matter of fact also tends to bring about the subjective conditions for revolution. My argument against this proposal rested on the historical evidence for the contrary view: When the productive forces have been developed so highly that communism could plausibly be superior for their further development, one can no longer count on alienation, poverty, or crises to generate revolution. The notion of backwardness enters into a possible rebuttal of this counterargument: Revolution could occur first in the backward countries, precisely because they are backward and therefore suffer more from the vicissitudes

---

[12]   Related to an argument sketched in Cohen (1978: 169–71 ff).

of capitalism, and then spread to the advanced countries in which a viable communist regime could be set up. To this my objection was again of an empirical character: The capitalist nations have resisted their historical mission of engaging in counterrevolutionary wars against the communist countries.

Finally I considered the possibility that a country, left to itself, might in fact experience a communist revolution at a time when it would have been economically ripe for communism, but that the existence of more advanced countries triggers a premature transition to communism. As I have stated, I do not believe that a country left to itself would find the narrow window to a viable communism, but those who believe in that possibility might find the argument worth considering. And in any case the backwardness might explain that a revolution took place at all, and so blocked the development to a viable capitalism. What Trotsky saw as an advantage of backwardness, viz., the creation of conditions that favor a communist revolution, may in the end turn out to have been yet another disadvantage.[13]

REFERENCES

Cohen, G. A. (1974). "Marx's Dialectic of Labor." *Philosophy and Public Affairs* 3: 235–61.
  (1978). *Karl Marx's Theory of History: A Defence*. Oxford: Oxford University Press.
Elster, J. (1975). *Leibniz et la Formation de l'Esprit Capitaliste*. Paris: Aubier-Montaigne.
  (1979). *Ulysses and the Sirens*. Cambridge: Cambridge University Press.
  (1983). *Explaining Technical Change: A Case Study in the Philosophy of Science*. Cambridge: Cambridge University Press.
Feuerwerker, A. (1968). "China's Modern Economic History in Communist Chinese Historiography." In A. Feuerwerker (ed.), *History in Communist China*. Cambridge, Mass.: MIT Press.
Gellner, E. (1980). "A Russian Marxist Philosophy of History." In E. Gellner (ed.), *Soviet and Western Anthropology*. New York: Columbia University Press.
Gerschenkron, A. (1966). *Economic Backwardness in Historical Perspective*. Cambridge, Mass.: Harvard University Press.

[13] To prevent misunderstandings, I should state that I have not offered the present argument as an objection to those who advocate the transition to some form of socialism or communism today. It is directed only against the classical doctrine that stresses (1) the technical superiority of communism, and (2) the need for a revolutionary transition. There are, however, other arguments for socialism and other ways of bringing it about.

Kaldor, N. (1954). "The Relation between Economic Growth and Cyclical Fluctuations." *Economic Journal* 64: 53–71.

Knei-Paz, B. (1977). *The Social and Political Thought of Leon Trotsky.* Oxford: Oxford University Press.

Maddison, A. (1971). *Class Structure and Economic Growth: India and Pakistan since the Moghuls.* London: Allen & Unwin.

Marx, K. (1962). Letter to the editors of "Otetschestwennyje Sapiski." In *Marx-Engels Werke,* vol. 19. Berlin: Dietz.

(1967). *Capital,* vols. I and III. New York: International Publishers.

(1969). *Theories of Surplus-Value.* 3 vols. London: Lawrence & Wishart.

(1971). Letters to Vera Zasulich. In D. Rjazanov (ed.), *Marx-Engels Archiv,* vol. I. 1881. Reprint. Erlangen: Politladen.

(1973). *Grundrisse.* Translated by M. Nicolaus. Harmondsworth: Penguin Books.

(1975). "On Friedrich List's book *Das Nationale System der politischen Oekonomie.*" In Marx and Engels, *Collected Works,* vol. 4. London: Lawrence & Wishart.

(1976). *The German Ideology.* In Marx and Engels, *Collected Works,* vol. 5. London: Lawrence & Wishart.

(1978). *The Class Struggles in France.* In Marx and Engels, *Collected Works,* vol. 10. London: Lawrence & Wishart.

(1979). "The Future Results of the British Rule in India." In Marx and Engels, *Collected Works,* vol. 12. London: Lawrence & Wishart.

Polanyi, K. (1977). *The Livelihood of Man.* New York: Academic Press.

Roemer, J. (1982). *A General Theory of Exploitation and Class.* Cambridge, Mass.: Harvard University Press.

Rosenberg, A. (1976). "On Technological Expectations." *Economic Journal* 86, 525–35.

Ste Croix, G. E. M. de (1981). *The Class Struggle in the Ancient Greek World.* London: Duckworth.

Schumpeter, J. (1939). *Business Cycles.* New York: McGraw-Hill.

Schumpeter, J. (1961). *Capitalism, Socialism and Democracy,* 3d ed. London: Allen & Unwin.

Tang, A. (1979). "China's Agricultural Legacy." *Economic Development and Cultural Change* 28, 1–22.

Tocqueville, A. de (1969). *Democracy in America.* (Translated by George Lawrence. Garden City,) N.Y.: Doubleday (Anchor Books).

Trotsky, L. (1977). *History of the Russian Revolution.* London: Pluto Press.

Veblen, T. [1915] (1939). *Imperial Germany and the Industrial Revolution.* (Translated by Max Eastman. Reprint) New York: Viking Press.

Venturi, F. (1966). *The Roots of Revolution: A History of the Populist and Socialist Movements in Nineteenth Century Russia.* New York: Grosset & Dunlap.

CHAPTER 3

Producing change: work, technology, and power in Marx's theory of history

RICHARD W. MILLER

Of the many controversies about what Marx meant, the most intense concerns his general theory of history. In dispute is a special topic within this special topic: What is Marx's general theory of basic economic change? Clearly, this part of his theory of history is the foundation for all the rest. For Marx, political and ideological institutions and the climate of respectable ideas have their basic features because those features serve to maintain certain economic relations, what he calls "relations of production." The debate is over the foundational questions: Why do the relations of production in a given period have their basic features, and why do they sometimes change from one basic type to another?

The most influential interpretations of Marx's answers to these questions make Marx a technological determinist. On this view, Marx regarded history as the story of how social arrangements adapt to technological progress, facilitating the productivity of tools and techniques. Above all, the development of relations of production is to be explained as ultimately due to the pursuit of more material goods through improved technology.

There have, of course, been dissenters from this view. But they have not offered any decisive criticism or any plausible alternative. Often, opponents accord a larger role to class struggle than technological determinism allows. But they do so without explaining Marx's

Work on an earlier version of this paper was part of a sabbatical leave partly supported by a Rockefeller Foundation Humanities Fellowship. Parts of this essay appear in "Productive Forces and the Forces of Change." *Philosophical Review* 90 (1981): 91–117. Reprinted by permission of the publisher.

life-long concern with the development of productive forces as determining the direction of social change. Worse yet, dissenters from the dominant interpretation often dilute Marx's theory to a thin soup of truisms to the effect that technology influences change and people don't do much thinking if they cannot eat. Marx's practice as a historian is surely more distinctive than that, his general remarks more interesting.

Refuting a view of such a complex matter as Marx's theory of history means refuting the best version of it, the specification most likely to be correct if the general approach is valid. In the first half of this essay, I will construct this most defensible version of technological determinism and argue that it does not remotely fit Marx's historical writings. Then, I will develop an alternative, what I will call "the mode of production interpretation." In this interpretation, basic, internal economic change arises (whenever it does, in fact, take place) on account of a self-transforming tendency of the mode of production as a whole, that is, the relations of production, the forms of cooperation, and the technology through which material goods are produced. In these self-transformations, processes by which the mode of production initially maintained its characteristic relations of production eventually produce their downfall. This change need not overcome any barriers to material production. It may do so. Change may be based on developments in the forms of cooperation or in technology, giving enhanced productive power to an initially subordinate group and motivating their resistance to the old relations of production because the latter came to inhibit the further development of that new productive power. But in this broad mode of production theory, change may also be wholly internal to the relations of production themselves. The patterns of control in the old relations of production may make it inevitable that an initially nondominant group will acquire the power and the desire to overthrow the old relations.

Admittedly, a somewhat narrower theory is expressed in some of Marx's general formulations, even though the broader account is entailed by several of his specific historical explanations. (For reasons of convenience, I will develop this narrower theory before the broader one.) On the narrower account, radical internal economic change is always the result of the first of the two processes I have sketched, namely, the acquisition of increased productive power by a subordinate group and the inhibition of further productive growth by the old relations of production. But even in this

60

narrower theory, Marx is not a technological determinist. The growth of productive powers is not primarily based on an autonomous drive toward technological progress. The enhanced productive powers almost always result from changed forms of cooperation, not new technology. The new relations of production need not be the most productive framework for the development of technology.

In short, in the theory that Marx actually applied, productive enhancement has no primary role among processes of internal change. And even in the narrower version to which he sometimes commits himself, productive enhancement lacks the particular primacy and the technological character assigned it by technological determinism.

I. MARX AS TECHNOLOGICAL DETERMINIST

Many technological determinists have obviously not been Marxists. For example, the anthropologist Leslie White claimed that institutions all evolve in such a way as to maximize "the amount of energy harnessed per capita per year" (1959: 368). In his theory, political and cultural institutions can adjust to productive needs quite directly, without any priority for relations of production. Change that is qualitative, structural, or relatively rapid plays no special role.

What specific version of technological determinism could have been Marx's theory? In effect, the answer to this question has consisted of a technological determinist gloss of a celebrated passage from the Preface to Marx's book *A Contribution to the Critique of Political Economy* (1859). In this passage, Marx says that people's

relations of production correspond to a definite stage of development of their material productive forces. The sum total of these relations of production constitutes . . . the real basis on which rises a legal and political superstructure.

More precisely, this correspondence and support occur in relatively stable social situations:

At a certain stage of their development, the material productive forces of society come in conflict with the existing relations of production. From forms of development of the productive forces these relations turn into their fetters. Then begins an epoch of social revolution. With the change of the economic foundation the whole immense superstructure is more or less rapidly transformed. (1969: 503–4)

Other statements by Marx suggest a technological determinist interpretation. But the passage from the Preface has played a special role. Every classic systematic exposition of Marxist technological determinism, from Plekhanov's *The Development of the Monist View of History* at the turn of the century to Cohen's recent *Karl Marx's Theory of History: A Defence,* returns to the scaffolding of this passage. (I have not quoted every important sentence in it.) This habit makes some of us suspicious. The passage is part of a short autobiographical sketch. It follows a modest introductory sentence: "The general result at which I arrived and which, once won, served as a guiding thread for my studies, can be briefly formulated as follows." I can think of no other major theorist whose general theory is often reconstructed, in large part, by a close reading of a brief formulation embedded in an autobiographical sketch in a preface to a book that he gladly allowed to go out of print, as superseded by later writings. Still, the central text for technological determinism is one of Marx's few detailed and general formulations of his theory of history. And it does often sound like a systematic presentation of a technological determinist theory. In the interest of both clarity and fairness, I will construct the most defensible version of the technological determinist interpretation by finding the best reading of this passage in which crucial terms are interpreted in a technological determinist manner.

In technological determinism, "productive forces" are best interpreted as tools, techniques, and knowledge by which matter is made usable by human beings, tools, techniques, and knowledge meeting two further constraints. Productive forces must be means to overcome physical obstacles, as against the obstacle of resistance by other human beings. On this reading, a gun used to kill deer for venison is a productive force, but not one used to conquer territory. A foreman's knowledge of how to cut sheet metal is a productive force, but not his knowledge of how to maintain labor discipline. This restriction is required by Marxist technological determinism, since the productive forces are supposed to be the autonomous technological factor that, on the whole, explains basic changes in social and political processes, not the other way around. Obviously, the development of means of control over other human beings has, to a large extent, been determined by social and political processes of domination and conflict that the technological factor is supposed to explain.

Also, the most defensible technological interpretation must exclude from the scope of productive forces what Marx calls "modes of cooperation" and Cohen calls by the short and evocative phrase "work relations": relations of cooperation between people engaged in production, defined apart from control over people or means of production. Again, the productive forces must be so restricted, or the claim that they are the autonomous basis for change will be false to history, both history as it obviously is and history as Marx obviously sees it. Typically, changes in work relations are due to new social relations of dominance. The labor gangs of the Pharaohs, the teamwork in medieval corvée labor on the overlord's demesne, and the dissociation of craftwork through the "putting-out" system in the preindustrial stage of capitalism are a few examples. Moreover, changed patterns of work relations rarely involve the development of *new* ways to produce efficiently, as they would have to if they were instances of technological progress. Virtually all work relations are already depicted on the walls of ancient Egyptian tombs.

In the Preface, "the sum total of . . . relations of production" are said to be the basis for political and ideological institutions. Much else is said of them: They find a legal expression in property relations; productive forces are normally at work within them; they may inhibit the productive forces; an era of social revolution is required to transform them. To play these roles, the relations of production are best construed as relations of control over people, labor power, or productive forces within the process of material production. People's positions in the network of relations of production define their class. For example, if someone controls productive forces and the use for a contracted period of the labor power of others, while the others sell their labor power because they lack control of substantial productive forces, the former are capitalists, the latter proletarians.[1]

---

[1] This conception of production relations is, I think, accurate as far as it goes, but incomplete and potentially misleading. We also need a means to individuate relations of production, so that, for example, owners of pretzel factories and owners of automobile factories are put in the same class, but a different one from mere owners of labor power. Marx individuates production relations, not just according to different objects of control in the production process, but also according to the political nature of the means of control and the use to which control is put in the political and commercial spheres. For instance, late feudal overlords are distinguished from capitalist farmers by the dependence of the former on the direct exercise of military power, the commitment of the latter to commercial expansion through competition (n.d., vol. III: 334, 790–1). The distinctive economic ruling class of traditional Chinese society is identified as a state directly extracting a surplus from relatively isolated villages (ibid.: 791). Thus, reference to political and commercial processes cannot ultimately be avoided when production relations are defined. Marxist technological determinists try to avoid such conceptual interdependence between

In the Preface, a network of relations of production is said to change when it fetters the "development of the productive forces." In interpreting this metaphor of fettering, any defensible version of the technological determinist interpretation will have to depart from a strict and literal reading of the Preface. Marx says, there, "No social order ever perishes before all the productive forces for which there is room in it have developed." If we take this to be Marx's strict and settled view, production relations fetter productive forces only when they exclude all further improvements in productivity. A theory of history that insists on this fettering must deny, for example, that feudalism was ever overthrown so long as it permitted any improvement in the productive forces. The implication concerning capitalism flies in the face of Marx's view that capitalist competition will always stimulate some technological progress, together with the fact that Marx was a socialist.[2]

Marx's extreme statement is an exaggeration to be understood in its political context. It reflects his polemics against Proudhon and the utopian socialists, who studied industrial development only to condemn it and would not realistically assess the material requirements of modern workers' needs. A more moderate standard for fettering is available, which fits Marx's practice much more closely. On this interpretation, the network of relations of production fetters productive forces when some alternative network would better promote the further development of those forces. Following Cohen's usage I will borrow Marx's concise label in the Preface for a whole network of relations of production, viz., an "economic structure." A defensible technological determinist reading of the Preface should understand the claim about fettering, metaphor and hyperbole to one side, as the claim that a basic type of economic structure only lasts as long as it is optimal for the development of the productive forces. It

production relations, politics, and commerce. For they seek to extract from the Preface and similar passages a set of empirical laws, on the basis of which political and commercial systems could, in principle, be predicted, given independent information about the nature of production. In a forthcoming book, *Analyzing Marx*, I argue that the "covering-law" model of explanation that underlies this demand is a main motivation for technological determinism as a whole.

[2] "The bourgeoisie cannot exist without constantly revolutionizing the instruments of production" (*Communist Manifesto*, in 1973a: 111). "Modern Industry never looks upon and treats the existing form of a process as final" (n.d., vol. I: 457).

perishes when the forces would develop more productively in a new structure, even if they could still develop to some extent within the old one.

Presumably, Marx is not proposing to explain every change in an economic structure, down to the smallest detail. In the Preface he is concerned with the disappearance of whole "social orders" or "social formations" and the appearance of new ones. Large-scale changes on the order of the transition from the feudal to the capitalist mode of production are his theme here, as whenever a theory of productive forces is brought to the fore. This less comprehensive aim of only explaining changes in basic type makes a technological determinist Marxism more plausible. But it raises one final interpretative question, the question of what counts as a basic difference in type. The difficulty arises because the statistically preponderant relation of production need not characterize the basic type of an economy, for Marx. For example, he was aware that most producers in sixteenth-century England and in the early Roman Empire were small peasant proprietors (1973: pp. 476–7, 487; n.d., vol. I: 671).

Fortunately, Marx states the standard of basic difference explicitly and emphatically in his later writings. "The essential difference between the various economic forms of society . . . lies only in the mode in which . . . surplus labor is in each case extracted from the actual producer, the laborer" (n.d., vol. I: 209; see also vol. III: 791). Marx identifies the basic type of an economic structure with the main way in which a surplus is extracted from the immediate producers, not with the relation of production that is statistically most pervasive in production as a whole. He does this because of the explanatory project of which the typology is a part. The most basic shifts in economic type are to explain the most basic shifts in political and ideological institutions. And Marx takes control over the surplus to be the most important single determinant of the latter. Once economic structures are distinguished according to the mode of surplus extraction, the Rome of Augustus and the England of Henry VIII become basically different in type, as they should be in any interpretation of Marx. In one, the surplus is extracted mainly through ownership of slaves, in the other, mainly through political domination of free farmers and craftsworkers.

The most defensible interpretation of Marx as a technological determinist is a gloss of the celebrated passage from the Preface with the crucial terms understood in the ways I have described. The general idea of technological determinism is that social structures evolve by adapting to technological change so as to increase its further productive growth. As a version of Marx's theory of history, technological determinism must answer three questions in ways that give primacy to tools, techniques, and productivity: What explains the main features of an economic structure during its period of relative stability? What causes basic changes among the productive forces themselves? What determines the timing and direction of change in economic structures? The Preface can be taken to yield technological determinist answers to all three questions. First, an economic structure is of its basic type because that best promotes material productivity given the productive forces at hand. Second, the kinds of productive forces available are mainly due to a human drive that is independent of the desire for power over other people, namely, the desire and ability to overcome material scarcity. Thus, in the causation of basic changes in type, the productive forces shape the relations of production and the commercial, political, and ideological processes to which the latter give rise, to a much greater extent than vice versa. Cohen usefully compares this primacy with a priority of the environment in Darwinian evolution, as traditionally understood: Environmental changes are the main influence on species transformations, not vice versa, though the latter obviously have some impact on the former. Similarly, in a Marxist technological determinism, economic structures and their concomitants have some impact on productive forces (otherwise they could not facilitate their growth), but the most basic changes in the productive forces are largely autonomous. Finally, basic instability in the economic structure is regulated by technological innovation, if due to internal causes. Such instability reflects the rise of new tools and techniques that would be more productive in a new basic type of economic structure. The period of change ends with a new economic structure that is the one best adapted to those new productive forces.

These three general claims certainly are a general theory of history that gives genuine primacy to technology and that is strongly suggested by the passage from the Preface and other texts. The theory is neatly summarized in Cohen's remark, "Forces select structures according to their capacity to promote development" (1978: 162).

II. THE STAKES ARE HIGH

When those who are sympathetic to Marx judge this most-defensible version of technological determinism, the stakes are extremely high,

for social science and for political practice. For one thing, technological determinism crucially affects the priorities of historical explanation, both priorities in research governing how much time historians should devote to various pursuits and priorities in assessment
determining what is a successful explanation and what is not, what is
a complete one and what an incomplete one. In a Marxist technological determinism, relations of production are as they are because
they promote productivity, given the technology at hand, and they
change because a new technology has arisen to which they are ill
adapted. Within this theoretical framework, the most important
question for a historian trying to explain the most basic social
changes is, "How did the new arrangement become the one promoting productivity in society as a whole?" Questions of how the change
affected the special interests of different classes and of what power
the various classes possessed, though crucial to understanding how
the change was brought about, are secondary in understanding why
it occurred.

As with all debates over the interpretation of Marx, this one has
important implications for political practice as well. Regimes in many
countries with little advanced technology, such as Angola, Tanzania,
and Afghanistan, call on Marxists to support a policy of modernizing
technology without instituting socialism, on the ground that this is a
necessary preliminary to socialism. Technological determinism is an
important basis for these appeals. The technological determinist emphasis on productivity also has poignant implications for such countries as South Africa, where capitalism is pushing per capita GNP
ahead by leaps and bounds, despite poverty, degradation, and repression. It does not seem that socialism would do a better job of increasing material productivity here, even if it eliminated much misery. A
technological determinist interpretation of Marx suggests a Marxist
argument against fighting for socialism now in such countries. "Capitalism is not yet obsolete here," is an argument that is, in fact, advanced by Communist Parties, both Moscow- and Peking-oriented.

In addition, the rationale for revolution has a very different position in technological determinism from its situation in the alternative
that I shall describe. Granted, a Marxist technological determinist is
free to say that the political superstructure stabilizing an economic
structure will always be so strong that large-scale organized violence
will be essential to basic change. But it is hard to see how the rationale for a general theory of the primacy of technology could include
a rationale for this general assessment. If anything, an argument

67

that change is based on a universal human drive for efficiency in production will suggest the effectiveness of an alternative to revolution, in which change is brought about by appeals to material desires common to all classes. Thus, if Marx does believe in the necessity of organized large-scale violence, this belief becomes detachable from the core of his general theory. Its position is analogous to Newton's corpuscular theory of light in contrast to his laws of motion, or to Darwin's semi-Lamarckian view of the mechanisms of heredity in contrast to his theory of natural selection. On the other hand, the general case for the mode of production interpretation will turn out to be a general case for the necessity of revolution.

III. MARX WAS NOT A TECHNOLOGICAL DETERMINIST

The dominant interpretation is wrong. When Marx writes history, he constantly violates the three distinctive principles of "Marxist" technological determinism. In history as he explains it economic structures do not endure because they provide maximum productivity. Productive forces do not develop autonomously. Change in productive forces, in the narrowly technological sense that excludes work relations, is not the basic source of change in society at large.

It will be convenient to start with the second thesis, that the development of the productive forces is, on the whole, autonomous, with the basic changes in economic and political processes ultimately due to changes in the productive forces, far more so than the other way around. Fortunately, everyone agrees on what text epitomizes Marx's work as an economic historian. It is the account in Volume I of *Capital* of how feudalism was first replaced by capitalism in Britain. Here are some crucial episodes in Marx's paradigmatic story of the shift from one basic type of economic structure to another. In all of these episodes, the economic structure and the commercial and political processes it generates play an independent role, crucially influencing all important changes in productive forces.

The old nobility is "devoured by the great feudal wars" and replaced by a new nobility of mercantile supporters of the competing dynasties (n.d., vol. I: 673). With this new nobility taking the lead, large landowners respond to Continental demand for wool by expropriating their tenants, converting peasant holdings to sheep pastures (ibid.). This change does not occur because it makes farming more efficient. Quite traditional methods of sheepherding have simply become more lucrative for landowners. The influx of gold from the New World causes long-term inflation, increasing agricultural prices and decreasing the real rents of relatively well-off peasants with long-term leases and the power to defend them in court. The latter become aggressive capitalist farmers (n.d., vol. I: 695). In manufacturing,

the discovery of gold and silver in America, the extirpation, enslavement and entombment in mines of the aboriginal population, the beginning of the conquest and looting of the East Indies, the turning of Africa into a warren for the commercial hunting of black skins [hardly: "the development of improved forces of production"!] signalized the rosey dawn of the era of capitalist production. (n.d., vol. I: 703)

Rich merchants who benefited from this pillage use their new financial resources to set up manufacturing enterprises, often employing desperate refugees from the rise of capitalism in the countryside. Their large financial resources are crucial to the rise of manufacturing, for nontechnological reasons. It is commercially risky to set up enterprises of a new kind serving new markets. In most branches of production, many wage laborers need to be employed in an enterprise to retain a total surplus attractive to an entrepreneur after each has been paid at least a subsistence wage (n.d., vol. I: 292, 305).

These episodes are not the whole story of the rise of capitalism, as told by Marx, but they are the lion's share. The rise of capitalism eventually includes substantial increases in productivity, through the consolidation of landholdings and the economies of scale of the factory system. In a broad sense, these are changes and improvements in productive forces. But these changes are not autonomous. In explaining this paradigmatic change in the level of productive forces, commercial and political processes are as important as the general desire to overcome material scarcity through technological improvement.

Actually, the situation for technological determinism is even worse than this. As we have seen, the new work relations in factories and in large-scale farms are not the sort of thing that technological determinism can afford to count as a productive force. Productive forces in the required narrow sense play no significant role in Marx's paradigmatic explanation of basic economic change. However, even if a broader construal could somehow be reconciled with technological determinism, the fact would remain that the development of the productive forces is not autonomous in the explanation of the rise of capitalism in *Capital*.

Wherever we look in Marx's economic histories, the relations of production and the processes they generate play a basic, independent role in explaining changes in productive forces. Marx's one extensive discussion of a technological change in a narrow sense of "technological" is his account of the new reliance on machinery in the Industrial Revolution. There Marx gives approximately equal emphasis to the greater efficiency of machine production and to its social advantage to the capitalist, as a means of reducing wages, extending the work day, and instilling labor discipline by destroying bargaining advantages of skilled craftsworkers (n.d., vol. I: 407–8, 410). In discussing the origins of a detailed and interdependent division of labor in society (surely the most basic influence on the subsequent development of tools), Marx suggests that contact and barter among social groups, not the pursuit of productivity, were its causes (ibid.: 91f., 332–3). The crucial influence on the shape of technology in late antiquity, the rise of aristocracies employing slave labor on a large scale, is traced, by Marx, to the domestic effects of expansion through conquest, the growth of commerce, and the power of money to "dissolve" traditional social relations (1973: 487, 493–5).

When we turn from the question of how productive forces change to the question of how they shape stable economic structures, the clash between technological determinism and Marx is just as jarring. According to technological determinism, an economic structure has its basic type because that type best promotes the productive forces. Marx, to the contrary, depicts both slavery and feudalism as structures maintained by the power of an economically dominant class in the face of a feasible alternative, at least as productive. Marx generally describes the feudal aristocracy as a fetter on technology, when feudalism flourished, an "organized robber-nobility" (1972: 46) whose economic obsession is prestigious consumption (1973: 507; n.d., vol. I: 672). Similarly, the basic tendency of the slave-based plantations in the ancient world is regressive, since the masters' aristocratic disdain for technology is matched by their slaves' unwillingness to perform novel or complex work (n.d., vol. I: 191). In both settings, the actual work of production is concentrated in "peasant agriculture on a small scale, and the carrying on of independent handicrafts" (ibid: 316). Feudalism and slavery do not persist because the productive forces would be weaker if farmers and artisans were to dispense with feudal or slaveowning aristocrats. The whole drift of Marx's comments is to the contrary. They persist because the farmers and artisans lack the means (above all, the unity and discipline throughout broad geographic areas) to overthrow the aristocratic ruling class. Indeed, Marx regards feudalism and slavery as triumphs of military, rather than productive, force in their very origins: "If human beings themselves are conquered along with the land and soil . . . then they are equally conquered as conditions of production, and in this way arises slavery and serfdom" (1973: 491).[3]

A third distinctive claim in the technological determinist interpretation of Marx is that fundamental social changes are basically due to changes in the productive forces. Accordingly, one would expect Marx frequently to describe changes in the productive forces in his account of how feudalism became unstable and gave way to capitalism. In my previous sketch of Marx's story of this transformation, I did mention several changes in productive forces in a broad sense of the term, a sense in which the organization of craftwork in factories and the organization of agricultural work in large-scale one-crop farms are themselves productive forces. But technological determinism requires a narrower usage, excluding work relations. Marx's writings on the rise of capitalism amount to a consistent, longstanding, and explicit denial that changes in the productive forces in this narrow, technological sense were the main stimulus to economic change.

When Marx describes the changes in production that initiated the rise of capitalism, he is almost entirely concerned with the spread of certain work relations, a change that is not based, in turn, on technological innovations. Production by craftsworkers in small, independent, specialized workshops is replaced by "manufacture," produc-

---

[3] Admittedly, feudal and slaveowning overlords may increase actual production by forcing workers to work harder. But the level of technological progress ought to be measured, not by the total output of the productive forces, but by their potential output per work hour, when employed most efficiently. A factory's technology does not become less advanced when a successful strike reduces the pace of work. In any case, it is not open to a technological determinist who wants to be a Marxist to make the ability to force people to work an aspect of technological progress. Marx regards it as a major limitation of capitalism that it prevents many people from choosing leisure or more interesting work over increased material output. It is supposed to be an advantage of socialism that workers can and often will collectively decide to shorten the workday or to make work more interesting, even if material production might otherwise increase more rapidly (see n.d., vol. I: chap. 10, "The Working-Day"; and vol. III: 820). If coerced intensity of labor were an aspect of technological progress, the technological determinist Marx would be arguing here against his own account of the inevitability of socialism.

tion by many interdependent craftsworkers of many specialties, assembled in one place. Farming of diverse crops on small family plots is replaced by one-crop farming on large plots. Technological change is scarcely mentioned. Indeed, Marx's general descriptions of the role of technological change, as against changing work relations, in the rise of capitalism are explicitly antitechnological. He says in *Capital:*

> With regard to the mode of production itself, manufacture, in its strict meaning, is hardly to be distinguished, in its earliest stages, from the handicraft trades of the guilds, otherwise than by the greater number of workers simultaneously employed by one and the same individual capital. The workshop of the medieval master craftsman is simply enlarged. (n.d., vol. I: 305)

In the *Manifesto,* Marx's summary of the change from feudal ways of producing things to capitalist ones is a description of how commercial activity produced changes in work relations:

> The feudal system of industry, under which industrial production was monopolized by the closed guilds, now no longer sufficed for the growing wants of the new markets. The manufacturing system took its space. The guildmasters were pushed to one side by the manufacturing middle class; division of labor between the different corporate guilds vanished in the face of division of labor in each single workshop. (1969: 110–11)

Marx does insist repeatedly that the development and subsequent fettering of productive forces are what initiate basic social change. Yet if productive forces are equated with technology Marx dramatically violates this principle when he writes history. Unless Marx had an enormous capacity for inconsistency, he must have been using the phrase in a broader sense.

The narrowly technological interpretation of productive forces not only fits Marx's historical practice badly. It also dramatically conflicts with many passages in which he explicitly classifies modes of cooperation as productive forces. For example, in *The German Ideology* he says,

> By social we understand the cooperation of several individuals, no matter under what conditions, in what way, and to what end. It follows from this that a certain mode of production, or industrial stage, is always combined with a certain mode of cooperation, or social stage, and this mode of cooperation is itself a "productive force." Further, that the multitude of productive forces accessible to men determines the nature of society. (1972: 50)

He also calls "the social . . . power which arises through the cooperation of different individuals as it is determined by the division of labor" a productive force (1972: 54). In the *Grundrisse*, roughly contemporary with the Preface, Marx says of work teams, "The unification of their forces increases their force of production" (1973: 528), speaks of "the association of the workers – the cooperation and division of labor" as a "productive power [an alternative translation of *Produktivkraft*, the word standardly rendered, "productive force"] of labor" (1973: 585), and speaks of "the productive force arising from social combination" (1973: 700). In *Capital,* he says of "the social force that is developed, when many hands take part simultaneously in one and the same operation": "Not only have we here an increase in the productive power of the individual, by means of cooperation, but the creation of a new power, namely, the collective power of masses" (n.d., vol. I: 308–9; as usual, "power" and "force" are alternative translations of *Kraft*). Indeed, he devotes two long chapters to the analysis of modes of cooperation, repeatedly describing them as productive forces (see, e.g., 312, 315, 316–17, 340, 344).

The prestige of Marx's writings among activists gives the question of defining "productive forces" great contemporary political importance. If changing work relations, not new technology, may be the means by which productive forces dissolve old economic structures, then Marx's general theories do not suggest that technological progress is a necessary means, or even an effective one, for a regime to advance a technologically backward region toward socialism.

In developing my own alternative to the technological determinist interpretation, I will adopt a broader reading of productive forces. These forces consist of the activities, tools, and materials through which material goods are created and made usable, so far as the existence of those activities, tools, and materials does not entail, in itself, rights and powers of control over people or things. This conception corresponds to Marx's description of the "elementary factors of the labor-process" in *Capital:* "1. the personal activity of man, i.e., work itself, 2. the subject of that work, 3. its instruments" (n.d., vol. I: 174).

IV. THE MODE-OF-PRODUCTION INTERPRETATION

There is a familiar picture of Marx as a superb practicing historian whose general theories departed enormously from his historical insights because he got involved in politics. If Marx's theory were technological determinist, we would now have grounds for accepting this diagnosis of Marx's sad case. But two alternative interpretations are available that make Marx's theoretical statements largely of one piece with his historical explanations. The first, which I will present in this section, fits all of Marx's general theoretical statements and nearly all of his specific explanations. In it, economic structures have great causal independence, while the growth of productive forces (in the broad, nontechnological sense) remains the basis for internal change. It is the general theory of history to which Marx explicitly commits himself. The second theory, which I present in the next section, fits all of his specific explanations and fits almost all of his general statements to a large extent, if not entirely. It is a broadened version of the first theory, one in which the growth of productive forces is not the only internal source of change. This is the theory that guided Marx in practice, when he wrote history.

In Marx's view, both stable social structure and dramatic social change are ultimately based on the mode of production, the activities, facilities, and relationships, material *and* social, through which material goods are produced. The mode of production includes productive forces in the technological sense, productive forces, such as work relations, in my broader sense, and relations of production. Although it plays no fundamental role in technological determinism, the concept of a mode of production is used throughout Marx's general statements concerning history, including a notable passage from the Preface: "The mode of production of material life conditions the social, political and intellectual life process in general."

Different features of the mode of production are primary, depending on what is to be explained, the features of a stable society, or the occurrence and direction of change. For stable societies, the basic type of economic structure is primary; for social change, productive forces (in the broader sense) are.

The most important features of a relatively stable society are largely explained by the needs and powers of what Marx calls "the ruling class," the group in the economic structure that, through its control of productive forces, mainly controls the surplus product of direct participants in production.[4] Because of ruling class dominance of the surplus, political and ideological institutions will operate to

---

[4] My interpretation will be directed at societies in which class divisions have already appeared. Technological determinism is obviously unsuited to account for Marx's discussions of pre-class societies. There he emphasizes two sources of change, neither constituting technological progress: conquest and exchange among social groups (see 1973: 471–513; n.d., vol. I: 91–2, 332–3).

maintain the economic structure, at least so far as it benefits this class.[5]

This framework for explaining features of a stable society creates a pressing problem about social change, all the more pressing for a revolutionary like Marx. If a society is dominated by a ruling class combining economic, political, and ideological power, how can processes internal to the society change its economic structure into another basic type, marked by the dominance of a different class?

With respect to his question of change, the productive forces are primary. Like Hegel before him, Lenin after him, and practicing scientists all the time, Marx treats primacy as relative to the question being asked.

A relatively stable economic structure may permit people to use new kinds of productive forces, or to employ old kinds in greater numbers, as they pursue greater control over material goods. This opportunity for change may have unforeseen revolutionary consequences. Although permitted, the additional productive forces may come to be fettered in that the old economic structure discourages their effective use or further development, where a new one would not. For example, as entrepreneurs were well aware in seventeenth-century England, the large fixed investment required for large-scale, one-crop agriculture or setting up a factory is discouraged by the risk that the investment may come to nothing because some court favorite had been granted a royal monopoly. At a certain point, these fetters on productive forces may be broken, and a new, better-suited economic structure set up, on account of quantitative or qualitative factors, usually both. Quantitatively, it may be that the new productive forces would be so much more productive in a new economic structure that a class that would dominate the new structure can organize successful revolution against the ruling class, based on a widespread hope for greater well-being. Qualitatively, it may be that the new productive forces – in particular, the new work rela-

---

[5] *The German Ideology* contains several neat descriptions of dominance by a ruling class; for example, "The ideas of the ruling class are in every epoch the ruling ideas, i.e., the class which is the ruling *material* force in society is at the same time its ruling *intellectual* force. The class which has the means of material production at its disposal, has control at the same time over the means of mental production, so that, thereby, generally speaking, the ideas of those who lack the means of mental production are subject to it" (1972: 64); "The state is the form in which the individuals of a ruling class assert their common interest" (1972: 80).

tions—are of a kind that gives a nondominant class new power to seize control of the surplus, quite apart from potential increases in the size of the social product. Marx gives approximately equal emphasis to both the quantitative and the qualitative factors in his account of how socialism will triumph. The deepening industrial depressions and increasingly violent wars characteristic of advanced capitalism limit society's ability to provide material well-being with the productive forces capitalism has developed. At the same time, the large-scale unity, discipline, and coordination produced by capitalist work relations give workers, for the first time, the ability to seize and control the productive forces. For example, both of these factors are emphasized in the famous descriptions of the triumph of socialism in the *Communist Manifesto* (1969: 119) and *Capital* (n.d., vol. I: 715). Marx emphasizes the quantitative factor in his account of the rise of the bourgeoisie, who were well organized internally in feudal society but needed the ties to larger groups afforded by the promise of heightened well-being through liberation from feudal constraints on production. He emphasizes the qualitative factor in his description of how a Greco-Roman aristocracy arose through the strategic advantages of larger farmers within the traditional apparatus for conquest, colonization, and trade.

Typical members of a subordinate class want to improve their well-being, powers, and opportunities, both in absolute terms and relative to the ruling class. Yet, as fetters tighten on developing productive forces, they limit the possibilities of improvement within the old economic structure of a subordinate class whose status depends on the development of those forces. As we have seen, the changes in productive forces that result in this fettering may, at the same time, give the subordinate class a new ability to change society, attacking the superstructure that maintains the old economic structure, and setting up a new, nonfettering structure over which that class presides. Since this process involves the overcoming of fetters on the new productive forces, the new society will be more productive than the old. In sum, change occurs when the productive forces have developed in such a way that (a) the old economic structure inhibits their further effective use, producing a new motive for structural change, and (b) the economic bases of class power are transformed, enabling a formerly subordinate class to set up a new economic structure, under its dominance, better adapted to the productive forces.

Purely for convenience, I will call the interpretation I have just sketched "the mode-of-production interpretation." Before, I summed up the technological determinist interpretation by listing its answers to three questions about stability and change. The difference between these interpretations is reflected in the different answers they yield.

According to the mode-of-production interpretation, the character of a stable society is explained by the economic dominance of the ruling class. In itself, this is perfectly compatible with the technological determinist interpretation, indeed implied by it. But there is a further element in technological determinism that is absent from the mode-of-production interpretation. There is no suggestion that a stable economic structure does a better job of promoting productivity than any alternative. Alternative economic structures, at least as productive as the triumphant one, may be ruled out by incapacities arising from the class situation of people who are quite adept at material production. This accords with Marx on feudalism and slavery. For example, so far as productivity is concerned, a structure dominated by peasants and artisans would have been at least as effective as the feudal economic structure. But sustained unity and collective discipline over large geographic areas would have been required to break the bonds that the overlords forged from the surplus they controlled. The social relations of peasants, by focusing loyalties on the family and the village, guaranteed that the needed class solidarity would not arise (see 1972: 45; 1969: 114–19; n.d., vol. I: chap. 32).

According to technological determinism, the development of the productive forces is the largely autonomous result of a general human tendency to use technology to overcome natural scarcity. The mode-of-production interpretation makes no such claim either in the broad usage of "productive forces" it typically employs, or in the narrow usage characteristic of technological determinism. The zigzag dialectic it permits between changes in productive forces and other, nonderivative changes in social processes is required by all of Marx's concrete discussions of major transformations of the productive forces. Moreover, since it does not assume a universal human drive for more advanced technology, the mode-of-production interpretation allows for the possibility that an economic structure might generate powers and attitudes that preclude substantial increases in productivity. This possibility is realized in Marx's account of ancient India and China (see 1973: 486; n.d., vol. I: 140, 330).

In the technological determinist interpretation, what initiates radical social change is change in the productive forces, conceived in a relatively narrow, technological way. The subsequent era of revolution ends with a society that is optimally productive, given the new productive forces. In the mode-of-production interpretation, changes in productive forces initiate social change. But productive forces are conceived in a much broader way and include work relations. Marx's paradigmatic explanation of social change, his discussion of the rise of capitalism, requires this broader reading. Moreover, the new society need not be optimally productive. Since it overcomes fetters on production, it will be more productive than the old. But further alternatives, at least as productive as the triumphant one, may be ruled out by differences in power based on historical differences in class situation. This is the possibility implied by Marx's discussions of feudal and slave societies.

An interpretation that unites Marx's general outlook on history with almost all of his specific historical explanations is surely preferable to one that splits him down the middle. I have argued that the mode-of-production interpretation is preferable on this ground. In addition, it fits several of Marx's general statements better than the technological determinist interpretation, and it is compatible with the rest.

Marx's first detailed description of his theory of history occurs in *The German Ideology*. There, Marx and Engels begin their most important summary of their theory of change with the sentence: "The form of intercourse determined by the existing productive forces at all previous historical stages, *and in its turn determining these*, is civil society" (1972: 57; italics added.) Quite uncontroversially, "civil society" here means the relations of production. At the outset, they are presented as the causal partner of the productive forces, not their servant.

Although Marx quietly let the Preface go out of print, he encouraged and often supervised the reissue of the *Communist Manifesto* throughout his lifetime. The general statements about history there emphasize the social aspect of production and do not give primacy to the technological. They are epitomized by the sentence introducing Marx's sketch of world history: "The history of all hither-to existing societies is the history of class struggle."

Marx's theoretical work was dominated by the writing of *Capital*. That work contains general statements about the nature of society and change that invite a nontechnological determinist reading; for example:

Producing change

The specific economic form in which unpaid labor is pumped out of direct producers determines the relationship of rulers and ruled, as it grows directly out of production itself and, reacts upon it [i.e., production itself] as a determining element. Upon this, however, is founded the entire formation of the economic community . . . thereby simultaneously its specific political form. It . . . reveals the innermost secret, the hidden basis of the entire social structure. (n.d., vol. III: 791. See also vol. I, 209 and the summary of the rise of capitalism in 1968, vol. I: 309)

Among the general statements by Marx that appear to support the technological determinist interpretation, the Preface is the most important and is highly representative of the rest. In showing how it can be accommodated to the mode-of-production interpretation, I hope I will provide the interested reader with ways of accommodating similar passages in *The Poverty of Philosophy*, the 1846 letter to Annenkov, and elsewhere.

Most of the Preface is obviously compatible with either interpretation. Two sentences do resist the mode-of-production interpretation. At one point Marx says, "No social formation ever perishes before all the productive forces for which there is room in it have developed." Literally understood, this is no part of the mode-of-production interpretation. However, as we have seen, it cannot be part of Marx's considered judgment. Marx did not believe that capitalism is, or that feudalism was, incapable of any technological progress at the moment of its death. This sentence, and similar ones from Marx's criticisms of Proudhon, must be a hyperbolic statement of the claim that a social formation is viable so long as it does not inhibit the development of productive forces, threatened once fettering begins. And this claim is very much a part of both interpretations.

Marx introduces his summary of his notion of history with the sentence: "In the social production of their life, men enter into . . . relations of production which correspond to a definite stage of development of their material productive forces." In his book Cohen notes, and rightly so, that this strong statement gives some kind of primacy to the productive forces. It certainly does in context, since no converse statement of the correspondence of productive forces to relations of production follows. But need this primacy be of the kind required by the technological determinist interpretation?

According to the mode-of-production interpretation, the productive forces (in the *broad* sense) play a unique role in the causation of basic social change. So far as factors internal to a society are con-

79

cerned, what causes the sum of relations of production to change from one basic type to another is the fettering of the productive forces. Changes in the relations occur as fetters on productive forces are overcome. This is naturally expressed by saying that the relations of production characteristic of a society correspond to (i.e., result from society's adjustment to) a stage of development of the productive forces.

Working in the other direction of causality, there is no universal phenomenon that would justify saying that productive forces correspond to a stage in the development of economic structures. There are, we saw, many social changes ultimately deriving from the economic structure that have a crucial impact on the productive forces. But these changes are not typically changes in the relations of production themselves. They are often new commercial needs and opportunities and new competitive pressures arising from the pursuit of interests determined by old relations of production, for example, the development of Continental markets for wool or rich peasants' exploitation of inflated food prices and fixed rents. In addition, many changes in productive forces are, of course, the result of the use of human know-how to overcome natural scarcity. Technological determinism is not all wrong. Finally, there remain cases in which new relations of production encourage changes in the productive forces relatively directly. This direct influence operated in the Industrial Revolution to the extent that machines were introduced by capitalist manufactures to destroy bargaining advantages of skilled wage earners. The same pressures had not existed within the guild-regulated workshop. Still, the impact of changes in the relations is only part of the story of why the forces change. The fettering of the forces is the basic story of why the relations change. We get symmetry only if we compare the impact of the forces with the impact of the relations plus the commercial and political processes independently shaped by the latter. The dominance of the forces also disappears if we ask what determines the direction of change, not just its occurrence.

Marx's statement about the correspondence of structures to forces is a synopsis of a specific scenario for change in structure, but not an assessment of the balance of ultimate causal influences. To this end it is entirely fitting, within the mode of production interpretation, that Marx should speak of the correspondence of relations to the development of forces, but not vice versa, in the course of a brief prefatory sketch of his basic outlook.

Producing change

The preceding version of the mode-of-production interpretation is meant to account for all of Marx's general statements about historical change, and almost all of his explanations of specific historical episodes. However, Marx sometimes offers specific explanations suggesting an even broader view of history, in which the growth of productive forces, broadly defined, is not the only internal source of fundamental change.

The *Grundrisse,* in effect Marx's notebook for *Capital,* contains an especially clear case of such an explanation, together with a fairly general description of the kind of mechanism for change on which these explanations rely. There, Marx examines the change from the early Roman society of independent household farms into a later society characterized by sharp class divisions among nonslaves (see 1973: 487, 493–5, 506). His speculation is that the earlier economic structure maintained itself by means that guaranteed its destruction in the long run. As the population grew, new households were given farms as a result of conquest and colonization, bringing land, slaves, and tribute. This process of expansion gave increased power to the richer farmers who dominated the army and the administration of public resources. They also specially benefited from the growth in trade produced by territorial expansion, since richer farmers were better able to switch to the raising of cash crops. Eventually, the better-off farmers used their accumulated control over land, slaves, and the political apparatus to become a new ruling class of large-scale absentee landowners. Other farmers became their exploited tenants, if they were not dispossessed entirely. "Thus," Marx concludes, "the preservation of the old community includes the destruction of the conditions on which it rests, turns into its opposite" (1973: 494).

The Preface and several other general statements about history make contradictions between the economic structure and the productive forces the basis for change. But in this explanation of change in the ancient world, contradictions within the earlier economic structure are themselves sufficient to bring about change. The earlier economic structure is maintained through processes that ultimately destroy it, quite apart from changes in the productive forces, even in the broad sense of the term. Indeed, Marx explicitly distinguishes the actual process of change, in which the maintenance of household farming by conquest proves self-destructive, from the process of change through productive growth. Immediately after the previously quoted remark about the preservation of the old community turning into its opposite, he adds,

If it were thought that productivity on the same land could be increased by developing the forces of production etc. (this precisely the slowest of all in traditional agriculture), then the new order would include combinations of labor, a large part of the day spent in agriculture, etc., and thereby again suspend the old economic conditions of the community.

The growth of productive forces is an imaginable but unlikely alternative source of basic economic change here.

Marx's speculation about the ancient world requires a broader outlook than that of the Preface. Social structure and social change are still based on the mode of production. The institutions of a stable society are still means of preserving ruling class control. Basic internal change still occurs because the mode of production as a whole encourages processes that eventually give a social group the ability and desire to destroy it, and create a new one. But this process of self-destruction may take two forms. As in the Preface, productive forces may grow until they encounter fetters. Alternatively, the economic structure may maintain itself through relations of power over people and productive forces that eventually enable a group to accumulate the power to remake society. Since these power relations (e.g., nonslaves' collective control of means to acquire new land and slaves for household farming) are themselves a part of the economic structure, an economic structure may be said to change as a result of conflict with itself, as well as with the productive forces. I will call this view of history the broader mode-of-production interpretation.

Although the *Grundrisse* discussion of class divisions in ancient Rome is uniquely clear and detailed in this regard, several other passages also appeal to the mechanisms for change characteristic of the broader view of history. The earliest is a brief discussion of ancient Rome in *The German Ideology* (1972: 445), in effect, a highly condensed version of the *Grundrisse* passage. A few years later, the *Communist Manifesto* traces the rise of capitalism to ultimately self-destructive conflicts inherent in the feudal economic structure. Escaped serfs form the basis of an urban bourgeoisie that unites with monarchs in the expansion of international trade and colonization, which so strengthens the bourgeoisie that it can dominate and transform society (1969: 109–10; see also 1978: 82–5).

In the *Grundrisse* as a whole, a long, self-contained discussion of precapitalist economic structures (roughly pp. 471–515 in the Nicolaus edition) is dominated by the idea that the total set of social relations of production may dictate the direction of social change, including change in those relations themselves. The possibility that these relations may be ultimately self-transforming is formulated in general terms in at least three passages (pp. 487, 493, and the previously quoted remark from p. 494).

In *Capital,* the explanations of some crucial episodes of economic change suggest the broader mode-of-production interpretation in that they appeal to a self-undermining tendency of an initial pattern of control over production. Capitalist manufacturing is initially characterized by a pattern of capitalists' control over factory buildings and raw materials, and workers' control over tools and technical knowledge. This pattern generates class struggles in which capitalists are driven to use their monopoly of surplus wealth to create a new industrial pattern. In this pattern, workers are deprived of old bargaining advantages, since they use capitalist-controlled machinery requiring relatively little technical knowledge (see n.d., vol. I: 407–10). Similarly, Marx speculates that a self-transforming pattern of control might have given rise to class divisions. A classless society organized into communities of farmers and artisans, independent but trading with each other, may acquire class divisions as contact between communities leads to increased reliance on large-scale production for trade, rather than subsistence farming and small-scale barter (n.d., vol. I: 91–2, 332–3). Finally, the self-destructive tendency of the feudal economic structure is implied by Marx's description of the first stage in the rise of capitalism: "The old nobility had been devoured by the great feudal wars. The new nobility was the child of its times for which money was the power of all powers" (ibid.: 672). The literal self-destruction of the old aristocracy and the rise of mercantile supporters of the great royal houses were not the result of productive growth. They were the result of a tendency toward civil war inherent in the feudal economic structure, where a surplus is mostly extracted through dominance over land and its tillers by means of military force possessed by independent family groups.

VI. MARX'S TWO MODELS

Which is Marx's theory of history, the broader or the narrower mode-of-production theory? In his explicit general statements, Marx commits himself to the narrower account. But the broader one is his essential theory, the one that guides his explanatory practice and the one that his theoretical arguments actually support. In practice, Marx is never constrained by the distinctive features of the narrower theory. When he develops an explanation that only fits the broader one, he adopts it, without any concern for the conflict. Indeed, in at least one passage (1973: 494), he acknowledges that an explanation appealing to the self-destructive tendency of an economic structure may be superior to explanations appealing to the growth of productive forces. As for Marx's general case in support of his theory of history, it may be meant to support the narrower theory, but it actually supports the broader one. The rationale for the claim that productive growth is the only internal source of change is that only productive growth and fettering can serve as an internal basis for the overthrow of a ruling class. But all of Marx's actual arguments to this effect are directed against efforts to locate a basic source of change outside the mode of production, for example, in independent cultural innovations or in military triumphs.[6] He never constructs an argument against the possibility that an economic structure might be inherently self-destructive in the long run. When he initially formulates this possibility, in the *Grundrisse*, it is to defend it. The logic of his argument does not require that productive forces be primary, whatever his own conclusions may sometimes have been.

Several compelling influences help to explain Marx's commitment to a theory that is narrower than his essential one. To begin with, the narrower theory is closer in form to Hegel's. For Hegel, peoples achieve and lose world-historical significance as their institutions embody, and then inhibit, the achievements of mind striving for freedom through reflection. Substitute "the achievements of people struggling for freedom from natural scarcity through production" and a basis for the narrower model, or for technological determinism, neatly results. Nothing is more common in the history of thought than the development of a new approach in forms derived from a great predecessor, by someone who is departing further from the predecessor than those forms suggest.

In the second place, as Engels notes in several biographical comments, Marx's political activities often dictated a heavy emphasis on the role of productive forces, not merited by less pressing, theoreti-

---

[6] As usual, *The German Ideology* (1972) contains vivid summaries of crucial arguments. See, for example, pp. 64–8 (on cultural change), 89–90 (on military conquest).

cal interests. In his debates with Left-Hegelian idealists and with anarchists, Marx is concerned to show that they neglect the material needs of modern workers, forget the social requirements of technology in their quest for ideal self-sufficiency, and substitute moral condemnation of industrialization for the study of its positive and revolutionary aspects.

Finally, Marx's reluctance to abandon in theory a model that did not constrain him in practice may have resulted, in part, from his commitment to a general principle regarding change. That principle is the assumption that social evolution always involves progress, at least of a certain limited kind. This equation of evolution and progress is entailed by the narrower theory, in which evolution always facilitates productive growth. It is not entailed by the broader theory, since an economic structure destroyed through self-generated conflicts need not give birth to a more productive society. The transition from the Roman Empire to feudalism might be an actual case of such self-destruction without productive progress.

Marx's autobiographical comments in the Preface suggest that the equation of evolution and progress had been extremely fruitful in his own development. It guided most of the best social science in his era. He might, then, quite reasonably have been reluctant to adopt a new theory of change in which the idea of progress is not so central.

If Marx did not really choose between his two models, that is because his need to choose was not urgent. Since he was using a very broad notion of productive forces, he may well have hoped that explanations that seemed to depart from the narrower mode of production theory could be reconciled with it, on further analysis. The political problems of the workers' movement, which always directed his theoretical interests, did not make it urgent to pursue this hope, or to choose between the broad and narrow theory, should reconciliation fail. In the late twentieth century, the political context has changed dramatically. At least in the so-called less developed countries, a frequent argument of self-described socialists against fighting for socialism now is, "The productive forces aren't ripe." This argument has much less initial plausibility in the broad mode-of-production theory than in the narrow one. On the broader view, even where capitalism does not inhibit productivity, it may have created a working class with the need and the power to overthrow it. Marx's reason for continued ambivalence between the two theories is no longer a good excuse.

Even if Marx had never stepped beyond the narrower theory, we would have a reason to regard the broader one as the Marxist theory of history. Since Marx's death, his writings have stimulated much productive historical research, uniform enough to constitute an approach to history and similar enough to Marx's work to be called Marxist. Lenin and Hilferding on late nineteenth-century imperialism, Hill on seventeenth-century England, Thurnwald and Meillassoux on the rise of class inequalities, Hilton on the decline of English serfdom, and De Sainte-Croix on the decline of the Roman Empire are a few examples. A model emphasizing the growth and inhibition of productive power is irrelevant to most of this historical work, inconsistent with much of it.[7] The broader mode-of-production theory describes the common features of the historical explanations that we naturally regard as Marxist.

The narrower mode-of-production interpretation expresses Marx's intentions in his general statements about history. The broader interpretation reveals the model of change that has guided the best history writing by Marx and subsequent Marxists. This is the more important task, since it makes Marx useful.

---

[7] For example, De Sainte-Croix (1975 and elsewhere) has argued that the Roman Empire maintained itself through a pattern of exploitative relations that ultimately destroyed it. A surplus product was extracted from the non-Italian empire through the co-optation of local elites and indirect rule. The material demands of co-optation and the presence of unsubdued and warlike peoples at the border required constant efforts at expansion. The basis for these processes was the farming population of Italy, used to support the core aristocracy, the farming population itself (imports could not do the job alone), and the constantly expanding military effort. As the frontiers enlarged, the working people of Italy could not support all these demands. Productive growth plays no role in this story. Similarly, in Hilton's work (e.g., 1969) the evolution of power relations yields structural change. The Black Death creates a labor shortage and a new level of domestic disorder giving rise to class struggles that ultimately destroy the classic form of feudalism, bringing England to the point at which capitalist transformation is a realistic prospect. As a final example, consider Thurnwald's sketch (1932) of a means by which class divisions might arise. Through location or traditional prerogative, some families administer exchange among family groups for whom exchange is, initially, a marginal and sporadic enterprise. As the advantages of exchange (*not* dependent on new technology) lead to more specialization and interdependence, these families achieve material preeminence, and eventual class rule, based on control of a surplus extracted from the exchanged product.

Producing change

REFERENCES

Cohen, Gerald (1978). *Karl Marx's Theory of History: A Defence*. Princeton, N.J.: Princeton University Press.

De Sainte-Croix, G. E. M. (1975). "Karl Marx and the History of Classical Antiquity." *Arethusa* 8: 7–41.

Hilton, Rodney (1969). *The Decline of Serfdom in Medieval Europe*. New York: Macmillan.

Meillassoux, Claude. (1960). "Essai d'interpretation du phenomène économique dans les sociétés traditionelles d'auto subsistance." *Cahiers d'études Africaines* 4: 49–67.

Marx, Karl (1968). *Theories of Surplus-Value*. 3 vols. Moscow: Progress Publishers.

(1972). *The German Ideology*. New York: International Publishers.

(1973). *Grundrisse*. Edited by M. Nicolaus, New York: Random House, (Vintage Books).

(n.d.) *Capital*, Vols. I and III. Moscow: Progress Publishers.

and Frederick Engels (1969). *Selected Works in Three Volumes*, Vol. I. Moscow: Progress Publishers.

Thurnwald, Richard (1932). *Economics in Primitive Communities*. London: Oxford University Press.

White, Leslie (1959). *The Evolution of Culture*. New York: Noonday Press.

CHAPTER 4

Marxism's central puzzle

PHILIPPE VAN PARIJS

At first sight, Marxist theories explain in very different ways. The explanation of the real wage level as the outcome of class struggle seems to have little, if anything, in common with the explanation of a society's religious beliefs by reference to its economic structure. And the explanation of the form taken by the capitalist state by reference to the structural imperatives to which it is subjected does not seem to share much, if anything, with the explanation of individuals' voting behavior by their class position. It is therefore by no means a trivial task to try to work out the nature of *Marxist causation*, that is, to identify whatever features are specific, whether conjunctively or disjunctively, to explanations put forward by Marx and the Marxist tradition.

Presumably a good way to start such an inquiry – and in this discussion I shall go no further than this start – is by looking closely at the central explanatory statements of what many view as Marxism's core: historical materialism. The choice of this starting point is particularly appropriate as G. A. Cohen's widely celebrated *Karl Marx's Theory of History: A Defence* (1978) has decisively clarified the explanatory status of these statements. In particular, Cohen has shown in all clarity how the explanatory framework provided by historical materialism unavoidably raises a (twofold) problem that I shall call the

I am very grateful to G. A. Cohen, Jon Elster, John Roemer, Robert van der Veen, Erik Wright, and the editors, who commented on an earlier version of this paper. A slightly different German version has been published in a topic issue of *Analyse und Kritik* (Vol. 4, 1982) devoted to Cohen's work. A reply by Cohen and a rejoinder have been published subsequently (Vol. 5, 1983, and Vol. 6, 1984).

primacy puzzle and that can be expressed as follows. First, how is it possible, at the same time, to claim that there is a causal primacy of the productive forces over the relations of production and to recognize that the development of the productive forces causally depends on the form taken by the relations of production? And second, how is it possible to assert the subordination of the superstructure to the economic base, while conceding that the latter is somehow controlled by the former? To this irritating puzzle, which threatens the very core of Marx's social theory, Cohen claims to have found a satisfactory solution, which follows directly from the central thesis of his book. He claims that the primacy puzzle is solved as soon as one realizes that the historical-materialist explanations of production relations by productive forces and of the superstructure by the economic base are *functional explanations*, that is, explanations by a propensity to produce certain consequences.

I shall challenge this claim by focusing on the first component of the primacy puzzle, namely, the relation between productive forces and relations of production. I shall argue that Cohen's solution, however helpful, rests on a fundamental ambiguity in the formula, "explanation of production relations *by* productive forces." Once this ambiguity is disclosed, I shall show, the historical-materialist "primacy thesis" and the closely related "development thesis" also turn out to be systematically ambiguous, whereas Cohen's claim that his functional interpretation constitutes the only way of solving the primacy puzzle turns out to be either trivial or wrong. What does solve the primacy puzzle (in its most sensible interpretation), and uniquely solves it, is what I shall call the coexistence of a *slow* and a *fast dynamics*. Realizing this is of crucial importance both if one is to vindicate the consistency of historical materialism and if one is to delineate the exact nature of Marxist causation.

I. TWO WAYS OF EXPLAINING RELATIONS BY FORCES

There is no question that historical materialism claims to explain the form of the relations of production *by* the development of the productive forces.[1] But this claim can be understood in two distinct ways. One may mean that the relations of production can be ex-

[1] For a precise definition of the "productive forces" and the "relations of production," I refer to Cohen's (1978: chaps. 2, 3) excellent discussions. Note that it will be assumed throughout here that both forces and relations admit of a classification into a discrete set of "levels" or "forms."

plained by reference to *the level currently achieved by* the development of the productive forces. But one may also mean that they can be explained by reference to *their ability to enhance* this development. In symbols:

(a) $PF \rightarrow RP$,

that is, the level reached by the productive forces (PF) determines ($\rightarrow$) the form taken by the relations of production or economic structure (RP); and

(b) (RP is best for $\triangle PF$) $\rightarrow RP$,

that is, the form of the relations of production (RP) that is best for the development of the productive forces ($\triangle PF$) determines ($\rightarrow$) the form the relations of production will actually take (RP). The remainder of this analysis will simply consist in following up the consequences of this distinction.

Before doing so, however, let us make the latter more intuitive by imagining situations in which one of the two senses of the explanation of relations by forces is present while the other is not. Suppose, for example, that the level of development achieved by the productive forces determines which relations of production are best for the sake of maintaining *cohesion* in the society under consideration: At a fairly low level of development of the productive forces, it is, say, slavery that secures the smoothest running of society, whereas at a very high level of development only socialism can free society from endless strife. Suppose further that whatever relations are most conducive to cohesion will tend to prevail. In such a hypothetical situation, one can correctly say that the form of the relations is explained by the current level of the forces. But the form of the relations is not explained by its ability to enhance productive development (rather, by its ability to maintain cohesion). The structure of such a situation is expressed by the following (somewhat excessively) compact formula:

(c) $PF \rightarrow$ (RP is best for SC) $\rightarrow RP$,

that is, the level of productive development (PF) determines which economic structure (RP) is best for social cohesion (SC), and this structure determines in turn the structure that will actually prevail (RP). Clearly, by transitivity, (a) is satisfied in (c), whereas (b) is not.

Next, let us turn to a scenario that will sound familiar to those acquainted either with Wallerstein's (1974) analysis of the origins of capitalism or with the so-called dependency theory of underdevelopment (e.g., Frank 1979). Let us suppose that it is the position in the world system (say, center or periphery) that determines which relations of production (say, capitalist or socialist) are best for developing the productive forces, and that whatever relations are best from this angle tend to prevail. In this second hypothetical situation, it is correct to say that the form of the relations is explained by its ability to enhance productive development. But one cannot say that it is explained by the current level of the productive forces (rather, by the society's current position in the world system). The structure of such a situation can be expressed as follows:

(d) $WS \rightarrow (RP$ is best for $\triangle PF) \rightarrow RP,$

that is, the position in the world system (WS) determines which economic structure (RP) is best for productive development ($\triangle PF$), and this in turn determines which economic structure will actually prevail (RP). In this case, (b) obviously holds, whereas (a) does not.

What is thus made plain is the possibility of having each of the two senses of "explanation by the development of the productive forces" without the other. Perhaps the chief (though not fully explicit) achievement of Cohen's book has been to demonstrate that these two senses, however distinct, are not incompatible, indeed that one very plausible interpretation of historical materialism corresponds precisely to the case where they go together. The structure of this case can be depicted as follows:

(e) $PF \rightarrow (RP$ is best for $\triangle PF) \rightarrow RP,$

that is, the level currently achieved by the productive forces (PF) determines which form of the relations of production (RP) is best for productive development ($\triangle PF$), and the best form from this angle tends to prevail (RP).[2] Here, clearly, one explains the form taken by the relations of production both by the current level of the productive forces and by its propensity to enhance the latter's development: (a) and (b) both hold.

[2] Here are some of Cohen's most synthetic formulations: "The favoured explanations take this form: the production relations are of kind R at the time t [RP] because relations of kind R are suitable to the use and development of the productive forces at t [RP is best for $\triangle$ PF], given the level of development of the latter at t [PF]" (1978: 160); "forces [PF] select structure [RP] according to their capacity to promote development [RP is

Though this will not retain us in the sequel, note that a somewhat more complicated structure preserves the truth of (a) and (b), while providing a more convincing interpretation of both historical materialism and the relevant historical evidence. The level achieved by the forces, rather than the form of relations that is optimal for productive development, may well determine, which forms of relations are currently possible. What happens at the end of the Middle Ages or under late capitalism, in this account, is not that capitalism or socialism, which had been possible all along, becomes more productive than feudalism and capitalism, respectively. What happens is rather that capitalism or socialism, which would at any time have performed better than feudalism and capitalism, then becomes possible. In short:

(f) $PF \rightarrow (RP$ is possible)
$\left. \begin{array}{l} (RP \text{ is best for } \triangle PF \\ \text{among possible forms)} \end{array} \right\} \rightarrow RP,$

that is, the level of productive development (PF) determines which forms of relations (RP) are possible, and whatever form of relations is both possible and optimal for productive development ($\triangle PF$) will tend to prevail (RP). In such a situation, the form of the relations can still be said to be explained by the level of the forces (a) and by its propensity to develop them (b), though in both cases only partly.

II. THE PRIMACY THESIS

Bearing in mind this distinction between two senses of the "explanation of the relations by the forces," and the ways in which they can be combined, we can now examine what the primacy thesis is supposed to assert. Cohen, I shall argue, uses this notion in two different senses, which correspond to the two senses in which an explanation of relations by forces can be understood. In a first sense, "The primacy thesis is that the nature of a set of production relations is explained by the level of development of the productive forces embraced by it (to a far greater extent than vice versa)" (Cohen 1978: 134). A shorter formulation is also sometimes used: "The nature of the production relations of a society is explained by the level of development of its productive forces" (ibid.). In short:

best for $\triangle$ PF]" (1978: 162); or "the character of what is explained [RP] is determined by its effect [RP is best for $\triangle$ PF] on what explains it [PF]" (1978: 278).

(PTo) $PF \rightarrow RP$,

which exactly amounts to the claim that the forces determine the relations in sense (a). However, Cohen warns us in a footnote that the qualifying phrase appearing in parentheses in the first of the two sentences just quoted "is always to be understood whenever the primacy thesis is asserted" (Cohen 1978: 134 n. 1). This first sense of the primacy thesis can then roughly be pictured as follows:

(PT1) $PF \rightarrow RP$ to a far greater extent than $RP \rightarrow PF$.

If there remains any doubt as to the sense of the "explanation of relations by forces" involved here, the following clarification removes it completely: "The primacy thesis implies that changes in productive forces bring about changes in production relations," or, more precisely, that "for any set of production relations, there is an extent of further development of the productive forces they embrace which suffices for a change in those relations" (Cohen 1978: 135). Clearly, the explanation involved is an explanation by the level achieved by the forces (a), not an explanation by the propensity to favor productive development (b).

Cohen, however, does not stick to this interpretation of the primacy thesis. Unambiguous evidence is provided by the following conclusion he draws from the "somewhat naive story" with which he illustrates "the nature of the primacy of the forces":

One may now say that the relations have changed (in a way required to ensure an efficient operation of the newly invented treadmills) because otherwise the forces would not have progressed, and that the forces do progress because the relations have changed. But it is clear, despite the second part of the last sentence, that the change in the forces is more basic than the change in relations: the relations change *because* the new relations facilitate productive progress. The story illustrates the type of primacy the forces have in the Marxian theory of history. (1978: 162)

Primacy, here, makes no reference to an explanation of the relations by the current level of the forces (a). Rather, it is closely linked to the claim that relations are explained by their propensity to further the development of the forces (b). Indeed, in this second sense, the primacy thesis reduces to this claim and can therefore by symbolized as follows:

(PT2) (RP is best for $\triangle PF$) $\rightarrow RP$.

PHILIPPE VAN PARIJS

In words: The reason why the prevailing relations do prevail is that they facilitate the development of the productive forces.[3]

III. THE DEVELOPMENT THESIS

Before discussing where this distinction of two senses of the primacy thesis leaves the formulation of the primacy puzzle, we need to clarify the closely associated *development thesis:* "The productive forces tend to develop throughout history" (Cohen 1978: 134). According to Cohen (1978: 158), the development thesis is what needs to be added to the purely symmetrical "facts of constraint" (the fact that not every combination of forces and relations is possible or stable) in order to get the primacy thesis.[4] However, two very different inter-

---

3 Some critics of Cohen have adopted the first interpretation of the primacy thesis. Levine and Wright (1980: 52) insist, for example, that the "compatibility thesis" (to the effect that a given level of development of the productive forces is compatible with only a limited range of relations of production) "is plainly essential for the Primacy Thesis," which makes sense only if the latter is taken in the first sense. Others have adopted the second interpretation. According to Elster, for example, "Cohen explains and defends the thesis that the productive forces have primacy over the production relations [. . .] in the sense that the latter are what they are because of the kind of influence they exert on the former" (1980: 123; see also 1981: 639 and 1983: chap. 6).

4 Note, incidentally, that the "facts of constraint," as specified by what Levine and Wright call the compatibility thesis, i.e., the claim that "a given level of productive power is compatible only with a certain type, or certain types, of economic structure" (Cohen 1978: 158), are *not* symmetrical in the sense that the reciprocal of this claim (a give type of economic structure is compatible only with a certain level, or certain levels, of productive power) automatically follows, contrary to what Levine and Wright take for granted. This is easily shown by the following counterexample. Suppose we have two levels of forces 1 and 2 and three forms of relations A, B, and C, with A or B "coresponding to" 1 and B or C "corresponding to" 2. In this case, it is true that any level of forces is compatible with only certain forms of relations, but it is false that any form of relations is compatible with only certain levels of forces, since B is compatible with both 1 and 2. And it is therefore false to say that the compatibility thesis, as stated, "involves" both claims (Levine and Wright 1980: 60). (It would do so if the initial "a given" were to be understood as "some given" rather than as "any given," but I am sure this weakening of the claim would be endorsed by neither Cohen nor Levine and Wright as an interpretation of what historical materialism asserts). The symmetrical character of the facts of constraint, consequently, must lie elsewhere, namely, in their failure to specify the direction of causation.

94

pretations of the development thesis can be given, which are connected, again, to the two senses in which one can speak of an explanation of relations by forces.

The first interpretation is strongly suggested by the following passage: "Given the constraints, with sufficient development of the
forces, the old relations are no longer compatible with them. Either
they will have changed without lag along with productive development, or – the theoretically prescribed alternative – there will now be
'contradiction' between forces and relations. But if contradiction ob-
tains, it will be resolved by alteration of the production relations"
(Cohen 1978: 158). What the development thesis asserts, this suggests, is that

(DT1) There is an autonomous tendency for the forces to develop.

Such an assertion can only give a causal direction to the "facts of
constraint" between forces and relations, thereby generating PTo,
that is, the claim that the form taken by the relations is determined
by the current level of the productive forces. This interpretation of
the development thesis is clearly embraced by the bulk of Levine and
Wright's review article, whose very structure is strongly influenced
by the foregoing passage.[5] Drawing on the way in which Cohen
(1978: 150–7) argues his case for the development thesis, they construe the latter as asserting that rational adaptive practices tend to
develop the productive forces, whatever the form taken by the relations of production. All the latter can do is brake or accelerate, but
not alter the basic trend.[6]

When interpreted in this way, however, the development thesis
seems to contradict Cohen's (1978: 278) emphatic claim that "production relations profoundly affect productive forces." If one takes
this claim seriously, that is, if one assumes that the development of
the productive forces is genuinely controlled by the relations of pro-

[5] What they call the contradiction thesis and the transformation thesis are
just meant to spell out the path that unavoidably leads from the facts of
constraint (compatibility thesis) and the assumption of an autonomous
tendency for the productive forces to grow (development thesis) to (the
initial segment of) the primacy thesis: $FP \rightarrow RP$. See Levine and Wright
(1980: 51–6).
[6] Levine and Wright's conception of the role played by the development
thesis is neatly depicted in their diagram (1980: 54), where "rational adaptive practices" are shown to determine the forces "from outside," independently of the relations of production.

duction, there is still another way of construing the development thesis, which can be phrased as follows:

(DT2) There is a tendency for those relations to prevail which are best for (or facilitate) the development of the forces.

Whereas DT1 assumes some search-and-selection process that operates directly on the productive forces, DT2 assumes one that operates on the relations of production, which in turn then control the search and selection of productive forces. In both cases, it is possible to say that there is a tendency for the productive forces to develop. But only in the second case is it also possible to say that whether the productive forces develop fully depends on the nature of the production relations. In this second interpretation, the development thesis (DT2) is obviously very close to the second interpretation of the primacy thesis (PT2). Indeed, the only significant difference between the two theses is that the latter makes fully explicit the causal claim that is only hinted at in the former. Whereas both PT1 and DT1 are directly relevant to the explanation of relations by the current level of forces, both PT2 and DT2 are directly concerned with the explanation of relations by their propensity to further productive development.

IV. TWO PRIMACY PUZZLES

Perhaps the most original feature of Cohen's reconstruction of Marx's theory of history, and certainly the feature that has attracted the most critical attention, is his *functional* interpretation of the central propositions of historical materialism: These propositions explain the forms taken by the production relations and the superstructure in terms of their functions of facilitating productive development and stabilizing the production relations, respectively. The most interesting argument Cohen puts forward in favor of this functional interpretation is that it enables him to solve what can be called the *primacy puzzle:* "Construing [Marx's] explanations as functional makes for compatibility between the causal power of the explained phenomena and their secondary status in the order of explanation" (Cohen 1978: 278). Or, as he puts it even more explicitly elsewhere, "No other treatment (but a functional one) preserves consistency between the explanatory primacy of the productive forces over the economic structure and the massive control of the latter over the former, or between the explanatory primacy of the economic structure over the superstructure and the latter's regulation of the former" (Cohen 1980: 129–30). However, since the primacy puzzle, thus phrased, is nothing but the problem of reconciling the primacy of the productive forces (and the economic structure) over the production relations (and the superstructure) with the recognition that the latter also control the former, what the primacy puzzle means will depend on which interpretation the primacy thesis receives.

As far as the explanation of relations by forces is concerned, we have seen that the primacy thesis, as formulated and illustrated by Cohen, can mean two different things. Let us take the second sense first. The primacy of the forces then consists in the fact that the reason why the prevailing relations do prevail is that they facilitate the development of the forces (PT2). How is this primacy to be reconciled with the fact that the relations control the forces? Clearly, there is no problem whatsoever about such a reconciliation, as the primacy thesis, in this sense, *presupposes* that the forces are controlled by the relations: If the relations did not determine the evolution of the forces, they could not be selected in such a way that they facilitate their development. Consequently, as primacy is here understood, there is no primacy *puzzle* for which a functional interpretation could provide a solution. Moreover, as the primacy of the forces consists, *by definition*, in the relation being functionally explained by reference to them, the claim that a functional explanation is necessarily involved becomes plainly trivial.

We may be able to make better sense of Cohen's justification of his functional interpretation of historical materialism if we turn to the other sense of the primacy thesis. The latter asserts that the form taken by the relations is explained by the level of the forces embraced by it to a far greater extent than vice versa (PT1). Strictly speaking, it is here again possible to argue that there is no primacy *puzzle*, no paradox to dissolve, as the primacy thesis (thus formulated) presupposes some sort of causation from the relations to the forces. But this is sophistry. Though inaccurately formulated, the underlying problem is clear: Granted the assumption of two-way causation, what sense can be made, if any, of the primacy of the forces (or the subordination of the relations), as caught by the expression "to a far greater extent"?

One possible, though farfetched, interpretation of this expression takes us straight back to the second interpretation of the primacy thesis (PT2). The "greater extent" could reflect the fact that although the relations control the development of the forces, they are in turn explained by the forces *twice over:* by reference to the level achieved by the forces (PTo) *and* by reference to their ability to facilitate the latter's development (PT2). I have mentioned that it does not make much sense to ask how the control of the forces by the relations can be reconciled with the primacy of the forces as expressed in PT2, which presupposes such control. But it does make sense to ask how this primacy (and its presuppositions) can be reconciled with the logically independent claim that the level reached by the forces explains the form of the relations (PTo). What enables us to perform such a reconciliation, Cohen's answer would be, is our recourse to a functional interpretation of the core of historical materialism. Clearly, not any functional interpretation would do. The "social cohesion" (c) and "Wallersteinian" (d) scenarios both involve a functional explanation.[7] But whereas the former fulfills PTo, not PT2 (relations are explained by their ability to maintain social cohesion, not by their ability to facilitate productive development), the latter fulfills PT2, not PTo (relations are explained by the society's current position in the world system, not by its current level of productive development), and neither therefore performs the required reconciliation of PTo and PT2. What we need, obviously, is a scenario of the kind actually put forward by Cohen (e), which also involves a functional explanation, but of a particular form. The functional nature of the interpretation proposed, therefore, is not sufficient for the required reconciliation. All Cohen claims, however, is that it is necessary. But as pointed out earlier, the latter claim is plainly trivial, since PT2 on its own *already* asserts that the relations are functionally explained by reference to the forces.

V. THE GENUINE PRIMACY PUZZLE AND ITS SOLUTION

Is there any way of saving Cohen's claim from triviality? At the beginning of the previous paragraph, I warned that the interpretation I there chose for the expression "to a far greater extent" was

[7] A *functional* explanation is the explanation of the presence of an item by the fact that it has some differential consequences (compared to its absence or the presence of some alternative item). This fact, which is a dispositional feature of the context in which the item appears, is sometimes in turn explicitly accounted for by reference to some structural (or nondispositional) feature of the context. Hence the general structure of a functional explanation, which can be (loosely) represented as follows: $S \rightarrow (i \rightarrow C) \rightarrow i$, and is illustrated by (c) and (d) as well as by (e).

farfetched. I believe that a different interpretation, though nowhere discussed by Cohen, has the twofold advantage of being closer to the sense in which historical materialists grant primacy to the forces (when they do so) and of saving from triviality Cohen's claim that only a functional interpretation can solve the primacy puzzle. The primacy of the forces, according to this interpretation, is fully contained in the fact that when there is a *contradiction* between the level currently achieved by the forces and the form taken by the relations, the latter adjusts to the former, and *not* the former to the latter. When used in this way, the notion of contradiction clearly presupposes the existence of *laws of correspondence* between various levels of development of the forces and various forms of production relations.[8] What the primacy thesis does is specify the causal direction of the adjustments that make it possible for these *laws of correspondence* to hold at equilibrium, that is, when the adjustment mechanisms have had time to operate. And it thereby enables historical materialism to provide a comparative-static theory of changes in the relations of production by reference to changes in the levels achieved by the productive forces. Put differently, each of these levels defines an *attractor* in the space of possible forms of production relations, a position in which the latter will eventually settle until the forces move on to a different level.

But here comes the genuine primacy puzzle. Does not the primacy of the forces, understood in this way, prevent the forces from being explained to *any* extent by the relations? Does not the claim that in case of contradiction, the relations always adjust to the forces and never the other way around undermine the very possibility of two-way causation? This is not the case. For a recourse to (equilibrium) laws of correspondence is not only legitimate when one of the two variables is exogenously determined. It is also legitimate (at least as a useful approximation) when there is, in most possible combinations of their values, a significant difference in the *speeds* at which the two

---

[8] As illustrated by Cohen's (1978: 198) Table IV:

Level of productive development	Form of economic structure
No surplus	Pre-class society
Some surplus, but less than	Pre-capitalist class society
Moderately high surplus, but less than	Capitalist society
Massive surplus	Post-class society

variables affect each other's level, here between the (higher) speed at which the relations adjust to the current level of the forces and the (lower) speed at which they carry the forces from one level to another. Somewhat more specifically, the situation envisioned can be depicted as follows. For most possible combinations of levels of forces and forms of relations (those of "noncorrespondence"), there is hardly any movement in the level of the forces compared to the much faster change (toward "correspondence") in the form of the relations. In a small area (of correspondence), however, there is no tendency for the relations to change, and the speed of the change in the forces (whose development is facilitated by "corresponding" relations) ceases to be insignificant in comparison. In other words, whenever the form of the relations "contradicts" the current level of the forces, the latter can be viewed as (nearly) fixed and as exerting on that form a (nearly) exogenous pressure toward change. But as soon as correspondence is restored the forces lose their (near-) fixity and start progressing, while the relations could now be viewed as exogenously fixed. To the extent that most possible combinations of levels of forces and forms of relations are contradictory, the adjustment of the relations to the forces can be referred to as the *fast* dynamics (though it slows down at or near the correspondence point), whereas the furthering of the development of the forces by the relations can be labeled the *slow* dynamics (though its speed ceases to be negligible at or near a situation of correspondence).[9]

When this fast and this slow dynamics coexist, it thus turns out, it is possible for the relations of production both to invariably adjust to the level of the forces in case of contradiction and to determine whether the forces will develop or stagnate. Such coexistence, in other words, solves the genuine primacy puzzle, the problem of reconciling the primacy of the forces, as interpreted here, and their control by the relations of production.

VI. IS A FUNCTIONAL EXPLANATION NECESSARILY INVOLVED?

In this light, we can return to Cohen's claim that his functional interpretation of the core of historical materialism, as captured in (e) or (f), enables him to solve the primacy puzzle. Note, first of all, that

[9] For illustrative diagrams and further discussion, see Van Parijs (1979: 89–92).

his functional interpretation implies the coexistence of a fast and a slow dynamics. His functional explanation is an explanation of the presence of some item *at equilibrium,* assuming all relevant parameters (here the level of development of the forces) are fixed.[10] And being a functional explanation by the ability to facilitate productive development, it also assumes a relaxation of this fixity when the relations take on their equilibrium form. However, it is not by virtue of its involving a functional explanation alone that Cohen's interpretation of historical materialism combines a fast and a slow dynamics. Take scenario (c), where the forces determine the form of the relations (at equilibrium) by picking out the form most conducive to social cohesion. There is a functional explanation of the relations (by their ability to preserve social cohesion), and a fast dynamics from the forces to the relations is clearly implied. However, though not ruled out (the relations may well affect *both* social cohesion and productive development in a situation in which only the former influence is relevant to the explanation of the form they take), a slow dynamics from the relations to the forces is not necessarily involved. Or take scenario (d), where a society's position in the world system determines the form that is best for productive relations (at equilibrium) by picking out the form best for productive development. Here again, there is a functional explanation of the relations, and this time a slow dynamics from the relations to the forces is clearly implied. But unless the position in the world system is in turn ("quickly") determined by the level of development of the forces, no fast dynamics from the forces to the relations is involved.

Consequently, the functional nature of the explanation does not suffice to guarantee that a fast and a slow dynamics are combined or, therefore, that the primacy puzzle is solved. Cohen's claim, in any case, is not that the functional nature of the interpretation is sufficient, but that it is necessary for the primacy puzzle to be solved. But this is wrong too. Suppose, in the usual way, that the form taken by the relations of production determines whether the forces develop or stagnate (slow dynamics from the relations to the forces) and also that the level reached by the forces determines which form the relations will take at equilibrium (fast dynamics from the forces to the relations). By no means does this imply that the form that prevails at equilibrium has been chosen because it facilitates produc-

---

[10] For an argument to the effect that functional explanations are necessarily static in this sense, see Van Parijs (1981: 40–4).

tive development. Indeed, the determination of the relations by the forces may proceed without involving any functional selection. As Veblen suggests, for example, the use of certain instruments of production may shape the producers' minds in such a way that their relations to one another are profoundly altered (1970: 208, 215–16). Given this scenario, it may be the case that the relations which prevail at equilibrium further the development of the productive forces, but this fact has no role here in explaining why those relations prevail. What the Veblenian scenario shows is that one can have primacy and two-way causation with no recourse to a functional explanation. All a functional account does is *embed* the slow dynamics in the fast one, as in (e), by stipulating that the reason why a particular level of the forces picks out a particular form of the relations involves the effect of these relations on the development of the forces. But this embedding is in no way required for primacy to be reconciled with two-way causation.[11]

VII. COHEN'S DILEMMA

I began by pointing out that there are two senses in which one commonly speaks of the explanation of the relations of production by reference to the productive forces. Corresponding to these two senses, there are also two senses, both explicitly used or strongly suggested by Cohen, in which one can understand what he calls the primacy thesis and the associated development thesis. In one sense, the primacy thesis asserts that the form taken by the relations is explained by its ability to further the development of the forces (PT2), and the primacy puzzle, understood as the problem of reconciling the primacy thesis and the control of the forces by the relations, then fails to make any sense, since the primacy thesis in itself presupposes such a control. In the other sense, the primacy thesis asserts that the level of the forces explains the form of the relations to a far greater extent than the other way around (PT1), and the primacy puzzle then becomes the problem of reconciling this "greater extent" with a (full) control of the development of the forces by the relations. When construed in this way, the primacy

[11] This embedding may be required, however, for primacy to be reconciled with two-way causation *and* other views Marx or Marxists hold. But (1) these other views would have to be specified, which Cohen does not do, and (2) my guess is that, once these views are stated explicitly, the alleged solution will become tautological.

puzzle makes much more intuitive sense and is clearly central to historical materialism. Cohen's interesting claim is that this puzzle can be solved only if the core of historical materialism is interpreted as a set of functional explanations.

Much hinges, we have seen, on how we interpret "to a far greater extent." What is meant might simply be that the relations are explained by reference to the forces in the two ways mentioned (PT0 and PT2). But as one of these ways (PT2) essentially involves a functional explanation, the claim that only a functional interpretation of historical materialism can solve the primacy puzzle becomes altogether trivial. More plausibly, the primacy of the forces may consist in the fact that in case of contradiction, the relations adjust to the forces and not the other way around. There is a general way in which such a primacy can be reconciled with the control of the forces by the relations. It is by building a dynamic model in which a fast and a slow dynamics can be distinguished. Cohen's functional interpretation presupposes such a model. It corresponds to the special case in which the slow dynamics is *embedded* in the fast one. But precisely because it is but a special case of a more general solution, Cohen's claim that it provides the only way of solving the primacy puzzle (in the most plausible interpretation of the latter) is plainly false.

Thus emerges Cohen's dilemma. His functional interpretation of historical materialism is certainly exciting and possibly correct. But the justification he gives for it by arguing that it provides the only way of solving Marxism's central puzzle is, depending on how the latter is construed, either trivial or false. My claim is that the more general model somewhat abstractly sketched here not only helps in displaying the structure of a remarkable pattern of "Marxist causation." It also covers all possible solutions of the primacy puzzle in its most relevant interpretation. This claim, I venture, is neither trivial nor false – and is the only way out of Cohen's dilemma.

REFERENCES

Cohen, G. A. (1978). *Karl Marx's Theory of History: A Defence*. Oxford: Oxford University Press.
    (1980). "Functional Explanation: Reply to Elster," *Political Studies* 28, 129–35.
Elster, Jon (1980). "Cohen on Marx's Theory of History," *Political Studies* 28, 121–8.
    (1981). "Clearing the Decks," *Ethics* 91, 634–44.

(1983). *Explaining Technical Change: A Case Study in the Philosophy of Science.* Cambridge: Cambridge University Press.

Frank, Andre G. (1979). *Dependent Accumulation and Underdevelopment.* New York: Monthly Review Press.

Levine, Andrew, and Erik O. Wright (1980). "Rationality and Class Struggle," *New Left Review* 123, 47–68.

Van Parijs, Philippe (1979). "From Contradiction to Catastrophe". *New Left Review* 115, 87–96.

(1981). *Evolutionary Explanation in the Social Sciences: An Emerging Paradigm.* Totowa, N.J.: Rowman & Littlefield.

Veblen, Thorstein (1970). *The Theory of the Leisure Class.* London: Allen & Unwin.

Wallerstein, Immanuel (1974). *The Modern World-System. Capitalist Agriculture and the Origins of the European World Economy in the 16th Century.* New York: Academic Press.

CHAPTER 5

Marxian functionalism

JAMES NOBLE

Many people associate functional explanation with structural functionalism and find the idea that it has any bearing on Marxism quite
implausible. Typically, structural functionalism relied on the Parso-
nian idea that social systems are held together by common social
values.[1] This, clearly, is at odds with a basic thesis of Marxism: All
societies are class divided. Furthermore, to an extent that is rare in
the social sciences, structural functionalism is agreed to be a dead
letter. Seemingly, Marxism and functionalism are as unalike as night
and day.

It is a thesis of Gerald Cohen's *Karl Marx's Theory of History: A
Defence* (1978) that Marx's fundamental theoretical claims are best
understood in functional terms.[2] My concern here is both to criticize
and develop Cohen's views. For although Cohen has clarified many
of the issues, I shall argue that his views are misleading in some
respects. They are based to too great an extent on positivism, which
is as poor a guide to functional explanation as it is to Marxism. I
agree with Cohen that Marxism *can* be revealingly analyzed in terms
of functional explanations. However, I disagree with some of his
claims about how functional explanations can be justified. One of

[1] As I use the term, structural functionalism refers to a theoretical approach in the social and cultural sciences in which elements of social
organization are explained by their contribution to the stability or viability
of the society as a whole. Structural functionalism was an attempt to
construct a model of society in general so that a general theory of social
organization could be developed. In its nature, it was anti-historical.
[2] But see Cohen (1982), where an agnosticism about functions and functional explanation is announced. I shall still use the term, as indeed
Cohen himself does, to present his views.

the legacies of structural functionalism is considerable doubt about whether functional explanations can be justified at all, and I hope to use Marxism to show one way in which such explanations *can* be justified.

First, I shall discuss and criticize Cohen's account of functionalism. Cohen's views nonetheless provide a basis for the rest of the essay in that they make possible a statement of the problem of functional explanation. Second, I shall examine Marx's explanation of the surplus laboring population in capitalist societies and use it as a basis for a statement of the *adequacy conditions* that functional explanations must meet if they are actually to account for social phenomena. And finally, I suggest that Cohen's positivistic idea that historical materialism is an "infant science" (1978: 27) misconceives Marx's intentions and accomplishments, and I propose an alternative understanding.

I

One task Cohen sets himself is to formulate an account of functional explanation that is not vulnerable to well-known philosophical criticisms. I shall begin with a discussion of Cohen's philosophical defense of functional explanation before turning to his views about the Marxian version of functional explanation.

According to Cohen, functional explanation is "a single, properly distinctive form of explanation," and although it is broadly causal, it is so in a "special sense" (1978: 250). Functional explanations invoke a special kind of law: a consequence law. Its form is: "IF it is the case that if an event of type E were to occur at t_1, then it would bring about an event of type F at t_2, THEN an event of type E occurs at t_3" (1978:260). The antecedent attributes a disposition to E-type events to cause F-type events. The statement as a whole says that this disposition causes an E-type event. An example Cohen gives is: If a rain dance would reinforce group identity, then a rain dance is performed (1978: 274).

Cohen argues persuasively that although explanations invoking consequence laws involve explaining something in terms of its consequences, they involve no commitment to the idea that something can cause something that is temporally prior to it. For a consequence law explains something in terms of a preexisting disposition of that something to have a certain consequence.

Cohen (1978: 272) represents a consequence explanation in a scheme derived from the covering-law model:[3]

L: IF it is the case that if an event of type E were to occur at t_1 then it would bring about an event of type F at t_2, THEN an event of type E occurs at t_3.

C: Were an event of type E to occur at t', it would bring about an event of type F at t''.

E: An event of type E occurs at t'''.

This says: The disposition of E-type events to bring about F-type events explains the occurrence of an E-type event on a particular occasion. Cohen's argument is that functional explanations have the form of consequence explanations (1978: 264). I think that this construal of functional explanation is promising and shall depend on it in subsequent analysis.

However, to *defend* functional explanation we must also show that explanations of this type can *justifiably* be given of social phenomena. I think Cohen errs when he writes:

It is of the utmost importance to note . . . that a consequence explanation may be well confirmed in the absence of a theory as to *how* the dispositional property figures in the explanation of what it explains . . . We may have good reason for thinking that a functional explanation is true even when we are at a loss to conjecture by what means or mechanism the functional fact achieves an explanatory role. (1978: 266)

Cohen does admit that "when B functionally explains A, there exists a mechanism by virtue of which it does" (1982: 51). But he insists that a functional explanation can be justified without such a theory. It is odd that in a book devoted to the detailed explication of historical materialism, Cohen does not expressly advance the thesis that historical materialism *is* the theory that justifies the application of functional explanations to social phenomena.

In the absence of a justifying theory or mechanism, it appears that any feature whatsoever of a society would be "explained by" the disposition of that society to be, say, viable, if, in fact, (1) the society is viable, and (2) it has that feature. For, absent a justifying theory, the sole evidence for (C) in the foregoing schema is the empirical

---

[3] Indeed, at many points Cohen lets the full elaboration of his analysis depend on the resolution of outstanding problems of the Hempelian analysis. He develops his analysis by analogy with straightforward causal explanation. See, for instance Cohen (1978: 256).

observation that the society is (or does) *F,* and also has *E*. If (E) – the *explanandum* – is true, as is typical in the context of explanation, and if (C) is true by virtue of this empirical evidence, it follows that (L) has both its antecedent and consequent satisfied. Thus, given *any* actual *E* and *F,* an "explanation" can be constructed. Clearly, more than empirical observation is necessary to justify a functional explanation. That something more, I suggest, is showing *how* the contribution of E to F brings E into being.

In response to similar criticisms by Elster (1980: 126), Cohen has conceded that exhibiting the underlying mechanism is *one* way to back up a functional explanation, but it is not the only one. The other is to look for "appropriately consonant and discrepant parallel instances" of the phenomenon (1978: 51). But Cohen does not say what counts as an *appropriately* consonant parallel instance. Appropriately in terms of what? This problem will not go away when the *explanans* is a dispositional property. Without an account of the underlying mechanism, it is hard not to agree with Elster that "the sluices are wide open for all sorts of pseudo-explanations" (1980: 126).

The problem can be seen in the following claim by Cohen:

If a Marxist says that the bourgeois media report industrial conflicts in a style which favours the capitalist class *because* the style of reportage has the asserted tendency, he may be able to justify his explanatory claim even when he cannot yet display *how* the fact that reportage in the given style favours the capitalist class explains the fact that industrial conflicts are reported in that way. (1978: 271–2)

Although I do not doubt that unions get less favorable press than management during a strike, recognizing that fact is not the same thing as explaining it. Clearly, Cohen's proffered explanation *hints* at some mechanism of social control. But until we have an account of that mechanism, we just do not have an explanation. Neither our understanding nor our ability to change the role of the press in capitalist society has been advanced.

Another example Cohen offers of a functional explanation in Marx concerns the passage of the Factory Acts in England in the 1840s and 1850s. On Cohen's analysis, that is, fitting it into the foregoing schema, Marx's explanation rests on the following generalization:

Substantial changes in economic structure which favour the immediate welfare of the subordinate class occur when the class fights for them *and* they increase – or at least preserve – the stability of the system (for reasons independent of allaying a felt grievance of the exploited). (1978: 295)

This generalization is of little use in explaining why the Factory Acts were passed in the circumstances in which they were passed. What *is* useful is what Marx in fact provides: a complicated historical narrative that includes shifting political coalitions, support by the Tories, the need of Liberals to enlist working-class support for the Free Trade Acts, the role of the judiciary, and the revolutions of 1848. Against this narrative, Cohen's generalization, riddled as it is with qualifications such as "increase – or at least preserve," lacks the requisite sharpness, something Cohen seems now to acknowledge (1982: 53). While it is reasonable to suggest that Marx has a functional explanation in mind, it is not reasonable to suggest that *this* is that functional explanation. As I shall explain, Marx recognized that the working of a law is always modified by circumstances.

Cohen's analysis of functional explanation is simply too derivative from the covering-law model of explanation. It is unusual, to say the least, to develop a defense of a style of explanation in the philosophical framework of one of the leading critics of that style of explanation. Was Carl Hempel simply wrong about the implications of the covering-law analysis for functionalism (1965: 297–330)? I suggest that we would do better to set aside the covering-law analysis and pose the question differently. If a person were offered the following functional explanation, "Poverty persists in advanced capitalist societies because its continued existence facilitates the accumulation of capital," what would that person want to know before he or she would be reasonably convinced by this explanation? The statements that would answer the questions that would occur to a reasonable person when presented with this explanation constitute its *adequacy grounds*. What are the adequacy grounds of a functional explanation of a social phenomenon?

II

I shall try to answer this question by generalizing from a passage in which Marx states one of his more important contentions.

If a surplus labouring population is a necessary product of accumulation or of the development of wealth on a capitalist basis, this surplus population becomes, conversely, the lever of capitalistic accumulation, nay a condition of existence of the capitalist mode of production. It forms a disposable industrial reserve army . . . that . . . creates, for the changing needs of the self-expansion of capital, a mass of human material always ready for exploitation. (1967: 632)

The basic idea here is obviously functional and readily cast as a consequence explanation: The contribution of the surplus population to capital accumulation leads to its ongoing formation. But Marx *also* says that the surplus labouring population is "a necessary product" of capital accumulation and "becomes . . . a condition of existence" of capitalism. These latter two contentions, I submit, refer to the adequacy grounds of the functional explanation apparent in this passage.

Marx shows that surplus population is a necessary product of accumulation by an argument, the fundamentals of which are as follows:

1. Insofar as the means of production have been appropriated by private persons, production becomes the production of surplus value (1967: 624).
2. The production of surplus value is maximized by improving the social productivity of human labor.
3. The social productivity of labor is increased when the mass of labor employed decreases in proportion to the mass of means of production moved by the labor (equivalently, when the technical composition changes in favor of the mass of means of production) (1967: 612).
4. Since there is a "strict correlation" between the technical and value composition of capital, the increase of the productivity of social labor leads to a decline of variable capital in proportion to constant capital (1967: 612).
5. Since the total demand for labor is determined by the variable portion of total social capital alone, it follows that the demand for labor falls progressively with increasing social productivity of human labor and the increase of total social capital (1967: 629).

Thus, a population is increasingly produced that is superfluous relative to the total demand for labor power. Marx also argues that the process is accelerated by the centralization of capital, but I shall ignore this for the purposes of the following discussion.

Marx's argument consists of a series of causal or quasi-causal statements that, taken together, relate private appropriation of the means of production to the production of surplus population. Private appropriation is the "historic basis" of capitalist production and necessarily, given the theory of surplus value, proceeds apace with the accumulation of capital (1967: 624). Private appropriation is thus the historic process that is definitive of the capitalist mode of production. Since the production of surplus population is shown to be a result of this process, it can fairly be said to be the necessary product of the capitalist mode of production. Because surplus population is related to the historic process of private appropriation, we can call this argument a *genetic theory* of surplus population.

Marx's second contention is that surplus population "becomes . . . a condition of existence of the capitalist mode of production." The surplus population is the social basis of the industrial reserve army. To describe it this way is to give a functional description, that is, one in terms of tasks it performs for capitalist production. The industrial reserve army is functional for further capital formation in two main respects. First, it makes it possible for capital to grow suddenly because it has a mass of "disposable human material" that can be thrown into new lines of production without disrupting already established production (1967: 632–3). This provides capital with disposable labor power beyond the natural increase of population. Second, the division of the labor force into an active and reserve army perpetuates the conditions for exploitation of labor power. The threat of competition to active workers by the reserve labor army compels the former to submit to overwork. General trends of wages are "exclusively regulated" by the expansion and contraction of the reserve army (1967: 637). Thus, says Marx, "Relative surplus population is . . . the pivot upon which the law of supply and demand of labour works" (1967: 639). In both these respects, the existence and increase of surplus population make possible further capital accumulation than would be possible in its absence.

It is fair to say that the production of surplus population *functions* to facilitate capital accumulation. As in the case of the genetic theory, Marx is considering the matter as an *evolving historical process.* But, unlike the genetic theory, the concern here is not with the operation of mechanisms in the historical development of capitalism. Rather, Marx is looking at capitalism as a social formation with a long-term propensity or end: the accumulation of capital. I shall call this demonstration of the consequences of surplus population for the accumulation of capital Marx's *functional theory* of surplus population.

Marx's discussion of the creation and role of surplus population is, in its general outlines, an adequate functional explanation. That is, it contains the relevant statements, which, if true, would justify a functional explanation of surplus population. Of course, I have only stated Marx's explanation in summary form, so it is not, as stated, a completely elaborated functional explanation. My thesis is that a rational person would accept the explanation if she or he were convinced that the genetic and functional theories were true.

The adequacy grounds suggested by Marx for this functional explanation of surplus population can be represented as follows, let-

111

ting E denote surplus population, E_f the industrial reserve army, and F capital accumulation:

E's disposition to cause F explains E, only if:

1. There is a social system, S, of which
2. E is a structural tendency, and,
3. There is a set of laws, L, that characterize S, and by virtue of which E is a necessary product, and
4. F is an end (or among the ends) of S, that is, by virtue of L, there is a selection process that produces F, and
5. E is E_f, and E_f contributes to the realization of F.

I shall discuss these adequacy conditions seriatim.

ad 1: The force of (1) is to say that functional explanation is relative to a system. For Marx, of course, the concrete subject matter is the capitalist mode of production. In saying this, however, there is already an element of idealization, for capitalist production was most completely developed in Marx's day only in England (1967: 648). Beyond this, Marx's discussion of the general law of capitalist accumulation, of which the formation of surplus population is an aspect, is premised on a simplified conception of capitalist production, based on several abstractions. First, Marx averages the individual capitals invested in a particular branch of production and then averages across branches of production to form the concept of "the composition of the total social capital of a country" (1967: 613). This implies a correlative conception of the total labor power of a country. Second, at this stage of his argument, Marx ignores the effects of circulation of commodities. Thus, the general law of capital accumulation is based on a conception in which the capitalist class exchanges wages for the labor power of the working class.

To say that a functional explanation is relative to a system is to say that one cannot demand an explanation of phenomena that were left out of the underlying conception. If, for example, we abstract away from particular branches of production, we cannot demand that the explanation we develop apply, by itself, to employment trends among coal miners. To explain the latter would require substantial historical information. But this is only to recognize, as Marx does, that the working of a law "is modified . . . by many circumstances" (1967: 644). Another way to put the basic idea is to say that the relativity of functional explanation to a system means that the explanation carries with it a *ceteris paribus* clause. In the case of surplus population there are three categories of *cetera* that have to be *paria:* noncapitalist features of the country, social divisions within the capitalist and working classes, and effects of circulation of commodities. Thus, to explain particular historical situations, account of these factors must be taken, and this is essentially a matter of historical analysis.

I fear Cohen fails to appreciate this when he tries to explain the passage of the Factory Acts in terms of the general stability of the capitalist system. This ignores the substantial degree of abstraction incorporated into the concept of the capitalist system. Of course, we can add limiting assumptions to our systemic conception, but this further specificity often comes at the price of loss of generality. This is not a problem that is specific to functional explanation; in all forms of explanation, specificity tends to come at the price of generality.

ad 2: "Relative surplus population" has both theoretical and observational content. It has the former in that it is related by way of propositions of the genetic theory to the historic process of private appropriation. Marx says that the tendency toward relative surplus population is "a law peculiar to the capitalist mode of production" (1967: 632). That is, it presupposes certain social conditions for its validity. On the other hand, relative surplus population has observational content: "Every labourer belongs to it during the time when he is partially employed or wholly unemployed" (1967: 640). Unemployment and underemployment are observable. Marx differentiates the surplus population into the "floating form," rural population displaced by commercial argiculture, and the "stagnant" form that enjoys "extremely irregular" employment.[4] The actual process that fills these ranks is "always connected with violent fluctuations and transitory production of surplus population" (1967: 643). In light of all this, relative surplus population is best said to refer to a structural tendency of capitalist society: structural in that it is a necessary product of capitalism, a tendency in that it is the underlying trend in the constant fluctuations of actual history.

I believe that the typical *explanandum* of a functional explanation is a structural tendency. Cohen says that there is no reason why functional explanations of historical events cannot be given. However, he supports this contention with his example of the passage of the Factory Acts, which I do not find persuasive as an explanation. In

---

[4] Today Marx's floating form is known as frictional unemployment, while the stagnant form is called structural unemployment. That the problems are still with us is shown by the fact that the level of unemployment deemed to be full employment is continually revised upward. This historic process of displacement of rural population only recently ended in Europe. It partially explains rising wages.

favor of the position that the object of a functional explanation is a structural tendency is the degree of abstraction built into such a concept. This abstraction makes it more likely that clear relationships can be found in the genetic and functional theories. At the least, it is quite clear that this is Marx's approach to the matter.

ad 3: One of the traditional criticisms of functional explanation is that even if it could be shown that a particular social practice contributes to, say, social viability, that by itself would not explain the presence of that practice. For unless this practice is the only one that would contribute to social viability – a dubious proposition – it follows only that this practice *or some other* will exist. This is the problem of functional equivalents and is the cutting edge of Hempel's argument against functional explanation (1965: 308–14). There is something to this argument. But it does not show that functional explanations are not really explanatory; rather it shows that adequate functional explanations require a genetic theory.

Marxian functionalism is not vulnerable to this line of criticism. Marx does not simply show that capitalist society has an abstract need for surplus population. He shows that it produces the surplus population that fulfills its need. Presented with a functional explanation, a reasonable person asks how it comes about that the item that fulfills the need is there in the first place. The genetic theory answers this question and therefore is among the adequacy conditions of the explanation. The structural functionalists paid scant attention to genetic theories, and this is no small part of the explanation of the abstractness and sterility of their theoretical fomulations.

It might be objected that if this is so, there is no need to cast the explanation of surplus population in a functional form at all. After all, in a genetic theory do we not have a perfectly respectable causal explanation of E? This misses an essential point about Marxian functionalism: The formation of surplus population is a continuing historical process. And the genetic theory that accounts for the continuing generation of surplus population is itself related to the process of capital accumulation. In the foregoing propositional representation of the genetic theory, the first proposition refers to the process of private appropriation. But private appropriation is a continuing process and an aspect of capital accumulation. It continues at the close of each working day with the conversion of surplus value into capital. But capital accumulation is the basic process in the functional theory as well. Therefore, the genetic theory is not a *replacement* for the whole explanation, for it is dependent on the functional theory.

ad 4: Marx's explanation depends on a conception of the capitalist mode of production as a social formation that evolves so as to achieve its ends. In the nature of the case, functional explanations can only be offered in the context of systems that can meaningfully be said to have ends. For to say that something is functional for a social system is to say that it contributes to the achievement of the ends of that social system. The problem of how ends are ascribed to social systems is a topic to which justice cannot be done in a short space. I hope only to indicate in general terms how I think it can be done.

A non-Marxian example will serve as the starting point. Aristotle said that to determine the ends of something we must "consider things in the process of their growth" (1962: 3). That is, the historical development of something is the basis for ascribing goals to it. Aristotle says that the polis exists for the sake of a good life. How does he know this? Human society did not remain just a collection of families and villages because these forms of society lacked self-sufficiency, that is, the possibility of a good life. Because people have a natural impulse for a good life, they will not be satisfied with the more basic societal structures and will leave them for the polis. What Aristotle is driving at is that the desire for a good life is learned. As a result of a process that leads from the family to the village and then to the polis, that is propelled forward by needs—first "daily, recurrent needs" and then something more than this—human beings are led to the polis and, once there, tend to stay there (1962: 4).

Aristotle is describing a rudimentary selection process. In general, a selection process exists when (1) there is a range of possible states, or variations within the phenomena under study, of which (2) some one, or ones, tends to prevail with a certain frequency, by virtue of (3) the operations of some mechanism (Wimsatt 1972). When a selection process exists, thus, it tends over time to produce certain preferred states or conditions. These states themselves can be said to be the end(s) of the process. In these terms, Aristotle's ascription of the end of a good life to the polis rests on a showing that of the range of possible human societies—family, village, polis—the latter comes to predominate because people have a natural impulse for a good life. Thus, the mechanism of the process is human choice.

The capitalist mode of production has an end: capital accumulation. The underlying selection process is well described by Marx in the following:

The development of capitalist production makes it constantly necessary to keep increasing the amount of capital laid out in a given industrial undertaking, and competition makes the immanent laws of capitalist production to be felt by each individual capitalist, as external coercive laws. It compels him to keep constantly extending his capital, in order to preserve it, but extend it he cannot, except by means of progressive accumulation. (1967: 502)

Individual capitalists really have no choice in the matter: They must accumulate capital in order to preserve their capital. Since this is the situation facing all individual capitalists, the sum total of their decisions in the face of economic competition creates a process with a direction and an end. To ascribe the end of capital accumulation to the capitalist mode of production is to say that it is produced by the consequences of the decisions of individual capitalists in conditions characteristic of capitalist production.

Clearly, many of the same laws that are invoked in the genetic theory also appear in the description of the selection process that is the basis for the ascription of the end of capitalist accumulation. Indeed, it is a matter of looking at the operations of capitalism from two different points of view: its consequences for the working class, and its long-term propensities. Thus, in fact, what I have separated as grounds (4) and (3) for purposes of discussion are related in that both presuppose many of the same laws for their delineation. The Marxian concept of the capitalist mode of production includes both these aspects.

ad 5: This restates what I previously called the functional theory. It consists of two parts: a redescription of surplus population in functional terms as the industrial reserve army, and a showing that the industrial reserve army contributes to the end of capital accumulation. The industrial reserve army makes possible greater capital accumulation by allowing capital greater flexibility and by disciplining the working class. Because it expands the possibilities for capital accumulation, it is eminently functional for capitalist society.

Summing up, if the conceptual elements provided in (1) and (2) are well formulated and adequately capture the phenomena they are meant to conceptualize, and if the statements comprising (3), (4), and (5) are true, then Marx has produced a rationally persuasive functional explanation of surplus laboring population. For this would show how surplus population comes into being in the first place, and why it persists and increases. It persists and increases *because* it functions to facilitate capital accumulation, which in turn reinforces the processes that produced surplus population in the first place. Marx's explanation achieves this persuasiveness because it rests upon logically related genetic and functional theories. My suggestion is that this is the hallmark of an adequate functional explanation. Conversely, without these logically related theories, the explanation would remain speculative and unpersuasive. Contra Cohen, we cannot have good grounds for accepting a functional explanation in the absence of theories that show how the functional fact explains what it does. This is Marx's practice, and I believe this practice is methodologically persuasive.

Functional explanations, if they are adequate, show the dependence of social phenomena on larger social processes in the social systems in which they occur. By showing this dependence, they indicate what practical interventions are likely to succeed in changing the phenomena, and which are bound to fail. Marx suggests that one effective intervention would be to "organize a regular cooperation between employed and unemployed in order to destroy or weaken the ruinous effects of this natural law of capitalistic production on their class" (1967: 640). This can be effective because it recognizes the consequences of competition between the active and reserve labor armies and counteracts its effects. On the other hand, directing educational programs at only the reserve army, of which the poor are a part, is bound to fail as a long-term solution. Given Marx's analysis, its predictable effect, even if the programs were successful, would be to intensify competition within the working class and thereby depress wages. Such a program, which is near to the hearts of American liberals, would amount to a subsidy by means of state action of further capital accumulation, which produced the problem in the first place. Similarly, the favored strategy of American conservatives of facilitating capital accumulation by means of, for example, tax credits for investment, can have no lasting effect on poverty. Though it may stimulate the economy in the short run, and thereby stimulate wages, it does not affect the basic process that produces the poor in the first place. Indeed, by encouraging a change in the technical composition of capital in the direction of a greater mass of means of production, it tends to exacerbate the problem. As this brief discussion shows, although they rest on a basis of abstractions, functional explanations have important political implications.

III

Cohen suggests that historical materialsm is an "infant science" that makes general functional theoretical claims about human history (1978: 27). In other words, according to him, Marx has a general theory of history that consists of a number of functional propositions. It is an implication of the analysis I have just given that this view should be rejected. I conclude with a brief discussion of this point.

As I see it, functional explanations are inescapably relative to a system. The relevent system in Marxism is the mode of production. Although Marx does, at times, formulate concepts that are applicable across modes of production, such as production in general, or the production of use values, these are far too abstract to be useful in explaining anything concrete. Thus, Marx concludes his discussion of the labor process in general by saying:

> As the taste of the porridge does not tell you who grew the oats, no more does this simple process tell you of itself what are the social conditions under which it is taking place, whether under the slave-owner's brutal lash, or the anxious eye of the capitalist, whether Cincinnatus carries it on in tilling his modest farm or a savage in killing wild animals with stones. (1967: 184)

If we are to generalize across modes of production in order to formulate general functional laws of history, it is inevitable that we must abstract away from the social conditions that alone give concrete meaning to the concepts of Marxism. If, as I have tried to show, functional explanation is relative to a system, such an abstraction would involve forming a conception of a generic human mode of production. But surely this transhistorical conception flies in the face of Marxism.

It is better to say that historical materialism is a conception of history, not a theory of history. A conception, or *Auffassung* as Marx calls it, is a set of related concepts that affords a point of view; a theory is a set of statements that, in principle, can be accepted or rejected on the basis of experience. What Marx actually accomplishes is the production of a theory of the capitalist mode of production. Historical materialism is the conceptual foundation of this theory of capitalism. It is inevitable, I believe, that if we try to reconstruct historical materialsim as a general functional theory of history, we will leave out the adequacy grounds that alone make functional explanations persuasive.

REFERENCES

Aristotle (1962). *Politics*. Translated by Ernest Barker. Oxford: Oxford University Press.
Cohen, Gerald (1978). *Karl Marx's Theory of History: A Defence*. Princeton N.J.: Princeton University Press.

(1982). "Functional Explanation, Consequence Explanation, and Marxism." *Inquiry* 25: 27–56.

Elster, Jon (1980). "Cohen on Marx's Theory of History." *Political Studies* 28: 121–8.

Hempel, Carl (1965). "The Logic of Functional Analysis." In Hempel, *Aspects of Scientific Explanation.* New York: Free Press.

Marx, Karl (1967). *Capital,* vol. I. Translated by Samuel Moore and Edward Aveling. New York: International Publishers.

Wimsatt, William (1972). "Teleology and the Logical Structure of Function Statements." *Studies in History and Philosophy of Science* 3: 1–80.

Morals and politics

Is there in Marx's writings an implicit or explicit political or ethical theory? Considerable controversy continues to surround this question. At least part of the answer depends importantly on what is meant by speaking of an ethical or political theory. If by the former one means a set or system of ethical norms defining our duties and imperatives for guiding individual conduct, then the answer is that Marx never in fact formulated an ethical theory; nor, given his premises and presuppositions, could he have done so. But if by a moral theory one refers to some conception of the good life, of human happiness, fulfillment, and autonomy, then it is at least arguable that Marx not only subscribed to some such theory but that he *had* to do so.

Much the same can be said about Marx's political theory. Certainly he advanced no theory of (say) political obligation and was indeed inclined to regard such theories as having served the patently ideological function of masking and legitimating the exploitation of one class by another. Hence, Marx had no political theory, at least in this traditional sense. But if by political theory we mean a more or less comprehensive vision of political possibility and of the good society, then Marx did indeed have such a theory.

But the question of whether, or in what sense, Marx can be said to have had a *political* theory is more complicated still. For if the state and its subsidiary institutions are merely expressions of class interest and therefore destined to wither away, there would in classless communist society be little if any room for activity that is recognizably political. But this objection merely takes for granted the conception of politics characteristic of capitalist "civil society." Paul Thomas examines Marx's reasons for regarding such politics as having an "alien" aspect. The politics of civil society precludes the possibility of meaningful political participation and citizenship, in no small part because its conception of politics presupposes an abstract and alienated misdrawing of the boundary between the public and private spheres of human life. Humanly speaking, politics, thus (mis)conceived, becomes the problem instead of the solution. Only when public and private are rendered concretely complementary, not abstractly contradictory, can politics be reconstituted as a humanly meaningful activity fit for free citizens.

To the jaundiced eye of modern political scientists Marx's conception of politics and citizenship will doubtless appear hopelessly utopian and manifestly unscientific. Drawing on Engels's rather too facile distinction between utopian and scientific socialism, C. B. Macpherson contends that many modern democratic theorists have, in effect, drawn an equally facile distinction between "utopian" and "scientific" views of democracy. And they, like Engels, unstintingly condemn the former as impractical, visionary, and hopelessly at odds with the facts of economic and political life. Macpherson criticizes this still-dominant variant of democratic theory by calling into question the distinction on which it rests. If science at its best is visionary, then the best scientific theory of democracy will itself be visionary; it will question and criticize the postulates and assumptions on which more conventional theories rest and trace out the political possibilities of unconventional ones. A genuinely democratic polity, Macpherson maintains, will not be one whose political arrangements are dictated by a particular economic system, but rather the reverse. What is needed, he concludes, is a new and genuinely *political* economy. Upon that foundation it may be possible to build a genuinely democratic society fit for active citizens rather than, as at present, for passive consumers of material goods. The good society is not reducible without remainder to the affluent society.

One cannot, of course, speak of the good society without presupposing some notion of goodness. Or, put differently, one's vision of the good society must be predicated on and justified by reference to a moral theory. But this, some commentators contend, is precisely what Marx did not have (see, e.g., Edgley 1982; Wood 1980). Marx, they maintain, was a moral relativist or conventionalist with no substantive moral theory of his own; hence, he had no warrant other than personal preference for speaking of one kind of society as being better or worse than any other. Alan Gilbert disputes this oft-cited criticism, showing that Marx's theory of social progress presupposes an implicit moral theory, the premises of which somewhat resemble those of Aristotle. By partially reconstructing this theory, Gilbert demonstrates that Marx was rather more of a moral realist than an ethical relativist. Marx's moral concepts and categories—justice, for example, or exploitation—are meaningful, not as abstract or asocial ideas or ideals, but only within the context of actual social relations and historical possibilities.

If Marx had remarkably little to say about "justice" directly, he nevertheless said a great deal about injustice, albeit recast as the ostensibly "economic" category of exploitation. The concept of exploitation has been the main focus of several recent Marxian explorations (Cohen 1980; Elster 1978). John Roemer attempts to set the Marxian notion of exploitation within the context of a more general theory. Marx's theory of capitalist exploitation thus becomes, in Roemer's reconstruction, a special case of a general theory. All systems of production—slave, feudal, capitalist, even socialist—are in some sense exploitative, but the *way(s)* in which they extract value varies from one system to another. By constructing simplified models of these different economies, Roemer is able to show how each is exploitative in different ways, and why Marx's theory of *capitalist* exploitation takes the form it does.

REFERENCES

Cohen, G. A. (1980). "The Labor Theory of Value and the Concept of Exploitation." In Marshall Cohen, Thomas Nagel, and Thomas Scanlon (eds.), *Marx, Justice, and History*. Princeton, N.J.: Princeton University Press.

Edgley, Roy (1982). "Revolution, Reform and Dialectic." In G. H. R. Parkinson (ed.), *Marx and Marxisms*. Cambridge: Cambridge University Press.

Elster, Jon (1978). "Exploring Exploitation." *Journal of Peace Research* 15: 3–17.

Wood, Allen W. (1980). "The Marxian Critique of Justice." In Cohen, Nagel, and Scanlon, eds. (1980).

CHAPTER 6

Alien politics: a Marxian perspective on citizenship and democracy

PAUL THOMAS

Liberal societies are commonly held to depend on a distinction of public from private spheres of existence or activity. How this distinction is to be drawn, along what lines, and to what end are questions that do not admit of a uniform answer, and the precise lineaments or coordinates of this distinction have been drawn differently by different liberal theorists. Yet the distinction itself is supposed to matter, wherever the lines are finally drawn. And so, within limits, is the weighting of the categories. It is common to regard the preservation, enrichment, or extension of private life as a goal, or (*ceteris paribus*) *the* goal of state action and public policy. Negative theories of liberty are commonly invoked to this end. The private is to be guarded against the encroachments of the public. It may be conceived of as a sanctuary, a refuge, or simply as a platform, the source of individual opportunity. But whichever of these is subscribed to, the vision of the private and its ultimate preeminence is held to with some tenacity. It is defined against the public or the political: It is for the sake of the private, and for no other legitimate reason, that the public realm exists and is permitted to operate. These priorities, which do not in themselves solve all the political problems that have a habit of arising – indeed, it could be argued that these priorities create more political problems than they can solve – are nevertheless characterized by an enormous resiliency. The pursuit of happiness seems to be more positively valued the more elusive and fugitive it becomes. The goal may of course be more than happiness – the sphere of spontaneous, or authentic, feelings, emotions, and actions may encompass fulfillment of the kind that cannot be reduced to anything so mundane as happiness – but the priorities remain the same. Something, defined privatistically, is separated more or less rigidly, but always decisively, from something else, which is defined publicly and politically. The latter, political realm exists on a spectrum stretching from deliberation, on the one hand, to coercion on the other, and this spectrum does not reproduce itself, apparently, within the former, private realm.

Doubt has, of course, been cast on this polarity of private and public. Rousseau, for example, was either strikingly original or rather old-fashioned in reversing them. It is public life that needs protecting against the alluring siren calls of private interest (including that of the family). Hegel approached the polarity somewhat differently, not only by redefining it so that the family, as well as civil society, becomes an officially sanctioned realm within the general area of "private" life, but also by insisting that the private is the sphere of material necessity as well as spontaneous feelings and actions. The public realm, to Hegel as to Rousseau, was conversely the realm of freedom. It is to this tradition that Marx belongs, yet Marx goes further than Hegel and Rousseau. Indeed, it is in Marx's critical comments on Rousseau in his essay "On the Jewish Question" (1964) and on Hegel in his *Critique of Hegel's "Philosophy of Right"* (1970) that some of his most significant contributions are originally to be found. What concerned Marx was not the weighting of terms within or across a public–private polarity, but what had happened with the onset of capitalist society to this polarity itself. The relevant questions to be posed about it include not only What does it mean? and What does it entail, in human terms? but also Why did it arise when it arose in the first place (and at no other time)? To what needs or interests does it speak?

These are broad questions that do not admit of easy answers. Without suggesting we should be satisfied with the answers Marx gave, I do want to suggest that there is nevertheless something about the way these questions (and questions like them) are posed that speaks to a dilemma he identified. Marx criticized the private–public dichotomy in order to try to overcome it. The "splitting of man into public and private," he wrote in 1843, has the effect of dividing and debilitating both individual *and* communal existence by setting them up against each other, as though they were zero-sum categories that could exist only at each other's expense. Marx looks forward to a time when "social force is no longer separated from [the individual] as political power" (Marx 1964: 15, 31). It is important that we get the sense of this. Nancy Schwartz has recently argued on the basis of Marx's *Grundrisse* that Marx does not ultimately reject "politics" or "the political" and does not seek to "dissolve it back into the economy . . . or society." I find this argument convincing and would like to support it through a reading of some of Marx's earlier writings, particularly those I have already mentioned. In particular, I should like to register my agreement with Nancy Schwartz's assessment that Marx's "critique of the public/private dichotomy was specific to bourgeois society, that he appreciated other forms of the dichotomy in the past, and . . . could conceive of its existence" in future society (Schwartz 1979: 246). Bourgeois society, Marx argues in "On the Jewish Question," redefines the public–private split in an original and unprecedented manner, and although this redefinition does bring in its train a particular way of looking at questions about citizenship and democracy, it by the same token offends against something that, being less historically specific, may be more humanly important.

Marx argued in "On the Jewish Question" that with the advent of modern, bourgeois society "man" was no longer, and was no longer treated, as a generic social being; that people's powers were no longer apprehended as social powers; that their political existence, the realm of their social, moral, and collective being, was alienated in relation to the more immediate demands of their concrete material existence; and that there was, in human terms, an immense loss involved in the historical process that had instituted and was to sustain these changes. But what had changed, what had been lost? Marx's answer, which is sketched out in his *Critique of Hegel's "Philosophy of Right,"* is suggestive. During the Middle Ages, "the classes of civil society and the political classes were identical because the organic principle of civil society was the principle of the state . . . the political state in distinction from civil society was nothing but the representation of nationality." The modern age is by contrast characterized by "the separation of civil society and the political state as two different spheres, firmly opposed to each other." Faced with this separation, appeal across the Middle Ages to ancient models is in a sense doubly misleading, since "with the Greeks, civil society was a slave to political society" (Marx 1970: 72–3), whereas, in modern, bourgeois society the opposite is the case. In the Greek polis, no specifically and exclusively political sphere existed apart from the daily conduct of life and work; public life was the "real content" of individual life, and the person who had no political status was a slave, an *Unmensch*. "In Greece the *res publica* was the real private concern, the real content of the citizen . . . and the private man was slave, i.e. the political state as political was the true and sole content of the citizen's life and will."

In the Middle Ages the "private sphere" came to acquire political status. "Property, commerce, society, man (i.e. private man, the serf) were all political; the material content of the state was fixed by reason of its own form; every private sphere had a political character or was a political sphere" directly (Marx 1970: 32). Property was paramount in feudal society but was so because its distribution and transmission were directly political matters. Although the medieval period produced an integrated way of life in which "the life of the people" and "the life of the state" were congruent, this congruence was made possible only because feudal societies were unfree, and because the medieval world was – as Marx puts it in a striking paradox – the "democracy of unfreedom, accomplished alienation," and as such no model for the future.

The old civil society [in the Middle Ages] had a directly political character; that is, the elements of civil life such as property, the family and types of occupation had been raised, in the form of lordship, caste and guilds, to being elements of political life. (Marx 1970: 128)

But what "On the Jewish Question" called "political emancipation" (coincident upon bourgeois revolution) released the political spirit, which

had been broken, fragmented and lost, as it were, in the various culs-de-sac of feudal society. It gathered up this scattered spirit, liberated it from its entanglement with civil life, and turned it into a sphere of the community, the general concern of the people independent of these particular elements of civil life. A particular activity and situation in life sank into a merely individual significance, no longer forming the general relation of the individual to the whole. (Marx 1964: 28)

What this means is that "political emancipation is a reduction of man to a member of civil society, to an egoistic independent individual on the one hand and to a citizen on the other" (Marx 1964: 31). The establishment of this polarity is of vital importance. It is by being one that one becomes the other; the categories are interdependent and mutually reinforcing. "The abstraction of the state belongs to modern times because the abstraction of private life belongs only to modern times." Not only is it true that, in consequence, "the abstract, reflected opposition" between civil and political life "belongs only to modern times"; it also follows that what "distinguishes the modern state from those states in which a substantial unity between people and state obtained is . . . that the constitution itself has been

127

formed into an actuality alongside the real life of the people" (Marx 1970: 32). The state cannot reconcile divisions in society – reproduced within the individuals who make up society, who are socioeconomic actors *and* citizens – since it is itself a term and product of these same divisions. The emergence of the modern state presupposes a radical and historically unprecedented separation of politics from society. The modern state cannot liberate people from the disastrous effects of predatory social agencies – bureaucracy, private property, the division of labor, religion, money. It permits, and to a considerable extent must permit, them to flourish freely.

What this means is that the split between the citizen and the adherent of a particular religion is part of a more fundamental schism. "The contradiction in which the adherent of a particular religion finds himself in relation to his citizenship is but one aspect of the universal secular contradiction between political state and civil society." If religion, no longer officially sanctioned or promulgated by the modern state, is displaced so that it becomes a purely individual concern, this does not mean that the hold of religion on people is in any way lessened (except in imagination). Political emancipation from religion, the emergence, in other words, of a secular state, leaves and must leave religion in existence. "The emancipation of the state from religion is not the emancipation of actual man from religion" (Marx 1964: 21).

It is property that provides the most immediate point of comparison. The abolition of property qualifications for the franchise does not, according to Marx, abolish property. It presupposes the continued existence and importance of property, together with distinctions among people based on the degree and kind of property they hold. "Political emancipation" frees property from political restraint without freeing people from the restraint imposed by property. This point can be put more strongly. Once the amount and type of property held are declared to be politically irrelevant, property becomes responsible to nothing outside itself, and its newly oppressive, because newly unrestrained, nature becomes clearly exposed and keenly experienced by those persons who in their everyday life bear the brunt of its free play. Property and religiosity are reentrenched, not abolished, by the transition from medieval to modern state forms. Any medieval state form, using religion for its own purposes, obscures what are at root the human bases of religiosity. The modern state that does not profess any particular creed – or which professes its lack of profession of any creed – is not the abolition but the consummation of religion. Religion is displaced from the orbit of government to that of everyday life. The emancipation of the state from religion, like its emancipation from property, will in and of itself solve nothing. Religion "only begins to exist in its true scope when the state declares it to be non-political and thus leaves it to itself" (Marx and Engels 1975, vol. iv: 117), and the same freedom is accorded property.

In making these claims Marx is identifying a defining feature of the modern state. With the collapse of feudalism—a process that in Germany was far from complete, as Marx was well aware—civil society and the state become discontinuous in an unprecedented and radical way. Civil society and the property relations that animate it become wholly emancipated from all political restraint or regulation for the first time in history. This freedom, which is, of course, freedom of a very specific sort, is on the social agenda for the first time. Private life, or for that matter life in society, becomes independent of any consideration of the common good, or of public purpose; political limitations on economic activity give way, and the market becomes "self-regulating." Emancipation from feudal and communal restrictions (usury, guild regulations, sumptuary laws, censorship by ecclesiastical fiat, and other aspects of feudal politics) has the effect of formally freeing society from state control. The removal of political limitations on economic activity is decisive. It was signified most dramatically by (without, of course, being limited to) the French Revolution. The *Déclaration des droits de l'homme et du citoyen* of 1789, which marked the emancipation of civil society from the purview of the state, is doubly significant. Just as the state became ideologically universal, out of the control of king, aristocracy, and priesthood, proclamations of the "Rights of Man" recognized the citizenship of the individual *qua* individual, the individual as such, rich or poor, Jew or Christian. Citizenship no longer depended on birth, rank, status, or occupation. All such "accidental" attributes were no longer to operate as political qualifications or disqualifications. They were instead relegated to the level of purely individual concerns. This fundamental shift, Marx pointed out, had political and social implications that, although crucial, might not initially be apparent.

The emergence of bourgeois society that is signaled by the *Déclaration* and other, similar, documents bifurcates human existences in a fundamentally new way. Once bourgeois society had established itself, "private" and "public" were no longer in any sense contiguous terms, as they had been in the past. In the Middle Ages, to take the most available example, the dominant persons in society were ipso facto politically dominant. The privileges of the feudal landowning aristocracy linked the form of the state with the structure of society. Society therefore had a "directly political character," albeit an unfree political character. But "political emancipation" detaches political significance from private condition. Citizenship and private life become mutually exclusive spheres of activity for the first time. One is now a capitalist or a worker or whatever *and* a citizen. Vocation and political status are no longer linked organically. Each is counterposed to the other; there is no possibility of anything more than an unstable equilibrium between the two. Occupational category and political activity at best coexist uneasily alongside each other.

Not only do these two newly counterposed areas of human existence not overlap. Their confrontation has a more than conceptual existence. It is expressed within each individual as a rigid distinction between exclusive roles. The schism of state and society constantly reproduces itself within each individual, in a distilled, concentrated form. Marx extended this particular aspect of political emancipation not in "On the Jewish Question" so much as in *The German Ideology:*

In the course of historical evolution, and precisely through the inevitable fact that within the division of labour social relations take on an independent existence, there appears a division within the life of each individual, in so far as it is personal and in so far as it is determined, by some branch of labour and the conditions pertaining to it. (We do not mean . . . that, for example, the rentier, the capitalist, etc., cease to be persons; but their personality is conditioned and determined by quite definite class relationships and the division appears only in their opposition to another class and, for themselves, only when they go bankrupt). In the [feudal] estate, this is as yet concealed; for instance a nobleman always remains a nobleman, a commoner always a commoner, apart from his other relationships, a quality inseparable from their individuality. The division between the personal and the class individual, the accidental nature of the conditions of life for the individual, appears only with the emergence of the class, which is itself a product of the bourgeoisie. (Marx and Engels 1965: 93)

It is the newly "privatized" individuals who, denied any real participation in the conditions governing their existence, seek solace. The state is awarded the consolatory functions once monopolized (according to Feuerbach) by religion. People seek solace in a realm of universality, a realm separate from and counterposed to the limited sphere of the individual's mundane, finite existence. This realm is no longer just religious. It is also, and more nearly, political. As Marx puts it in a much-quoted passage,

By its nature the perfected political state is man's species-life in opposition to his material life. All the presuppositions of this egoistic life remain in civil society outside the state but as qualities of civil society. Where the political state has achieved its full development man leads a double life, a heavenly and an earthly life, not only in thought or consciousness but also in reality. In the political community he regards himself as a communal being; but in civil society he is active as a private individual, treats other men as means, reduces himself to a means and becomes the plaything of alien powers. The political state is as spiritual in relation to civil society as heaven is in relation to earth . . . In the state where he counts as a species-being, he is the imaginary member of an imaginary universality, divested of his real individual life and endowed with an unreal universality. (Marx 1964: 13–14)

The "unreal universality" of the citizen and of the state are connected. Taken together, they are coextensive in an unprecedented, and ominous, way. The remoteness and abstraction of political life, or what passes for political life, from ordinary, profane individual pursuits in society over which the state has relinquished control have distinct political consequences. Universality and communality remain part of people's lives in a "Feuerbachian"-compensatory fashion if their attainment – an attainment that speaks to a real and fundamental human need – is impossible in reality. The Feuerbachian viewpoint that what people lack in fact they attain in fancy still applies but needs refocusing. If meaningful political participation is withheld or denied, it turns abstract and fanciful, and thus newly appropriate to the fantasy world of citizenship. The state, to put it simply, becomes a kind of religious fetish. The division of people's social nature into separate, exclusive spheres of privacy and universality means that the latter is fictitious. To say this is not simply to assert the proposition that universality minus something is no longer universality. It is to underscore the historical point that the state was first presented as "universal" at the very time when the relations of production in society began to make the state the surrogate of the bourgeoisie. Political emancipation is in other words by its very nature bound to have the effect of displacing and negating the very satisfactions and needs in whose name it justifies itself. What Hegel had put forward as the human need for the universal (*das Allgemeine*), corresponding to the communal side of human nature, or to what Marx called "species-being" (*Gattungswesen*), is bound to remain unsatisfied. Once civil society was emancipated, freed from political restraint for the first time, property relations were enabled and encouraged to penetrate every crevice of the supposedly transcendent political realm.

The state's abstract, idolatrous universality and economic laissez-faire are of course linked. Political emancipation replaced the impact of personal power with the impersonal arbitrariness, the repressive anonymity of Adam Smith's "hidden hand." The illusion of liberty that the modern state creates and sustains is appropriate to the state's inability to liberate people from the disastrous effects of predatory social agencies (religion, property) it allows to flourish freely. The ideological expression and celebration of this state of affairs was the doctrine of the "Rights of Man" enunciated by the American and French revolutions.

None of the supposed rights of man go beyond the egoistic man, man as he is, man as a member of civil society; that is, as an individual separated from the community, withdrawn into himself, wholly occupied with his private interest and acting in accordance with his private caprice. Man is far from being considered, in the rights of man, as a species-being; on the contrary, species-life itself, society, appears as a system that is external to the individual and as a limitation of his original independence. The only bond between men is natural necessity, need and private interest, the preservation of their property and their egoistic persons ... The political liberators reduce the political community to a mere means for preserving these so-called rights of man ... The citizen is declared to be the servant of the egoistic man ... The sphere in which man functions as a species-being is degraded to a level below the sphere where he functions as a political being ... it is man as a bourgeois and not man as a citizen who is considered the true and authentic man. (Marx 1964: 26)

The "Rights of Man" refer to people as though they were self-sufficient, self-motivated atoms closed to one another. This portrayal leads by extension to a social system close to the Hobbesian *bellum omnium contra omnes.*

This is the liberty of man viewed as an isolated monad, withdrawn into himself ... [it is] not based on the association of man with man but rather on the separation of man from man ... The practical application of the right of liberty is the right of private property ... it lets every man find in every other man not the reality but the limitation of his own freedom. (Marx 1964: 24–5)

Yet in portraying the ideology and the reality of modern civil society as "atomistic" Marx was claiming not that people were in fact reduced to the status of atoms but that their behavior in certain respects was atomistic. To derive the former from the latter proposition would be to fall prey to the illusion of theorists such as Hobbes. Civil society in Marx's view was not a simple aggregate of human atoms unrelated to one another, as some British economists and utilitarians imagined, but a state of mutual dependence of all on all. As Marx put it in *The Holy Family:*

It is natural necessity, essential human properties, however alienated they may seem to be, and interest that hold together the members of civil society; civil, not political life is their real tie. It is therefore not the state that holds together the atoms of civil society but the fact that they are atoms only in imagination, in the heaven of their fancy, but in reality beings tremendously different from atoms, in other words, not divine egoists but egoistic human beings. Only political superstition today imagines that social life must be held together by the state . . . [in] reality the state is held together by civil life. (Marx and Engels 1975, vol. iv: 120–1)

I have argued elsewhere (Thomas 1980: 56–122) that Marx's theory of alien politics – his notion of the modern state as the fake, ersatz universal, based not on the expression but on the alienation of people's communal capacities – and his better-known characterization of the modern state as the far-from-"neutral" instrument of bourgeois predominance, are connected in significant ways. To enter into these connections with as much detail as would be required is an enterprise that would take this analysis too far afield. But even if neither theory resolves itself into or can be reduced to the other, to exclude alien politics from Marx's theory of the state is to misplace one's emphases. Some of the reasons for this were pointed out in passing by Georg Lukács, here as elsewhere an astute and creative reader of Marx:

Many workers suffer from the illusion that a purely formal democracy, in which the voice of every citizen is equally valid, is the most suitable instrument for expressing and representing the interests of society as a whole. But this fails to take into account the simple – simple! – detail that men are not just abstract individuals, abstract citizens or isolated atoms within the totality of the state, but are always concrete human beings who occupy specific positions within social production, whose social being (and mediated through this whose thinking) is determined by this position. The pure democracy of bourgeois society excludes this mediation. It connects the naked and abstract individual directly with the totality of the state, which in this context appears equally abstract. This fundamentally formal character of pure democracy . . . is not merely an advantage for the bourgeoisie but is precisely the decisive condition of its class rule. (1970: 65)

Lukács's perception helps explain why Marx predicated even his most programmatic revolutionary injunction – the need for political action on the part of the proletariat – not simply on his ruling-class theory of the state, but also on his perception of the modern state as the ideological representative of the alienated communal capacities of those beneath its sway. These capacities are deflected and even parodied in and through the modern notion of citizenship and the formal equality ("equality before the law") it brings with it. Such equality, being formal, masks but does not conceal the division of modern bourgeois societies into social classes. The principles of private property, freedom of contract, equal opportunity are upheld by the state but by their very nature are unequally distributed. The state maintains inequality, failing as a rule to act decisively against the private interests that animate civil society in the name of some public interest. Public interests in any genuine sense may actually be prevented from emerging. Class interests masquerading as public interests are made free from state interference and are encouraged to take center stage.

Yet the divisions such pretenses stimulate are not necessarily beneficial to the individual bourgeois. The hard-and-fast distinction of citizenship from private life entails the continual triumph of the latter, of the private over the public. This means that the bourgeois has at best what Marx calls a "sophistical" participation in the life of the state. Nancy Schwartz has perceptively indicated some of the untoward results of this participation. The state, we may recall, is presented as a, or the, "universal" category at the very moment when it is at once the surrogate of the bourgeoisie, and necessarily remote from ordinary, everyday, profane pursuits. Both what it *does* and what it *is* vitiate its claim to completeness, and the fact that abstract or unconnected universality and economic laissez-faire are historically connected does nothing to lessen the cynicism that results. But the paradoxes here go beyond cynicism and have considerable bearing on the themes of equality and citizenship. Given the formalism of either category, it is certainly not fanciful to suppose that considerable confusion is likely. What modern society defines and must define as moral life, or as authentic moral consciousness, is refracted into the transcendent but elusive, even chimerical, concept of citizenship. This is supposed to be validated, but is not. On the other hand, what society finally *does* validate, namely, individual privatized existence that sees in other existences nothing more than obstacles, it is supposed to devalue as being ethically unworthy. "This leads," in Nancy Schwartz's words, "to a divided consciousness and a widespread sense of inauthenticity and powerlessness even worse than the egoism and loneliness of private man, for now even in his solitude man negates himself. He judges himself by impossible standards and thus inevitably finds himself lacking. So not only for the worker is it true that 'the more values he creates the more worthless and unworthy he becomes' " (Schwartz 1979: 248). And if we ask where such a person is to turn for solace, an ominous answer is provided, again by Lukács: Even if we stop short of state worship, scientific and philosophical abstractions have a logic of domination of their own.

"The Antinomies of Bourgeois Thought," as Lukács (later) conceived of them (Lukács 1971: 110–49), cannot be entered into here in any adequate sense. But what is posed, I hope, by the foregoing discussion is a series of questions that go beyond what is normally thought of as Marxian state theory, and that at least connect with Lukács's "antinomies" in significant ways. The fundamental – though not according to Marx and Lukács, irreversible – change in the meaning of the terms "public" and "private" that is ushered in by bourgeois society entails the displacement of public functions onto the rarefied and abstract level of the modern state. Only a fetishized concept of citizenship can be appropriate to a fetishized state; each becomes complicit in the operation of the other. The stage appears to be set for the ratification, by means of law, of the purely formal equality and freedom of unequal and unfree citizens, and for the reproduction of capitalist social relations by a state institutional apparatus that plays on the distinction of "public" from "private" in order to appear as the neutral arbiter of social conflict. The effect of these developments might be to make these capitalist social relations seem obvious and noncontingent, in such a way that capitalism could present itself (in Lukács's striking phrase) as a kind of "second nature," or as what Guillermo O'Donnell once called an "obvious prolonging of yesterdays" in which "each yesterday was capitalist."

But (as I write) the prolonging of capitalist yesterdays is less in prospect than an intensification of capitalist todays. To the extent – a considerable extent – that the current "crisis of Keynesianism" is also a "crisis of democratic capitalism" (Przeworski and Wallerstein 1982: 57), we are witnessing today a possibly decisive shift *within* the "second nature" that capitalism has become, a shift that obliges us to reexamine the coordinates of capitalism and democracy. If we do so, we find that "alien politics" does much to explain the unexpected intrusion of blatantly post- (and anti-) Keynesian regimes in the evolution of contemporary capitalism. Even though Marx developed the concept of what I am calling alien politics to characterize the emergence of a certain kind of relationship between state and society, between private and public, and even though this relationship, broadly speaking, is one that has endured, it is my concluding contention here that alien politics has not for these reasons lost its relevance today. To the contrary, in a certain sense it has become more pointedly relevant than ever a full century after Marx's death.

Since the Second World War liberal-democratic capitalist states had more to do than simply represent the interests of a capitalist class and more to do than simply ensure the reproduction of capitalist relations of production. States, as Marxist theorists, to their credit, all too frequently came to acknowledge, had also to legitimate themselves. This they could do, not through inaction, but only by acting, positively, on society. Besides being anxious not to offend the electorate at large, states had to incorporate and integrate powerfully placed social classes, including the working class, and had to see to it that their demands and interests attained some degree of recognition and satisfaction.

With varying degrees of success, states endeavored to balance these demands according to the precepts of a broadly Keynesian settlement. State management of the level of aggregate demand in the economy was geared to the maintenance of full employment; increased social and welfare expenditures were traded against the promise of (relative) social harmony and industrial peace; and the demands of producer groups (trades unions and employers' associations) were channeled—to an extent that has been exaggerated among academics—through nonmarket political institutions that were designed as attempts to integrate the working class into the governmental process and thereby to contain industrial and class conflict.

There was a time, not so very long ago, when we, as citizens as well as theorists, had come to expect capitalist states to observe certain protocols. We had come to expect them to prefer compromise to conflict among contending producer groups; to fashion welfare policies that, besides aiding the state in its task of macroeconomic management, would integrate the dispossessed into the polity rather than alienate them from it; to forsake damagingly monetarist policies if beset by mounting unemployment; to implement wages policies (or, more rarely, price restraint) to offset inflation and to shape macroeconomic policy to fit the contours of the business cycle. That these policies were *not* the "neutral" initiatives of an impartial arbiter is the least of it. My main point, which is also concerned with a set of expectations we had come to entertain about the province of state action, is a much more ominous one. This is that it has taken the radical-right regimes of Ronald Reagan and Margaret Thatcher, which are committed to flying in the face of all these expectations, to show us how complacent we were in taking them for granted in the first place. Did not Marx more than a century ago chide the classical economists for treating then-existing social and economic relationships as though they were eternal, when in fact they were historical, that is, transitory and changeable? Should we not have done the same to those in our own day who preached the permanence, or evolutionary logic, of the Keynesian settlement? More to the point, what we overlooked was not just the possibility of economic downturn, a failure in civil society's capacity to reproduce itself that created an opening for radical-right regimes to exploit. We also overlooked the ever-present possibility of a recrudescence of alien politics.

Full employment, social security, adequate unemployment insurance, maintenance of the "social wage," guaranteed free collective bargaining, the provision of decent levels of health, education, and welfare – can we really still say that these areas of state action, these political aspects of the postwar Keynesian settlement, these struts and props of the political economy of the welfare state, are ineradicably inscribed in the logic of modern democratic politics? Have not all of them in Britain and the United States already proved their vulnerability and reversibility?

The central paradox of what Teresa Amott and Joel Krieger so aptly term the "hyper-capitalist" regimes of Reagan and Thatcher is that they intervene "powerfully to restructure capital, alter the balance of class relations, and actively promote particular outcomes in the economy, while simultaneously posing as the champion[s] of state withdrawal" (Amott and Krieger 1982: 14). These are strong regimes masquerading as weak; they are *dirigiste* regimes that stridently proclaim their desire for weakness vis-à-vis their respective societies. They act, not out of concern for the needs of any particular fraction of capital – indeed, the fragmentation of industrial and finance capital may well reinforce the conditions that sustain their rule – but on the basis of their own narrow, doctrinal and (above all) political panegyric on the virtues of the free market.

The paradoxes here run deep. According to supply-side economists, the state must intervene drastically within civil society if it is to find (or create) its mythical "free market"; only a thoroughgoing alteration of tax policies, which are to be weighted away from capital, can release the required, if elusive, torrent of economic activity in a magically revitalized "private sector," which only then will (no less magically) revitalize the rest of us. (The alchemists these days are evidently not those of revolution.) What we are currently witnessing, then, is not a form of pressure by civil society on the state. It is the state's revenge on civil society.

The vengefulness of the hypercapitalist regime expresses rather than conceals a contradiction between its political practice and its ideological representation of itself. The regime in its own estimation appears perilously close to what Marx attacked in his *Critique of the Gotha Programme:* It sees itself as "an independent entity possessed of its own intellectual, ethical and libertarian bases" (Marx and Engels 1962, vol. ii: 32). As Marx recognized in *The Eighteenth Brumaire of Louis Bonaparte* (another text that is connected in significant ways with "On the Jewish Question"), once a regime's power of initiative comes to seem largely unimpaired by the wishes or demands of any one class, or any fraction of a class, it can proceed to claim to represent all classes and fractions, to represent society (or the nation) at large. More pointedly still, the regime can purport to embody all social interests and transmute or project them into a higher, "general" interest counterposed to civil society, and can do so even though or *precisely because* it was called into being in order to maintain and strengthen the existing social order, one based on the domination of labor by capital.

Our hypercapitalist regimes, in Amott and Krieger's words, "parade the values of social cohesion and national unity, while [constructing] anti-integrative strategies which exacerbate class, racial and sexual divisions in society" (Amott and Krieger 1982: 14). The sheer revanchism involved in the Falklands War, together with attempts on the part of both hypercapitalist regimes to drum up public support for a recharging of the nuclear arms race, should on this view be considered alongside, and as counterparts to, these regimes' frontal attacks on trade union, working-class, and welfare constituencies amid mounting, state-induced unemployment. The now-surpassed Keynesian era was characterized by various integrative strategies: The articulation of sectional, corporate, and class interests was not only enjoined but also encouraged by the state, both as a way of legitimating itself and as a means of attempting to alleviate people's subjection to the fortunes and vagaries of the market. To the extent that hypercapitalist regimes uncritically celebrate the vagaries of the market and repudiate all such integrative strategies, their efforts are in the direction of depoliticization and disaggregation. They no longer need to acknowledge, but can dispense with, the power of organized labor, whose hard-won positions of access are no longer of much account; they freely introduce stark public policies that are designed to discipline and demoralize the working class and underclasses; and they proceed consciously to erode the egalitarian, universalistic claims and entitlements involved in postwar welfarism in favor of appeals for support that are nationalist and chauvinist, denominational, fundamentalist, and racist.

These are not welcome developments. But faced with them, how can we not think of alien politics, of the instances Marx provides of the state's disjuncture from society in such a way that "bourgeois society . . . attains a development unexpected even by itself" (Marx and Engels 1975, vol. i: 518), of the state as an "abstract totality" (Marx and Engels 1975, vol. iii: 205), superimposed upon a realm of private, self-interested activity, a realm that today is not just validated but actually revalidated by the state itself? An already alien politics is being realienated. If alien politics reminds us that the estrangement of the state from society proceeds apace under the (political) guise of a supposed reconciliation or resolution of the split; that at the level of individual existence our political significance becomes detached from our private condition; and that citizenship and private life become mutually exclusive, how can we avoid concluding that all these lines of division are now being redrawn? If the Keynesian settlement overlapped with what Sheldon Wolin once termed the "sublimation of politics" (Wolin 1960: 352), can we not conclude by purloining (and ripping from its context) a phrase from Marcuse and call urgently for a more searching analysis, not only of alien politics per se, but also what can only be called the "repressive desublimation" of politics?

REFERENCES

Amott, Teresa, and Joel Krieger (1982). "Thatcher and Reagan: State Theory and the 'Hyper-capitalist' Regime." *New Political Science* no. 8: 9–37.
Lukács, Georg (1970). *Lenin: A Study in the Unity of His Thought.* Translated by Nicholas Jacobs. Cambridge, Mass.: MIT Press.
    (1971). *History and Class Consciousness.* Translated by Rodney Livingstone. Cambridge, Mass.: MIT Press.
Marx, Karl (1964). *Early Writings.* Translated and edited by T. B. Bottomore with a foreword by Erich Fromm. New York: McGraw-Hill.
    (1970). *Critique of Hegel's "Philosophy of Right."* Translated by Annette Jolin and Joseph O'Malley; edited with an introduction and notes by Joseph O'Malley. Cambridge: Cambridge University Press.

Marx, Karl, and Frederick Engels (1962). *Selected Works in Two Volumes.* Moscow: Foreign Languages Publishing House.

(1965). *The German Ideology.* Translated by S. Ryazanskaya. London: Lawrence & Wishart.

(1975). *Collected Works,* vols. iii, iv. New York: International Publishers.

Przeworski, Adam, and Michael Wallerstein (1982). "Democratic Capitalism at the Crossroads." *democracy* 2: 52–68.

Schwartz, Nancy (1979). "Distinction between Private and Public Life: Marx on the *zoon politikon.*" *Political Theory* 7: 245–66.

Thomas, Paul (1980). *Karl Marx and the Anarchists.* London: Routledge & Kegan Paul.

Wolin, Sheldon S. (1960). *Politics and Vision.* Boston: Little, Brown.

CHAPTER 7

Democracy: utopian and scientific

C. B. MACPHERSON

When Engels published his *Socialism: Utopian and Scientific* in 1880, European socialism was in some disarray. He hoped to put it on the right track by making his readers think again about the then-competing doctrines of socialism. Now, a century later, European and American democracy is in such disarray that it is tempting to consider whether a parallel analysis of democratic theory could usefully be made.

Engels's division of socialist theory into utopian and scientific had the merit of throwing into bold relief the kind of theory required for moving ahead to a society more humanly acceptable than nineteenth-century capitalism. Can a division of democratic theory into utopian and scientific point us a way ahead now to something more desirable than our present precarious Western democratic systems? It seems a promising starting point for anyone who is looking for an improved democratic theory as a guide to a better democratic society. If utopian is taken to mean, as Engels used it to mean, nobly intentioned but unrealistic and therefore ineffective, then clearly those who want a change for the better must avoid the utopian and embrace the scientific.

We should, however, beware of that division into utopian and scientific when we reflect that the twentieth-century liberal-democratic theory that most claims to be scientific, and most denigrates earlier theory as utopian, concludes that no significant change for the better is possible. Its "science" tells us to stop dreaming and to be content with the democracy we have. One may suspect that there is something wrong with a distinction between utopian and scientific that makes the two terms mutually exclusive. There is perhaps a simple logical fallacy here: All utopian (i.e., unscientific) thought is visionary: therefore, all visionary thought is utopian (i.e., unscientific). The conclusion is surely false, for scientific thought also is visionary.

If we allow that empirical science and scientific vision are not incompatible, we shall have to be wary of Engels's division between utopian and scientific theory. For although he, like Marx, did not treat the empirical and the visionary as incompatible, he did lend some support to those who were to take that line later. For he drew the distinction between utopian and scientific theories entirely in economic terms: Marx's theory was scientific insofar as it was based on the advance Marx made in economic science over the classical economists. What Engels forgot, in making his case for Marx's theory at that particular political conjuncture, was that Marx's economic science was preeminently a *political* economy.

However, although Engels may be faulted for having reduced Marx's political economy and his political vision to narrowly economic terms, we may still hope to learn something from the contrast he drew between utopian and scientific theory.

Let us explore this by looking first at his criteria for distinguishing them from each other. He reduced the difference between the utopian theories (Fourier, St. Simon, Owen) and the scientific theory (Marx) to two points on which he held that Marx had surpassed all earlier socialist theory. First, whereas the utopians had based their theory on abstract ideas of truth, reason, and justice "independent of time, space, and the historical development of man" (Engels 1908: 74) and had tried to evolve a solution to the social problems "out of the human brain" (ibid.: 58), Marx had insisted that socialist theory be based on the real, historically changing, power relations of society, which were essentially economic relations. In short, Marx's first surpassing insight was to have seen that the power relations of existing society were transient, that they were a historical stage governed by its own internal laws of motion.

The second and equally important respect in which Marx had surpassed the earlier theory was in discovering the mechanism of exploitation inherent in capitalist society. The utopians had vigorously denounced the exploitative character of the nineteenth-century society but had been unable to explain it. Marx had discovered the secret of capitalist exploitation and had formulated it in his law of surplus value (Engels 1908: 92–3).

Thus, for Engels the two requirements of a scientific theory of socialism were (1) that it saw existing economic relations to be a transient historical stage, subject to its own internal laws of motion, and (2) that it comprehended and explained the necessarily exploitive nature of those relations.

Now if we were to take Engels as our model for assessing the scientific quality of democratic theory we should have to look for *parallel* insights into the *political* relations of existing society. We should have to ask how far, if at all, democratic theory has (1) seen the political relations of existing society as a transient historical stage with its own inherent laws of motion, and (2) understood the necessarily exploitative nature of those political arrangements.

To formulate the question in that way is already to expose its untenable narrowness. For there is no reason to expect that a political system as such, unrelated to the economic system that must serve it and that it must serve, will have its own inherent laws of motion, or its own inherently exploitive character. (Indeed, to assume that democratic institutions are exploitive in themselves would be to foreclose the question whether liberal democracy can survive exploitive capitalism or even be the mechanism for transcending it.)

But if we must abandon a political analogue of Engels's narrow economic criteria, we may still give a central place to laws of motion taken more broadly. We may take as a test of the scientific quality of a democratic theory the extent to which it sees inherently interdependent forces of economic and political change as setting the direction and limits of democracy. After all, neither an economic nor a political system can exist independently of the other. Strains or inadequacies in either will create problems for the other. The worry now in our Western democracies is not about democracy per se but about *capitalist* democracy: neoconservative (e.g., Samuel Huntington, Daniel Bell) and neo-Marxist (e.g., Jürgen Habermas, Claus Offe, James O'Connor) analysts are agreed that there is a crisis of liberal democracy and that the crisis arises from an increasing misfit between demand and supply, that is, between the increasing political demand for the goods of the welfare state and the decreasing ability of the capitalist economy to supply them. No clearer case for presuming the interrelation of political and economic forces need be offered.

So instead of asking how far democratic theory has thought in terms of laws of political motion and political exploitation, we may ask how far it has thought in terms of laws of political-economic motion and political-economic exploitation. We may ask both questions of both pre-liberal (seventeenth and eighteenth century) and liberal (nineteenth and twentieth century) democratic theories. I shall first look very summarily at some highlights of both periods down to the mid-twentieth century, then look more closely at the subsequent and now prevalent theory.

Democratic theorists of both periods have commonly seen the political relations of their own societies as a product of historical change, at least in the obvious sense of seeing that they had emerged from something different, but none saw that change as due to some inherent laws of motion or thought of such laws as still at work within the existing political system in such a way as to lead to that system being superseded. Pre-liberal democrats, notably Rousseau, confronted with a wholly undemocratic society, did demand that it should be surpassed by something democratic, but had no clear idea *how* it could be surpassed, that is to say, no idea of any inherent laws of motion that might make its superssession possible or probable. Rousseau called for a deus ex machina, a charismatic legislator.

In the nineteenth century, liberal democrats, at least those in countries that had already achieved some measure of democratic government, had no interest in inquiring into laws of motion of political society, for they thought the motion had virtually stopped or would stop with the achievement of a substantially representative governmental system and saw no need to surpass it. John Stuart Mill may be cited as the outstanding liberal democrat in the English tradition. It is true that Mill, following the insight of the classical economists, did see a law of motion of the capitalist economy whereby it would necessarily decline to a stationary condition of no growth, but he did not relate this to a possible decline in the democratic character of the political system: Rather, he applauded the prospect of "the stationary state" as an opening for a more humanistic society. And although he held that there had been some improvement in Western political institutions with the broadening of the franchise, and might be more improvement with some further adjustments of the franchise and other parts of the mechanism, he was content enough with the main lines of existing representative government that he did not think in terms of surpassing it. The existing system, with some adjustments, was about as democratic as could realistically be expected. There was no thought that it ought to be superseded, or that any laws of motion might lead to its supersession. Subsequent liberal democratic theory has generally followed Mill in that respect.

Our second question is whether any of the democratic theorists

have understood the necessarily exploitive nature of the political
structure of existing societies. The pre-liberal democratic theorists
(Winstanley, Rousseau) saw clearly that the political institutions of
the blatantly class-divided societies in which they lived had as their
main function the enforcement of class exploitation. And liberal
democratic theorists who wrote before any measure of democratic
institutions had been achieved (e.g., Bentham) were equally clear
that the political systems they confronted were essentially exploitive
in that they maintained the power of the great proprietors of land
and capital to exploit all the rest of the society. But from the time
that formal democratic institutions were achieved, liberal democratic
theorists have not generally seen capitalist democratic political institutions as similarly exploitive. Indeed, the very idea that they might
be so, by virtue of their maintaining and lending legitimacy to an
exploitive economic system, is scarcely entertained by liberal democratic theorists, for they do not generally consider capitalism to be
necessarily exploitive.

In this summary account, democratic theory – particularly twentieth-century liberal democratic theory – comes off badly. It neither
thinks in terms of laws of motion nor recognizes exploitation. It fails
because it does not give attention to the interrelation between economic and political motion.

But we have still to look at the school of liberal democratic theory
that has become dominant since the mid-twentieth century, which
makes some claim to be scientific in that it is based on empirical
observation and analysis of the actual functioning of Western democratic systems and does explain how they operate and what forces
move them. I refer to the pluralist–elitist equilibrium theory of
Schumpeter, the early Robert Dahl, the voting studies specialists,
and a whole host of followers.

They define democracy narrowly as simply a method of choosing
and authorizing governments, and see the democratic political process as a marketlike process in which the self-chosen leaders of political parties are the entrepreneurs offering competing parcels of
political goods (leaders whose skill lies in estimating the plural demands of the voters), and in which the voters are the consumers
whose role is simply to choose which parties' promised parcels they
will buy at election times (and in between elections to keep the successful parties up to their promises by acting in plural pressure
groups). This is said to produce an equilibrium between political
demand and supply, as evidenced by the fact that, at least when all

the players stay within the conventional rules of the game, the system does not break down into dictatorship or military rule or chaos. The additional claim made or implied by these theorists, namely, that it provides some measure of consumer sovereignty and is therefore a good thing, is not strictly part of its scientific claim and is indeed incompatible with it. As I shall suggest in a moment, the justificatory inadequacy of the theory follows logically from the extent of its scientific accuracy.

How strong is the scientific claim of this theory? We may grant that it does describe fairly accurately the way in which the political system in the developed capitalist democracies does operate: The voters do behave as consumers choosing between packages of political goods offered by competing parties, and the party directorates and managers do perform the entrepreneurial functions of judging what goods will be most in demand and then marketing the packages they have put together. And the theory can readily be made to cover some evident political facts that render the system less than ideally democratic. Thus it can recognize that the market in which the parties compete as sellers is oligopolistic, not perfectly competitive: There are only a few sellers, and consequently they need not be fully responsive to buyers' demands, as sellers in a perfectly competitive market must be. The theory can also accommodate the fact that political parties, as oligopolistic suppliers, can to a considerable extent create the demand. As Schumpeter (1942: 264, 282) put it, the people "neither raise nor decide issues but . . . the issues that shape their fate are normally raised and decided for them"; the wishes of the electorate "are not the ultimate data," the electorate's choice "does not flow from its initiative but is being shaped, and the shaping of it is an essential part of the democratic process."

The theory's recognition that the party system is structured in such a way that it need not be fully responsive to the voters' demands, and that it can even determine the demand, does severely damage its justificatory claim that the system provides a substantial measure of consumers' sovereignty but does not impugn the theory's descriptive accuracy. It is because and to the extent that the theory recognizes the imperfectly competitive nature of the party system that it can claim some scientific accuracy, but insofar as it does so it must logically give up much of its justificatory claim.[1] A measure of

[1] The equilibrium political theorists differ in the extent to which they recognize the imperfect party competition and to which they claim some measure of consumer sovereignty. On this, see Macpherson (1977: 81–2).

its scientific accuracy is the extent to which it takes as the model of the democratic political system the reality of a mature oligopolistic capitalist economy rather than the simple textbook model of a fully competitive economy.

All that I have said so far about the equilibrium theory gives it some scientific credit, but does not establish it as an adequately scientific general theory of liberal democracy, let alone of democracy as a whole. (I do not here deal with any such broader claim,[2] since the scientific claim of the equilibrium theory is tenable only in respect of existing Western liberal democracies. Its narrow definition of democracy as merely a mechanism for choosing and authorizing a government rules out any idea of democracy as a kind of society embodying equality of chances of a fully human life, i.e., rules out something that a scientific general theory of democracy as a whole would have to accommodate. The equilibrium theory praises liberty but forgets equality and fraternity.)

The scientific inadequacy of the equilibrium theory as a general theory of liberal democracy is attributable to its lack of a historical perspective. It situated itself firmly in its own time. Its formative period was the decades following World War II, when Western capitalism appeared to have made a stable recovery, and to be capable, for the foreseeable future, of maintaining a satisfactory rate of economic growth and meeting the expectations of the electorate. Even Schumpeter (1942: 163), who held (though not for the same reasons as Marx) that capitalism had a terminal illness, thought it might have another successful run for a further fifty or a hundred years.

The political scientists who developed the equilibrium theory after Schumpeter had much less doubt about the stability of capitalism and the adequacy of their model of capitalist democracy. They easily assumed that Western liberal democracies would maintain such an equilibrium as not to collapse into dictatorship or chaos. They could overlook the many instances in the mid-twentieth century when some had so collapsed, as in Italian and German fascism and military takeovers in other European and Latin American countries, which came when their economies could not meet popular expectations. They could overlook or discount those failures because the postwar revival of European capitalisms made any repetition of those failures seem unlikely. And that prognosis appeared to be confirmed by the subsequent restoration of liberal democratic institutions in Spain,

---

[2] On this, see Macpherson (1977: 86–91).

Portugal, and Greece. The future of liberal democracy on the equilibrium theorists' pattern seemed fairly secure. But it depended on the assumption that the rate of economic growth would hold up.

The now endemic slowdown of economic growth in the capitalist world as a whole has put the prospects of liberal democratic institutions in a different light and has revealed the shallowness of the equilibrium theory. That theory is static. It takes no thought for the possible outcome of a probably increasing inability of the capitalist economy to satisfy the expectations of both the electorate and the powerful pressure groups in its midst. A scientific theory of liberal democracy would have to consider at least two possible outcomes: that popular movements intent on transforming or transcending capitalism would demand and get more participatory democratic institutions, or that democracy would be effectively destroyed by some kind of corporatist plebiscitary state. The equilibrium theory considers neither possibility. Yet either outcome would spell the end of the equilibrium theory's scientific claim.

What the equilibrium theorists forgot was that the democratic franchise was won in the first place in most of the present liberal democracies by the irresistible pressures brought against oligarchic regimes by the new industrial working class and/or the farmers or peasants, who had had no effective political voice. Liberal democracy was founded by class pressure against class oligarchy: The democratic franchise was granted to forestall revolutionary activity by the classes that had been created by competitive capitalism. As long as the capitalist economies went on expanding, the democratic upsurge was tamed, chiefly by the operation of the party system, which was then more fluid than it has become (cf. Macpherson 1977: 64–9).

But now, in the measure that the capitalist economy has matured into oligopoly, *and* has begun to slow down to no-growth, the political and economic oligarchy will have to reckon with a new democratic upsurge, this time by the descendants of those who originally demanded and got a political voice. Such an upsurge is to be expected when those descendants come to recognize that they also are subject to an oligarchic regime. They may not appreciate that the two words "oligarchy" and "oligopoly" have the same Greek root; indeed, they may never use the words, but they are apt to appreciate the real connection. In the measure that they do so, the present ruling oligarchy, if it is unable to destroy the liberal democratic state (replacing it with some kind of corporatist state), will be compelled to submit to a more genuinely democratic participatory system.

Democracy: utopian and scientific

The equilibrium theory takes no thought of such a future. It sees that in affluent Western societies store clerks dress in the same style as the well-to-do; that industrial workers have their own cars and television sets, and are apt to be chiefly interested in leisure pursuits, as long as their income allows that indulgence; that their concern for their income is usually left to the trade unions, which seek to maintain the workers' slice of the pie but do not question the methods of the bakery; that even if their concern extends to some support for a regional economic pressure group or an ethnic or religious or moral or neighborhood pressure group, all of those still operate within the limits of the accepted economic and political system. Equilibrium theorists conclude that the class-divided society has been permanently replaced by a relatively complacent pluralist society. That is the limit of their science, and it is an increasingly damaging limit.

It might still be argued, in defense of the equilibrium theorists' position, that capitalism, having emerged successfully from the economic debacle of the Great Depression of 1929 by adopting Keynesian policies, may overcome its present decline by discovering some comparable new rejuvenating principle. But when one notices that the revival from the 1930s to the 1960s depended not just on Keynesianism but also, as is generally acknowledged, on the boost given the economy by World War II and subsequent lesser wars, and, as is less generally acknowledged, by the massive rearmament required by the continuing cold war, some doubts arise. Actual full-scale war has become too dangerous to be used again. And the rearmament budgets required by cold war are already seen to be, and must increasingly be, at the expense of the Keynesian welfare-state measures that have kept capitalism afloat until now. A further doubt arises if it is acknowledged that the buoyancy of the Western economies in the Keynesian period had depended on their continued exploitation of the Third World peoples. For it seems likely that that exploitation has nearly reached its limit, that is, a limit that could only be surpassed if the Western powers resorted to outright or concealed dictatorship at home as well as abroad. That also would spell the end of the equilibrium theory. I conclude that the equilibrium theory cannot claim more than a very short-run scientific validity.

We should notice finally what may be described as a conservative revision of the equilibrium theory, as in the work of Samuel Huntington (in Crozier et al. 1975) and Daniel Bell (1978). It does not seek to replace the descriptive content of the equilibrium theory, but, as mentioned earlier, it does find a crisis in current Western democracies and sees the crisis as due to the increasing difficulties of capitalism and the increasing demands of the people. It is not complacent about pluralist society or the viability of liberal democratic institutions. It sees plural demands putting an overload on capitalist democratic institutions and sees democracies becoming ungovernable.

To the extent that the conservative revisionists recognize an impending crisis in capitalist democracy they may be said to be more scientific than the mainstream equilibrium theorists. They do see some inherent motion in the politics of capitalism: They have gone beyond the static limits of the earlier equilibrium theory. But it is doubtful if they can be considered to be approaching a scientific theory of democracy, or indeed if they would make such a claim. They foresee an increasing inadequacy of Western party systems and governmental systems, an inability of the systems to go on providing acceptable government or providing government for an acceptable society, a breakdown of liberal democracy as we have known it. They offer us in effect the euthanasia of liberal democracy and the equilibrium theory. And on their own implicit premise of an unchanging human nature their sombre conclusions are realistic enough. But in the end it is the static quality of that premise that renders their theory unscientific. The theory is inadequate as science because it is not visionary. It sees little or no prospect of Westerners moving away from their present behavior as unlimited material desirers. It does not envisage that the demand for material satisfactions might give way increasingly to demand for a better quality of life and of work. But a theory that, although it sees democracy in motion, rules out such a possible basic change in the forces producing that motion, cannot be given much of a scientific rating.

We are left then with the position that neither the pre-liberal democratic theorists (Winstanley, Rousseau, Jefferson), nor the early liberal democratic theorists (Bentham, Mill), nor the twentieth-century followers of Mill, nor the equilibrium theorists, nor the conservative revisionists may properly be called scientific. They have all failed, in one degree or another, to take account of the necessary and possible forces of change inherent in capitalist democracy.

To say this is not to condemn them all as valueless. On the contrary, all of them have made a useful contribution to our understanding of democracy, however much the claim of some of them to be scientific has to be discounted and however much the others have been dismissed by the scientific claimants as utopian.

My appreciation of the democratic theories prior to the mid-twentieth-century equilibrium theory is rather similar to Engels's appreciation of the utopian socialists. He saw much that was good in their theories. He applauded their humanism, the grandeur of their vision, and their moral rejection of existing exploitive society. Their weakness he attributed to their having written at a time when capitalist relations had not yet fully worked themselves out, so that they were unable to grasp the necessary motion of capitalist society, and hence could not see any way ahead except to draw up blueprints of the good society and hope that the blueprints would be so persuasive, by their beauty and symmetry, that people of good will would adopt them and make them into a reality. We may make the same appreciation and critique of the pre-liberal democratic theory and the liberal democratic theory of Mill and his followers: They had the humanism and the vision of a better society but were writing too early to have understood the dynamics of capitalist society.

When we come to the twentieth-century equilibrium theorists there is not the same parallel. They are not evidently utopian. They have eschewed the humanism and vision of the earlier democrats. Nor are they totally unscientific. They have not altogether failed to recognize the change from early to mature capitalism: As we have seen, the more astute of them have taken account of the change from pure competition to oligopoly. Nevertheless there is some parallel between the weakness I have ascribed to them and the weakness Engels found in the utopians. The curious parallel lies in this: The utopians were writing at a time when capitalist relations had not yet fully worked themselves out; the equilibrium theorists have been writing at a time when the *breakdown* of mature capitalism has not yet fully worked itself out, so that they also see no way ahead, indeed see no need for a way ahead, and so are content with the logical beauty of their analysis and with their truncated democratic ideal. The parallel is in their failure to understand the dynamics of capitalist society.

Let us go back to Engels and consider the opening sentences of his *Socialism, Utopian and Scientific.* "Modern socialism," he wrote (referring to the whole socialist movement), "is, in its essence, the direct product of the recognition, on the one hand, of the class antagonisms, existing in the society of today, between proprietors and non-proprietors, between capitalists and wage-workers; on the other hand, of the anarchy existing in production. But, in its theoretical form . . . like every new theory, modern socialism had, at first, to connect itself with the intellectual stock-in-trade ready to its hand, however deeply its roots lay in material economic facts."

We may find another parallel here with democratic theory, though again not a complete one. The early democratic movement may also be said to be the product of the recognition of the same class antagonism and the same anarchy of production, and its theory too had to be built from an existing intellectual stock-in-trade. So the early democratic theory was utopian, celebrating liberty, equality, and fraternity and postulating an essentially moral rational man, without fully understanding the nature of the class anatognism or of the anarchy of production that were thwarting human beings in capitalist society.

But after that, the parallel fails. Nineteenth-century democratic theory still failed to see the source of the class antagonism and hoped it would be overcome by the plural society. And by the twentieth century, the equilibrium theory assumed that class antagonism *had* been swallowed up by pluralism. As for recognizing and understanding the anarchy of capitalist production, democratic theory appears to have gone backward between the nineteenth and twentieth centuries. Yet there is some excuse for the twentieth-century equilibrium theorists, for by their time the anarchy of competitive capitalism to which Engels had referred (where no producers could control the market) was giving way to the increasingly uncompetitive system where collaborating large capitals could control the market and, with some help from the state, could plan and administer it. Capitalist firms, and whole industries, now use the state and at the same time depend on it for favors—subsidies, tax exemptions, contracts, and favorable regulations of many kinds. The capitalist firms and consortiums have in effect become political pressure groups: They compete politically more than economically, and so they can be fitted into the equilibrium theorists' pluralistic political framework. What the theory overlooks is that this is not a very democratic pluralism. To the extent that the equilibrium theory is scientific, it is not democratic. It is neither a utopian nor a scientific theory of democracy. We still have no scientific general democratic theory.

What, then, must we do to move toward one? My analysis here suggests that the most needed step is to work out an adequate theory of the now-changing relation between the state and the economy and project it into the future. We need a new political economy, and we need to develop it without losing sight of the humanistic goals of earlier democratic theory. It was not its humanism that made the earlier democratic theory utopian: It was its faulty political economy. Without a humanistic goal, the scientific enterprise is scarcely worth undertaking; and if we see beyond the model of market man, nothing but a humanistic vision will make our theory scientific.

REFERENCES

Bell, Daniel (1978). *The Cultural Contradictions of Capitalism.* New York: Basic Books.

Crozier, Michel, Samuel P. Huntington, and Joji Watanuki (1975). *The Crisis of Democracy: Report on the Governability of Democracies to the Trilateral Commission.* New York: New York University Press.

Engels, Frederick (1908). *Socialism: Utopian and Scientific.* Translated by Edward Aveling. Chicago: Kerr.

Macpherson, C. B. (1977). *The Life and Times of Liberal Democracy.* Oxford: Oxford University Press.

Schumpeter, Joseph (1942). *Capitalism, Socialism, and Democracy.* New York: Harper and Brothers.

CHAPTER 8

Marx's moral realism: eudaimonism and moral progress

ALAN GILBERT

A dialectic of moral outrage and scientific analysis instigated Marx's political activity. But in reflecting on his theoretical works, Marx stressed science and was virtually silent about moral theory. And he broke this silence mainly to dismiss all manner of moralists, whether liberal, anarchist, or socialist. He rejected theories of "justice" and "fairness" that sought to repair or transform capitalism as misconceptions based on that system's standards of formal legal equality; he subjected prevailing conceptions of justice to historical debunking and sociological critique (1961, vol. 3: 339–40; Gilbert 1982). Not surprisingly, many interpreters have relied on this silence or dismissal to argue that in moral matters, Marx was a relativist or reductionist (Fisk 1975; Wood 1972). Yet his comprehensive, withering indictment of capitalist exploitation and his ennobling conception of a community of free individuals reveal a moral vision of great stature. The truth of this vision deserves to be assessed on its own terms, that is, as part of a debate about human needs and the possibilities and limits of social cooperation. To regard Marx's metaethical verdict on this vision as "just a matter of opinion, with no more justification than any other" or as "the sanctification in thought of rising forces of production" is to trivialize it. Such assertions are belied by the dedication, vehemence, and courage of Marx's extensive revolutionary activity, and by the fiery moral implications of his theory.

Elsewhere, I have suggested that Marx was a moral realist and that this metaethical view best accounts for the objectivity of his own

I am indebted to Richard Boyd, Richard Miller, and Harvey C. Mansfield, Jr. for enlightening conversations about Aristotle, Marx, and moral objectivity, and to James Farr and Terence Ball for acute editorial suggestions.

moral judgments (Gilbert 1981b, 1982). Moral realism recognizes progress in morality and advance in moral theory through successive approximations to the truth about human potentials for cooperation and freedom. Further, progress in moral theory rests heavily on progress in social theory. I want to show here that Marx had a more coherent (if implicit) *moral* theory underlying his judgments than is often thought. The first section examines the ways in which Marx adhered to and developed an Aristotelian eudaimonism. It casts new light on Marx's theory of alienation and the moral thrust of *Capital.* It also contends that his severe differences with Aristotle's particular judgments arose mainly from clashes over facts, including issues of social and biological theory, not disagreements about moral premises. The second section argues that Marx's scientific realism toward Aristotle's analysis of commodities and money requires an accompanying realism about ethics. The third section uses the eudaimonist and realist claims of the first sections to reject two sophisticated arguments advanced by Richard Miller that call into question both the moral character and moral objectivity of Marx's normative judgments.

I. THE ARISTOTELIAN LINEAGE OF MARX'S EUDAIMONISM

Marx characterized Aristotle as that "giant thinker" who "first analyzed so many forms of thought, society and nature" (1961, vol. 1: 59). His broad judgments about human goods resemble Aristotle's eudaimonism; his novel social theory reveals the appropriate social and political arrangements for furthering a good life. I will begin this section by highlighting the relevant similarities between the two thinkers and the impact of eudaimonism on Marx's critique of capitalism and vision of communism; I will then counter a leading relativist objection by tracing a strong historical progression in the theory of human cooperation and freedom.

Marx's *particular* views about such issues as justice, property, slavery, and the treatment of women differ dramatically from Aristotle's. If we were to remain at the level of particular disagreements, however, we would miss profound general similarities of ethical framework that qualify both thinkers as eudaimonists and moral realists. These thinkers share a philosophical recognition of diverse intrinsic human goods including life, knowledge, friendship, political community, and the like. They contend that happiness (in Aristotle's terms, *eudaimonia*) stems from activities which realize or participate in these goods, and that different kinds of happiness arise from diverse activities. For both, the appropriate reasons for activities contrast with corrupt external motivations, human qualities and relationships with those counterfeited by wealth. Both emphasize political association and action as an especially important good. Moreover, we can find four more shared notions about political life. They stress: (1) the importance of a cooperative and free political life, based on a common good, (2) the role of politics as an arena for the display and development of moral character, (3) the need to criticize and refine existing opinions about justice and other moral goods, and (4) the importance of practical deliberation and choice in serving the common good. Aristotle's and Marx's broad eudaimonism and common framework for studying politics separate their conceptions from utilitarian or rights-based ethical theories.

As a moral theorist, Marx's scathing repudiation of utilitarianism stems from a eudaimonist vision of the diversity of human activities and needs. In *The German Ideology*, for example, Marx condemned the utilitarian "stupidity of merging all the manifold relationships of people in the *one* relation of usefulness" or pleasure (Marx and Engels 1964: 449). Against that view Marx insisted on the "peculiarity" of activities such as speech or love as "definite manifestations of definite qualities of individuals," done on their own account, not as part of some alien, monetary "third relationship." In *Capital*, Marx mocked Bentham, who opposed aesthetic criticism on the grounds that it might disturb the many admirers of mediocrities. Marx also recognized the perversity of Bentham's endorsement of Christianity merely because of its "usefulness" in sanctifying the penal code. Bentham, he suggested satirically, had projected the needs of an English "shopkeeper" as a, in a harmful sense, *socially* determined ideal or "normal" human (*Normalmensch*); in contrast, Marx proposed a conception of genuine need based on "human nature in general and as modified in each historical epoch" (*menschliche Natur; in jeder Epoch historisch modifizierte Menschennatur;* 1961, vol. 1: 609–10). Marx's rejection of utilitarianism requires a clear distinction between the integrity of activities that express human nature and their corruption.

Aristotle's critique of pleasure in Book X of the *Nicomachean Ethics* explains and deepens Marx's argument. Aristotle maintained that an adult's happiness differs from that of a child, and an adult would never confine himself to childlike pleasures, whatever their intensity. Only malign pleasures (those of a sick man or woman), he insisted, accompany depraved activities. To be a good, pleasure must arise from the intrinsic merit of an activity. Thus, Aristotle contrasted genuine friendship, sustained by mutual concern, with defective friendships based on flattery or monetary gain, even when they generate like pleasures (1173b21–1174a13). Such a distinction would make Marx's point about the "definite" qualities of relationships and activities in *The German Ideology* more exact.[1] Furthermore, the happiness (or wonder) that arises from the search for knowledge is different from that of friendship or of sight or of political action. A good life includes different kinds of happiness. In addition, diverse justified needs stem from particular activities. The best flute players, not the handsomest, should get the finest flutes; olympic prizes should reward the swiftest, not the wealthiest (*Politics* 1282b38–1283a24). Although, for Aristotle, distortions of activities arose from status- and power-seeking, grasping after money was a general source of corruption. Aristotle's careful differentiation of appropriate and corrupt motivations for activities is consistent with Marx's indictment of utilitarianism. But, one might ask, did Marx regularly draw such a distinction? In fact, this distinction clarifies a number of the central themes of *Capital* and highlights the varied political impact of different features of Marx's theory of alienation. For instance, in the chapter on "The Results of the Immediate Process of Production," Marx contrasted productive labor in general with productive labor under capitalism in a precisely Aristotelian way. A great artist like Milton, Marx contended, created *Paradise Lost* as an "activation of *his own* nature," not to secure a few pounds. Marx likened Milton's activity to a silkworm's production of silk. This genuine or natural activity – unproductive from a capitalist point of view – contrasts with the "productive" work of a hack who grinds out a political economy text on commission from a publishing house. In the same passage, Marx distinguishes a singer who "sings like a bird" – again, the image of a natural activity – from one who sings for hire, and a genuine teacher from an employee of a "knowledge-mongering institution" (1977, vol. 1: 1044). Capitalism fuses material and social (value-producing) aspects; it is partly natural – expressive of human nature – as well as historical. Thus, Marx need not maintain that capitalist productivity corrupts all activities: Some may sing "like birds" or find aspects of their work consonant with their own nature, even though it also realizes profit for the capitalist.

---

[1] See also Richard Miller's fine article (1981) on Aristotle and Marx.

But the occasional existence of such consonance highlights its general absence; the capitalist system as a whole, he maintained, undermines such integrity.

An important feature of Marx's theory of alienation focuses on the impact of capitalism on motivations for work (Marx 1967: 281, 290). Productive activity in this system serves only as a means of life, not as an expression of life (Marx and Engels 1962, vol. 2: 24). As Marx put it in "Wage-Labor and Capital," "What he (the worker) produces for himself is not the silk that he weaves, not the gold that he draws from the mine, not the palace that he builds." Invoking an Aristotelian sense of natural justice, Marx characterized wage labor as "unnatural"; he compared it to the production of his favorite animal, the silkworm, but this time, to a perverse one that spun, not to become a butterfly, but to "maintain its existence as a caterpillar" (Marx and Engels 1962: vol. 1: 82–3).

A second, closely related feature of alienation, which also relies on eudaimonist arguments, highlights the perverse impact of great differences of wealth and poverty on human qualities and relationships (Marx 1967: 270–1). Money sometimes enables the rich to counterfeit qualities they lack. In *Capital,* Marx cited approvingly Shakespeare's *Timon of Athens:*

Gold, yellow, glittering, precious gold!
Thus much of this will make black, white; foul, fair;
Wrong, right; old, young; coward, valiant;
. . . This yellow slave
Will knit and break religions, bless the accurs'd
. . . place thieves
And give them title, knee and approbation (Marx 1961, vol. 1: 132)

A third feature of alienation is the isolation of individuals from one another and from their "species-being" (*Gattungswesen;* Marx 1967: 294–5). Aristotle had stressed the political association and activity of citizens, who rule and are ruled in turn, as a defining species characteristic. Similarly, Marx admired the participation of workers in the Paris Commune. Worker officials, he suggested, discharged their functions enthusiastically because they recognized their stake in the community as well as for justified instrumental purposes; their actions fused intrinsic and instrumental goods (Gilbert 1981b). They required neither special monetary rewards nor any "aureole" of prestige:

The whole sham of state-mysteries and state pretensions was done away [with] by a Commune, mostly consisting of simple working men, organizing

the defense of Paris . . . doing their work publicly, simply, under most difficult and complicated circumstances, and doing it, as Milton did his *Paradise
Lost,* for a few pounds. (Marx and Engels 1971: 153)

To highlight the good of political activity as an expression of human
nature, Marx recurred to Milton, one of his favorite human ana-
logues. Despite an inversion of the ancient scorn for manual work,
Marx gave a profound Aristotelian meaning to the Communard's
conception of a "republic of labor." The Communard was *a political
animal.*

Especially in the early manuscripts, the idea of species being has a
somewhat illusory quality. How can humans alienate, one might ask,
a species being that they have so far been unable to realize? As
Aristotle recognized, ancient political community had provided an
important example of such species being. Later egalitarian movements such as the Roman slave revolt led by Spartacus, the German
Peasant War, the Levellers in the Puritan Revolution, and the sans-
culottes in the French Revolution had pointed to further human
possibilities. But the social republican movement of the nineteenth
century, especially the Commune, gave a deep and more precise
institutional and political picture of what species being might look
like.

Marx had long seen such political potentials in the working-class
movement. Following his first communist meeting in 1844, he
praised the "nobility of man" (*Adel der Menschheit*) that "shone" from
these revolutionary artisans; they exemplified a human need for
association (Marx 1970: 1990–1). As a dialectical contrast, to satirize
the alien character or "zoology" of German feudal and bourgeois
life, Marx had found the Aristotelian conception of human nature
an apt benchmark: "A German Aristotle, who would derive his politics from our conditions, would start by saying: *man is a social but
wholly apolitical animal*" (1967: 206).

Marx's theory of alienation has two other, more familiar features.
First, workers in capitalism sell their labor power and carry out their
productive activity under the rule of another. Second, that alien
power, capital, the creation of accumulated labor, dominates the
workers (Marx 1967: 289–93). Although these aspects of alienation
interfere with choice, they are not distinctively Aristotelian. The centrality of these aspects at least partially accounts for the failure of
many scholars to see the striking affiliation of Marxian and Aristotelian conceptions (Avineri 1970; Kolakowski 1978; Ollman 1971).

Marx's mature economic theory in *Capital* traces the source, combination, and differential bearing of these aspects of alienation. According to Marx, capitalism fuses the material or physical labor process of human beings using land, raw materials, and machines (*Arbeitsprozess*) and the social process of extraction of value and surplus value (*Verwertungsprozess*) (Cohen, 1978: chap. IV). This distinction is originally nonmoral. In looking at these two features of the production of a commodity, Marx differentiates concrete labor, which produces particular useful things, from the abstract average (socially necessary) labor time, which produces values. But Marx's further explanation of capitalism reveals the *moral* cutting edge of this distinction. In the production of value, the achievements of science and effort – in the form of accumulated capital – come to dominate the living workers (1961, vol. 1: 607–8). The value process perverts the physical labor process and harms the producers:

If we consider the process of production from the point of view of the simple labor-process, the labourer stands in relation to the means of production, not in their quality as capital, but as the mere means and material of his own intelligent productive activity. In tanning, e.g., he deals with the skins as his simple objects of labor. It is not the capitalist whose skin he tans. But it is different as soon as we deal with the process of production from the point of view of the process of creation of surplus-value. The means of production are at once changed into means for the absorption of the labor of others. It is now no longer the laborer that employs the means of production, but the means of production that employ the laborer. *Instead of being consumed by him as material elements of his productive activity, they consume him as the ferment necessary to their own life-process,* and the life-process of capital consists only in its movement as value constantly expanding, constantly multiplying itself (*als sich selbst verwertender Wert*). (1961, vol. 1: 310, emphasis added)[2]

This image of the alien "life process" (*Lebensprozess*) of capitalist or value accumulation that uses up the workers is mirrored in the image of the "vampire" or "werewolf hunger" of capital for every last moment of the worker's time in the chapter on the working day, and in Marx's discussion of the monstrous social, political, and moral consequences of capitalism – war, unemployment, the ransacking of agricultural districts and special exploitation of immigrants, and so forth – in the chapter on the general law of capitalist accumulation (1961, vol. 1: 243, 302; Gilbert, in press). These arguments render the first two features of Marx's theory of alienation specific and vivid.

[2] Although Marx rarely used the term alienation in *Capital* (he speaks of capital as an "alien power" in 1961, vol 1: 571), his later theory emphasized features of alienation on pp. 360–1, 571, 573, 606–8, 615, and 621.

But the vampirelike features of alien domination in *Capital* mainly, though not exclusively, affect the goods of life and dignity; they are as easily condemned by a rights-oriented theorist or perhaps, by a utilitarian, as by a eudaimonist (Gilbert 1981b; Miller 1981). The robust material or natural relationships and qualities of individuals (as in the case of Milton or of love or friendship) highlight the dwarfing or impoverishing impact of the capitalist value process. But the eudaimonist arguments on alienation that Marx inherited from Aristotle – work only as a means of life, not as a varied expression of life; money as the forger of simulacra of human qualities; alien politics as a fundamental denial for human flourishing – pick out the central features of Marx's vision of social individuality in communism (Cohen 1978: 129–33; Marx 1973: 325).

Eudaimonist arguments cast new light on two other important themes in *Capital*, namely, the distinction between science and vulgar economics, and the contrast between the gigantic productivity of capitalism and the continuing denial of leisure to workers. First, Marx repeatedly contrasts reality and appearance, and science and vulgar economy. On Marx's theory, capitalism manufactures such strange characters as "Madame La Terre" and "Monsieur Le Capital," which seem to accrue an income out of their physical or particular characteristics (1961, vol. 3: chap. 48). Vulgar economy sticks to such appearances or "illusions," but Marx's theory shows that such incomes are forms of surplus value. Appearance and vulgar economy are explained by the alien features of the process of value creation; science, for Marx, grasps the inner connections or reality that render otherwise irrational appearances comprehensible. Thus, vulgar economy, a mistaken theory, is a social product, a creature of alienation and appearance. But a scientific theory of capitalism or of history is not a *social* product *in the same sense*. It is a refinement of a more general, natural human quest for knowledge; the collective or social contribution to it is important but nonnefarious. Like *Paradise Lost*, scientific achievement is an expression of human nature, a natural activity of the individual theorist. This eudaimonist argument strikingly demonstrates that Marx is *not* a relativist. A scientific theory may learn from history and may benefit the workers, but there is no such thing as a "proletarian" or "bourgeois" science.

Second, for Aristotle, the highest human activities – nonproductive ones – are conducted, not under the pressure of necessity, but by choice (*Nicomachean Ethics* 1105a30–b4). For Marx, likewise, work for subsistence is least characterized by choice; it is *necessary* labor.

But as *Capital* emphasizes, the vast expansion of productivity by capitalism increases potential disposable or free time that could serve as an arena of individuality and choice. This expansion and potential, however, lead to a deep moral paradox. For as it creates enormous potentials for disposable time, capitalism, unless checked by working-class movements, fights relentlessly to stretch out the workers' labor time and restricts leisure; it impoverishes the worker as a social individual. To drive home the *inhuman* character of capitalist production, Marx recalled Aristotle's dream of looms that would move of themselves like the sacred tripods of Hephaestus and release the weavers from slavery. Aristotle's general priorities were clear enough. He mistakenly justified slavery only because it served the "full development of man." Marx satirically juxtaposed Aristotle's vision to the narrowness of contemporary political economists, who, hypnotized by the appearances of the profit system, extolled wage slavery for its elevation of "influential shoe-black dealers" and "extensive sausage makers" (1961, vol. 1: 408–9). For Marx, by contrast, communism meant proletarian control over labor time, the forging of a nonexploitative social nexus, and the flourishing of human nature or *social individuality*. Some of Marx's most original, deepest arguments against capitalism are Aristotelian or eudaimonist in inspiration (Cohen 1978: chap. XI; Gilbert 1983).

In addition to his emphasis on political participation, Marx adopted four other features of an Aristotelian view of politics. First, Marx concurred with Aristotle's distinction between regimes that served a common good and those that did not. Studying a new political form, the polis, Aristotle offered a complex conception of such a good among citizens who shared in a cooperative and free political life. He differentiated rightly ordered regimes from tyrannical ones, dominated by particular interests. For Marx, all stable regimes in exploitative societies, whatever their forms, served particular, ruling-class interests. Thus, he saw Greek democracy as an unjustified despotism over slaves and modern liberal democracy as a social dictatorship over workers. To dominate the producers, such regimes require an *alien* repressive apparatus, revealed most sharply in the "parasite state" of mid-nineteenth century Europe (Gilbert 1981a: chap. 12). They debilitate political life. As an alternative, Marx admired the dictatorship of the proletariat, which adheres to a common good for the vast majority of its members. Thus, either a politics of a common good or a community beyond a need for (certain types of) politics contrasts with the corrupt politics of exploitative regimes.

Second, Aristotle envisioned politics as an arena for noble action. Marx likewise thought that revolutionaries would acquire a specific moral character, one involving sympathy and friendship for the oppressed, hatred for oppressors, dedication, enthusiasm, and willingness to learn from errors given fresh political experience. Though he rejected the haughtiness of Aristotle's "great-souled man," Marx maintained that a capacity to grasp and act decisively on great political issues distinguished women and men of real political ability such as Spartacus, Babeuf, and the "heavenstormers" of the Paris Commune from others. In the dedication of *Capital*, he memorialized his long-standing political associate, Wilhelm Wolff, as "intrepid, faithful, noble protagonist of the proletariat." Moreover, Marx's vision of revolutionary character stresses, in specific situations, the need for heroism and self-sacrifice (Miller in press). He scorned any merely egoistic or selfish model of human motivation such as Bentham's "shopkeeper." Marx's conception of individuality emphatically includes the good of others in one's own good.

His view thus recaptures a distinctive feature of the Aristotelian conception of social connectedness including, as its most intense form, friendship (*philia*). Marx saw the intrinsic value in activities that involved the solidarity of persons bound by friendship, political community, or internationalism. Informed by theoretical and strategic insight, these connections, not selfish calculation, inspired revolutionary action (see Shaw, chap. 1, this volume).

Third, for Aristotle, an understanding of the common good arose from a philosophical refinement of diverse claims about justice (*Politics*, 1282b14–1283a23). Ethics has a political or *conversational* quality in Aristotle; it is not arcane. Likewise, Marx criticized and refined existing ethical opinions. For example, in *Capital*, he indicted formally fair transactions, involving the private ownership of capital, on the consequentialist grounds that such contracts harmed workers and undermined a good life. Similarly, in a speech to leaders of the International Workingmen's Association (hereafter IWA) on "Wages, Price and Profit," he criticized the social theory implicit in the proletarian demand for a "fair day's pay for a fair day's work" (in Marx's terms, that "fairness" could represent only a better "rate of exploitation" from the worker's point of view); yet his own theory, embodied in the slogans, Abolition of the Wage System or Abolition of Classes, reinterpreted and extended the workers' moral claims (Marx and Engels 1962, vol. 1: 446). Though he and Engels hesitated to characterize their own claim as one of justice, his revolutionary demand coincides with a broad Aristotelian conception of a community based on a common good (Gilbert 1982).

Fourth, Aristotle emphasized practical deliberation about courses of action. Given the diversity of human goods, he recognized that moral choice often involves conflicts. One way of reading Aristotle's complex argument in Books VI and VII of the *Nicomachean Ethics* is to interpret failures of deliberation as the superimposition of the pursuit of one good (usually a lesser one) on another. Thus, in one of Aristotle's examples, Niobe placed love for her children above piety (1142a23–1143b3); life is a good, but cowardice in defense of a city is not. Deliberation and prudence play a decisive role in political action.

But deliberation is also central to Marx's conception of politics. Marx had extended the Aristotelian idea of a common good to include internationalism; the revolutionary movement had to make the *"common interests of the proletariat independently of all nationality"* the central aspect of its political strategy and (broadly speaking) conception of justice. Marx recognized that internationalism often required hard political and moral choices. Thus, in his "Inaugural Address of the IWA," Marx praised the "heroism" of English workers who vehemently supported abolitionism in the American Civil War (Marx and Engels 1962, vol. 1: 384). The English ruling classes campaigned for breaking the Northern blockade; they advertised the acquisition of Southern cotton as a supposed cure for widespread unemployment (Marx 1972: 112–13, 152–63). Though these workers needed jobs to stave off starvation (an important good), they were keenly aware that slavery was an unjustifiable evil, that they themselves would be asked to fight and pay for a war, and that the victory of a slaveholding republic in North America would push international politics in a reactionary direction and ultimately harm them. Their meetings and demonstrations thwarted an "infamous" crusade by the English ruling classes on behalf of slavery (Gilbert 1978). These workers had chosen a great international public good – one affecting the quality of their existence – over some short-run gains contributing to mere survival.

These four broad similarities, along with their common emphasis on political action as an intrinsic good, reveal the affinities of an Aristotelian and Marxian conception of politics. Yet, a critic might note, Marx envisioned a higher stage of communism in which the state had dissolved. His ultimate conception, in contrast to Aristotle's, is postpolitical. But Marx's argument on communism deserves clarification. A proletarian revolution overthrows only the "parasite state" and its alien politics (see Thomas, chap. 6, this volume). In its place, as the Paris Commune illustrated, workers and their allies reabsorb all the functions of political life. Officials, drawn mainly from the working class, would receive an ordinary wage; an armed citizenry would replace a standing army; political meetings and re-call would enable the workers to communicate their wishes and exer-cise authority. Thus, for Marx, such a regime, though strongly po-litical, already moves toward the abolition of the parasite state. An Aristotelian conception of the centrality and intrinsic good of politi-cal activity underscores the nonalien character of this political form. In the later stage of communism, the need for proletarian prepara-tion for war against external and internal counterrevolutionaries would cease. Yet dialectically, important features of association and solidarity would remain. The view that communism abolishes the politics of deliberation on common problems as opposed to the polit-ics of war and class war is misleading. Some of Marx's early com-ments on the dissolution of the (alien) political in the social are a mistaken, overly context-specific gloss on his argument (Gilbert 1981a: 36–40).

Furthermore, politics plays a decisive role for Marx in the triumph of communism and the emergence of its higher stage. The eudai-monist criticisms of alienation highlight the contrasting features of revolutionary motivation in politics, work, and social relationships. Together these aspects offset those survivals of capitalism, especially bourgeois "defects" involved in the maintenance of differential wages, which Marx saw as an obstacle to communism in his "Critique of the Gotha Program" (Marx and Engels 1962, vol. 2: 22–4). In addition, as the experience of the Russian and Chinese revolutions has shown, clashes over politics versus material incentives, foreshad-owed in Marxian and Aristotelian eudaimonism, have figured cen-trally in the conflicts and transformations of twentieth-century com-munism (Gilbert 1981b: sec. 3, 5). The arguments traced in the preceding discussion have had enduring practical significance.

At this point, many readers may still find these various similarities between Aristotle and Marx overdrawn. One must, after all, pit Aris-totle, leading defender of natural slavery, against Marx, the great opponent of exploitation. Aristotle never doubted the existence of a large number of humans who lacked sufficient mental capacity to govern themselves; he defended slavery as a necessary basis for the political action of leisured (in Marx's terms, parasitic) citizens. Yes Aristotle questioned slavery, not only for Greek males, but for many barbarians as well. He admired a barbarian city, Carthage, as one of the three best actual regimes. Aristotle even imagined an automated setting that would eliminate slavery in production (*Politics* 1253b33–1254a3). Thus, we might look at Aristotle's and Marx's clash about slavery as rooted in a factual disagreement over who counts as human rather than in conflicting moral premises.

But, a critic might add, Aristotle only held a conception of cyclical change and denied historical or moral progress. To many, and especially to the ethical relativist, these differences reveal the unbridgeable intellectual chasm between Aristotle and Marx, a chasm obscured by the abstract similarities allegedly overdrawn here.

I suggest, however, that Aristotle's central argument on citizenship and human nature includes an important example of moral progress and points to still further continuities with Marx. On Aristotle's view, human beings display their highest moral capacities through their actual political organization. In Book I of the *Politics*, Aristotle celebrated Greek political community and freedom – the capacity of Greek males for ruling and being ruled in turn – as a *natural* phenomenon, a manifestation of man's nature as a *zoon politikon*. Yet Aristotle recognized that freedom, as something distinctive and admirable, had emerged against the dark background of past despotism:

The most natural form of the village appears to be that of the colony or offshoot of the family . . . This, it may be noted, is the reason why each Greek polis was originally ruled – as the primitive peoples of the barbarian world still are – by kings. (*Politics* 1252b17–26)

Aristotle praised the legislator who first "constructed" the city as "the greatest of beneficiaries of mankind" (1253a30–31). In a realist vein, we might interpret Aristotle's argument on the emergence of the polis as a claim that human beings historically *discover* their highest capacities for political and ethical organization. By his own method, if, counterfactually, Aristotle could have forged a *political* theory before the existence of the polis, he might have said: Man is a *despotic* or patriarchal animal. Aristotle's own account of the transition from a defective patriarchal organization to a polis exemplifies historical progress in morality.[3] Such progress illustrated the real hu-

---

[3] If Engels's argument in *Origin of the Family* on the equality of women and men in early communism is right, a Marxian could dialectically reinterpret Aristotle's account of the progress of freedom (Marx and Engels 1962, vol. 2: 246, 266, 271). In that case, the first despotisms would represent a decline from more cooperative arrangements. This decline

man capacity for cooperation and freedom. Furthermore, in contrast to despotisms, the polis revealed the distinctive class conflicts and clashes of opinion over the common good that would characterize (comparatively) free regimes. As a result of these new political facts, Aristotle could first pose the main questions about human potentials for cooperation and freedom and found the scientific, or, to use a less loaded term, objective study of politics and ethics (Gilbert 1983).

Starting from the actual reorganization of European society sans slavery, liberal theorists like Montesquieu and Hegel denied the biological arguments Aristotle advanced to sanctify such servitude. In so doing, they identified and defended *further* moral progress. To put it in Hegel's terms, Aristotle had proclaimed that some are free as opposed to the earlier ("Eastern") conception that only one (i.e., the despot) is free. Modern liberalism went further and recognized that all (males) are (politically) free. Recalling Aristotle's view that man is a political animal, Hegel insisted: *"Man is by nature free* (Hegel 1975: 54–5). He might also have said: Man is an animal that can only individualize himself in society. Later liberals like Mill would challenge the subjection of women. But they often contended that capitalism is consistent with individuality. Marxian theory would go further still. Only when workers emancipate themselves from economic servitude ("wage slavery") and forge a genuinely cooperative society can further moral progress be made and social individuality or human freedom actualized.

Thus, both liberals and Marxians endorse Aristotle's view of the polis as an arena of partial human freedom, recognize its creation as an example of ethical advance, and acknowledge that Aristotle's ethics and political science illustrate progress in moral theory. Both contend that human beings can manifest their full capacities for cooperation, freedom, and individuality *only* in the course of a lengthy historical development. Further, whether liberals or Marxians are ultimately right about the potentials for cooperative organization, both theories rightly view the demise of slavery as morally progressive. Contrary to a relativist view, Aristotle's theory of freedom provides a framework for later liberal and Marxian advances. Far from revealing an intellectual chasm, the contrast of Aristotle

would be sustained in the exploitation of slaves and the subjection of women in the Greek polis. Yet, compared to original communism, that regime would still mark progress in freedom, human self-recognition, and the flourishing of higher, more diverse individual capacities.

and Montesquieu or of Aristotle and Marx highlights moral progress. Such contrasts show how strikingly some leading debates in ethics pivot on disagreements over *factual* matters, including social and biological theory, rather than on clashing *moral* premises. As opposed to relativism, this moral realist argument, in either a liberal or Marxian version, is historical, but not historicist.[4]

II. SCIENTIFIC AND MORAL REALISM

Metaethically, in committing himself to a transformed version of Aristotle's eudaimonism, Marx seconded Aristotle's judgment that there was objectivity in morals as well as in science. His complex realist interpretation of Aristotle's political economy underlines the role of *discoveries* about human capacities in science and, by implication, in moral theory.

Aristotle recognized the difficulties in defending moral objectivity. In Book V of the *Nicomachean Ethics,* he acknowledged the force of the conventionalist arguments that distinguish invariant nature from mutable political and moral practices. For, he noted, the laws of each regime combine natural and conventional justice and vary, whereas "fire burns here and in Persia." In this vein, Aristotle sarcastically compared conventional justice to wine and grain measures, which merchants adjust one way in wholesale and another in retail markets according to expediency; at best, he maintained, specific rules of conventional justice, for instance, the particular punishment for a crime or character of a religious sacrifice, are, before they are legally set, indifferent (*Nicomachean Ethics* 1134b18–1135a5).

Yet Aristotle viewed response to a type of crime – for instance, punishment for the taking of innocent life – or piety toward the cosmic order as matters of natural justice. Further, novel Greek political arrangements set a standard for the general distinction between regimes oriented toward a common good and corrupt, tyrannical ones. We might interpret his account of the emergence of the polis as an unusual example of his claim that *even* standards of natural justice vary (*Nicomachean Ethics,* 1134b23–32).

Marx's scientific and moral distinction between the (humanly) natural and the (distortedly) social aspects of activities and arrangements

---

[4] Historicists contend that ethical standards shift with prevailing interests or modes of production, that such standards are incommensurable, and hence, that nothing resembling moral progress exists.

recaptures this Aristotelian view. His critique of his predecessors relies on a realist conception of the advance of scientific investigation. In broad terms, scientific realists hold that the "natural kind" terms of mature scientific theories *refer* to features of the world and that, through a process of theoretical criticism, observation, and experiment, scientists accommodate such terms to the structure of the world. This view stresses continuities of reference across major theory changes and progress in scientific theory. In contrast to empiricism, the realist also insists that such nonobservable entities as electrons actually exist, even though they can only be identified via mature scientific theory and inferred from other phenomena. Marx makes a similar claim regarding the reality of surplus value (Gilbert 1982: 338–43)

As a realist, Marx carefully studied the theories of his predecessors in scientific political economy and sought to show how his own theory explained the insights of previous ones. Early in *Capital,* he criticized the political economy of that "giant thinker," Aristotle. Aristotle's "brilliance," Marx avowed, "shines" (*glänzt*) in three ways: first, in his discovery of the distinction between use value and exchange value; second, in his insight that money (what Marx called the money form) further developed the (value) form of commodities; and third, in his recognition that equality between two physically disparate commodities, subject to radically different uses, must embody some third, common characteristic. Mature or scientific political economy is founded on these three observations (1961, vol. 1: 60–1, 85).

Yet Aristotle provided no explanation for the equality between disparate commodities identified in his third discovery. According to Marx, he considered it "a makeshift for practical purposes" (*Notbehelf für das praktische Bedürfnis*). From the point of view of economic explanation, Marx's criticism was well taken. Yet Aristotle's analysis contained a deeper *moral* insight than Marx's gloss recognized. Aristotle viewed money, the medium of commensurability, as a political tool to knit together the complementary functions or activities necessary for any form of justice to work. He saw money (*nomisma*) as tied to law or custom (*nomos*), not to nature (*physis*). Aristotle's play on words prefigures the central distinction between conventional and natural justice in the same book of the *Ethics*. Although the use of money can corrupt, it can also unite diverse activities and needs (*chreia;* 1133a26–1133b10). In the latter case, it furthers *eudaimonia*, strengthens the life of the polis, and is, to that extent, natural. Although Aristotle never unraveled the source of monetary commensurability, he emphasized the ethical significance of the particular forms of human cooperation and achievement that underlie it.

On Marx's account, Aristotle's question about commensurability was scientific and profound, but his solution mistaken. Marx saw abstract human labor time as the source of this equality. The labor theory played a central role in the elaboration of a mature political economy. Since the Greek polis rested on a radical division of labor among humans – free males in politics, slaves in production – Aristotle could hardly have arrived at a solution that presupposed the comparability of *human* labor. Aristotle's discussion of reciprocity and equality in Book V of the *Nicomachean Ethics* underscored the theoretical and moral impact of this division: "The existence of the polis depends on proportionate reciprocity; for men demand that they shall be able to requite evil with evil – *if they cannot, they feel that they are in the position of slaves* – and to repay good with good" (1132a32–1133a2). In short, reciprocity and equality were not for slaves. Aristotle discerned no commonality in the activity of slaves and citizens (or, among citizens, between that of doers and makers; 1140a1–7). As Marx contended, investigators could unravel the "secret" (*Geheimnis*) of commensurability only in a historical context in which equality "possessed the fixity of a popular prejudice" (*die Festigkeit eines Volksvorurteils besitzt;* 1961, vol. 1: 61, 81). Though Marx's choice of the term "popular prejudice" seems tinged with relativism, the underlying claim about human capacities that determines the "fixity" of this view is an objective one. For Marx, *major social transformations,* such as the emergence of social organizations not based on slave labor, the Puritan and French revolutions, and working-class political movements like Chartism, had subsequently revealed Aristotle's error. Such changes alone provided the setting that made possible the adoption of an approximately true theory: the labor theory of value. Only on the basis of such a theory could political economists at last answer Aristotle's clearly posed question.

Morally speaking, the modern labor theory presupposed the distinctive liberal recognition (described earlier) that humans generally have sufficient capacity to participate responsibly in political life. Therefore, no society based on (legalized) human bondage can be justified. Thus, major historical changes played a decisive role in both economic *and* moral theorizing. But Marx's political economy accords even more deeply with a moral realist view of Aristotle than the argument about slavery would suggest. For as we have seen,

Marx's labor theory stresses not only the equality of alienated productivity (that of abstract labor, which yields exchange value); it also
emphasizes production for use and the perversion of the motivations
for work that characterizes capitalism. Following Aristotle, he suggested that humans must engage in activities *for their own sakes* if they
are to further happiness. If they cannot, the world of action is
turned upside down. Marx's aim was to set the world aright, to make
the social accord with the (*humanly*) natural. This eudaimonist view
underlies Marx's communist conception of social individuality that
measures out resources: "From each according to ability, to each
according to *need.*" Here Marx's view strikingly recalls and dialectically transforms Aristotle's insight into the relationships underlying
the appropriate functioning of money. In communism, use and
need, consonant with natural justice – not money and abstract equality – rule production and distribution.

In the natural sciences, social changes, however influential, are
external to the development of the theory. The needs of the industrial revolution spurred the expansion of research in chemistry and
physics, but did not contribute centrally to their theoretical content.
In the social sciences and morals, however, transformation in social
and political organization often play a more *internal* role. For instance, in Marx's critique of Aristotle's political economy, the abolition of slavery and the rise of egalitarian movements provided important background conditions for a revolution in the theory. But
moral theory, being concerned with human cooperation, freedom,
and individuality, pivots even more fundamentally on historical *discoveries* about the relevant capacities. Such capacities are often exemplified in radical movements and new social and political forms,
which thus serve as *evidence* for advances in moral theory.

Furthermore, given the fusion of the natural and social aspects of
human activity, there is a sense for Marx in which, following Hegel,
history just *is* the (nonrelativist) story of cooperation, freedom, and
individuality. History is the dialectical unfolding of material or natural human capacities, though in a setting of socially created distortion; the latter makes historical progress heavily dependent on class
struggle. Marx's theory of the production of value is so striking, as
an economic and moral explanation, because capitalism is the most
complex, *extreme* form of that social distortion, namely, "enchant-
ment" or "fetishism." Thus, Marx's theory of history unites scientific
discovery and moral discovery.

On a realist account, both Marx's theory of political economy and his (implicit) moral theory have an Aristotelian lineage. Yet his recognition and advances over Aristotle in the former contrast with his (comparative) silence about the latter. Marx's hesitancy about clarifying this relationship is part of a misplaced, metaethical caution that results in his occasional contrasts of his science to the moralizing of other radicals (1961, vol. 1: 84–5; Gilbert, 1982). Yet Marx's new historical theory identified the manifold character of capitalism's harms to human happiness; that theory justified Marx's opposed vision of the flourishing of social individuality in communism. In the marked divergences between Aristotle's and Marx's particular ethical judgments, disputes about facts, including social and biological theory – not clashes of underlying moral premises – play the pivotal role. These essentially empirical differences in social theory led to Marx's achievements and stature as a moral theorist. The dynamic character and profound moral impact of these differences help to explain, though they do not justify, Marx's failure to spell out the relationship of his conclusions to Aristotle's. But Marx's eudaimonism and moral realism dialectically incorporate and transform an Aristotelian inheritance.

III. MILLER'S CRITICISMS OF MORAL OBJECTIVITY

Although a Marxian eudaimonism and moral realism appear to be an impressive, (potentially) full-fledged moral point of view, not all proponents of Marxian social theory will be convinced. Indeed, Richard Miller (in press) has advanced two important and subtle criticisms of any such interpretation. The first, which I will call the *two-components objection,* contends that Marx's social theory lacks the distinctive general structure of a moral theory. His normative judgments depend too heavily on his theory of history and are too empirical or contingent to count as moral ones. The second – *the clash-of-goods objection* – maintains that extreme conflicts of goods pervade not only exploitative societies but even the first stage of communism. Such clashes are sufficiently serious to prevent unanimity of moral choice and consequent political action even among eudaimonists. In this section, I want to use two arguments based on the previous sections to respond to these objections, one on the role of empirical moral discoveries (such as the emergence of the polis and of non-slave societies) in moral theorizing, the other on a central expectation of Aristotelian practical deliberation that choices involving limited conflicts of goods do not undermine moral objectivity. This section will also show that Aristotle's and Marx's moral realism dovetails with and is amplified by current realist arguments in philosophy of science and language.

Miller has defended general views close to my own about Marx's historical theory, the importance of political activity and internationalism, and (ironically) the relation of Marx's to Aristotle's eudaimonism. In "Marx and Morality," however, Miller proposes a general conception of the distinctive structure of an ethical theory that, he suggests, conflicts with a Marxian social theory and political strategy. Here Miller's view is a variant of a more common philosophical position. Philosophers have often thought that moral knowledge must be a kind of a priori knowledge. Hence, moral theories involve two components. First, an ethical theory should discern the most general moral principles without regard to empirical circumstances or specific institutional practices. Second, the latter become relevant (as a subordinate, almost external component) only in applying the theory. Miller's own conception of moral theory makes a similar division:

> The validity of those (moral) norms is not subject to direct empirical controversy . . . Thus, whatever maximizes the general welfare is best, for the utilitarian. But he or she may claim to know little about what would actually maximize welfare. Factual questions about institutions and strategies largely, if not entirely, *belong somewhere outside moral theory*, in politics, social theory, or social engineering (emphasis added).[5]

In characterizing the primary component of moral theories, he identifies three broad features of morality as a basis for political decision (equality, an appeal to general norms, and universality). He contends that Marx's communism, like Nietzsche's aestheticism and Weber's nationalism, lacks just those features. Thus, the triumph of Germany in the struggle of the great powers in the early twentieth century was an overriding value for Weber against all three features of morality. Similarly, Nietzsche celebrated aesthetic achievement, which he saw as at odds with equality, and debunked *moral* norms as masks for a nonmoral "will to power." For Miller, Marx's position is closer to a moral one. At least full communism is a much more egalitarian and internationalist society than the preceding ones. Thus, he speaks of Marx as holding a *decent* or *humane,* but nonmoral, point of view in comparison to those of Weber and Nietzsche.

But Miller's concession about humaneness makes it unclear that

---

[5] The final pagination for Miller (in press) is not yet available.

Marx's conception is, by his standards, nonmoral. Given a recognition of the common features of an Aristotelian and Marxian eudaimonism (Miller 1981), one might see Marx's vision as moral. Yet Miller's two-components objection raises important questions about the structure of Marx's normative vision. For Marx's moral theory is not readily resolvable into a general definition of goodness and subordinate empirical claims. Furthermore, Marx's judgments about the fundamental conflicts of goods in exploitative societies – Greek political community at the expense of slavery, modern science and mechanization at the expense of gross inequalities – rest on contingent features of human history. Marx condemned the exploitation that accompanied alien or merely instrumental progress. A rhetoric of moral indictment imbues Marx's account of such episodes as original capitalist accumulation or colonialism (Gilbert 1981b: 180–2). Yet Marx concluded that over long periods of history, no social alternative to such progress existed: The propagation of reactionary ideas by the exploiters was too strong, the scale of production too narrow, the revolutionary experience of the oppressed too limited. Given these contingent features of historical development, Marx restricted his moral judgments of past social epochs to a specification of the conflict of goods involved in exploitative progress.

Moreover, Marx advanced specific empirical arguments on the contemporary possibility of a more cooperative society; those claims distinguished the present epoch from past ones and spurred revolutionary activity. The communist movement marked a great moral divide and initiated *"human history"* as opposed to preceding *"prehistory"* (Marx and Engels 1974: 183). But the fusing of diverse intrinsic goods in communism is also a contingent factual claim.

Miller rightly maintains that Marx's historical theory strongly governs his moral judgments. What Miller considers the secondary or external component of an ethical theory becomes primary; the distinctively analytic component drops out altogether.

Miller's two-components view, however, is far too sweeping. It rules out liberal moral theories, for example, John Rawls's theory of justice, not just Marxian ones. Thus, it can not do the work of discrimination that Miller wants it to do. In addition, as recent realist arguments in philosophy of science and language have shown, scientific terms do not have analytic or conventional definitions. Instead, scientific definitions are arrived at through a process of theoretical criticism and experimental discovery; investigators increasingly accommodate such definitions to the structure of the world. I will contend that definitions of the good are similarly empirical, that is, contingent on the way the world is.

On the surface, Rawls's theory of justice seems a likely candidate for a two-components distinction. First, Rawls offers a very general definition of the original position. Those principles are just, he contends, that individuals would adopt after negotiation in that ideal situation. Second, a Rawlsian can apply these principles only with the addition of specific factual statements pertaining to particular social configurations and moral dilemmas. But this description is an inadequate characterization of Rawls's moral theory. For even the general principles in the original position depend strongly on facts in two important ways. To be plausible as a device for moral reasoning, the original position requires empirical claims about the centrality of bargaining, contract, and consent in our conception of justice. Beyond this, no moral principles follow from the general definition of the original position alone. To adopt such principles, Rawls acknowledges, the individuals would have to know how human beings are constituted *psychologically* and have at their disposal *all true social theories* (1971: 137–8). Thus, Rawls's principles depend on controversial empirical claims. Similarly, utilitarianism initially appeals to empirical claims about what constitutes human happiness or welfare; so does Aristotle's eudaimonism. Now, Marx's ethical viewpoint does not look like that of Rawls or of utilitarianism; it is much more embedded in and dependent on the validity of particular empirical claims. But Miller's two-components criterion still rules out leading ethical theories rather than distinguishing them from Marxian normative arguments.[6]

The two-components interpretation is sometimes part of a general conventionalist view, which looks for analytic definitions in science as well as in ethics. Alternatively, one might hold the two-components

---

[6] Miller also claims that a Marxian view, unlike other moral arguments, violates a standard of equal treatment. For a revolutionary movement will act against some capitalists and police who have personally committed no wrong. But this *harm-to-innocents objection* once again rules out obviously moral arguments about other large-scale political conflicts. For instance, it would exclude those of Kant or Mill in justification of the French Revolution or the North in the U.S. Civil War (comparably innocent aristocrats and slaveholders would be affected) and even standard liberal defenses of the bombing of military targets in which some civilians will be killed. Miller's objection would pose a special problem for Marxians only if they were barred from taking the same steps as other justified political actors to limit such harm. But they aren't.

interpretation in ethics alone, contrasting that interpretation with a naturalist or realist view of scientific definitions, which are based on empirical discoveries. In opposition to both of these views, a moral realist takes the next step and asks: Can the definition of the "good" and other moral terms also be empirically grounded? This is the approach I favor, and the one most appropriate to Marx's scientific and moral realism.

As Kripke (1980), Putnam (1981), and Boyd (1979) have argued, it is routine in science for definition to rest on contingent discoveries about the way the world is. No one could know a priori, for example, that temperature is mean molecular kinetic energy (Putnam 1981: 206–8). Yet the term "temperature" *referred* to a certain feature of the world even though investigators needed a long period of discovery and theory change to ascertain the exact molecular property. Thus, the enterprise of scientific theory, including the search for adequate definitions, proceeds by providing successive approximations to the truth. To borrow another example from Putnam, a modern chemist can identify as fool's gold glittering specimens that would have deceived Archimedes. If we suppose a conversation in a possible world, the modern chemist could point out features of the sample that differed from those of gold even *without* persuading the ancient chemist of the truth of modern chemical theory. Gold is gold; fool's gold is not. In studying the history of science, we do not take as a defining standard the specific (operational) criteria that an ancient scientist used to define an element. Instead, we look at the overall project of ancient and modern chemistry: namely, to discover the nature of matter. Thus, we can see continuities of reference to gold even if the modern chemist has a more profound theory of its microstructure and even if the ancient chemist improperly identifies iron pyrites as gold (Putnam 1975: 153–7). Putnam's argument contrasts sharply with that of the conventionalist who seeks analytic definitions or takes contemporary scientific criteria to define a term. On the conventionalist account, in Greek chemistry, fool's gold just *was* gold; ancient definitions and modern ones are, to use a Kuhnian term, incommensurable. This general view leads directly to relativism regarding scientific knowledge and to the denial of scientific progress. As naturalists have shown, however, this view is a misleading portrayal of scientific practice and purposes and leads to utterly implausible consequences.

Given Miller's emphasis on the role of analytic definition in moral knowledge, Miller, like the conventionalist, strongly denies progress in moral theory. For instance, he asserts "that Aristotle would have changed his mind about slavery if he had appreciated some fact or argument does not fit with what we know of Aristotle and his contemporaries." According to Miller, we cannot hold both that Aristotle is rational and that moral progress has occurred since the ancient polis; so much the worse, he concludes, for moral progress. Miller's argument rejects any notion of moral objectivity. But Miller's contention about Aristotle seems wrong on the face of it. For, as I noted earlier, given the facts of his day, Aristotle already challenged slavery for Greek males and many barbarians as well; despite contemporary stereotypes, he insisted, these men were not incapable of self-government. In addition, Aristotle's idea of a citizenship and the role of political action in a good life depend on an *empirical moral discovery:* the emergence of the polis. Aristotle's own account reveals the existence of moral progress. Given Aristotle's view of human moral and political capacities and confronted (hypothetically) with nonslave societies, Aristotle could have denied the existence of natural slavery without the adoption of any particular modern social and political theory. By his own argument, he would probably have concluded that man is *not* a despotic (i.e., slaveholding) animal. Alternatively, as we will see later, even if Archimedes or Aristotle had failed to draw the relevant conclusions, scientific and moral rationality do not require consensus.

A moral realist conception deepens this point. For example, in a manner paralleling Kripke's and Putnam's arguments about science, a moral realist would contend that Aristotle's ideas of justice and a good life *referred* to human capacities for cooperation and freedom. Liberal and Marxian criticisms of Aristotle – for instance, the rejection of Aristotle's theory of natural slavery or of the subjection of women – rest on subsequent *discoveries* about the extent of such capacities. Yet, as I noted previously, we can still see the *broad* continuities between Aristotle's and modern conceptions, despite the modern denial of specific features of Aristotle's view. If we see these theorists as engaged in a moral project that has a common *reference* to human capacities and needs, we will not be overly beguiled by the dissimilarities in *meaning* of *dikaiosune,* liberal conceptions of justice, and the Marxian abolition of classes that have led some philosophers to conventionalism. For the realist, Aristotle's error about slavery, despite its more severe human consequences, is comparable to Archimedes's misidentification of fool's gold. And Aristotle's own definition of the good life is strongly empirical. Thus, contingency and discovery are, contra conventionalism and the two-components theory, part of morality.

Miller's second objection to moral objectivity, which I call the *universality of the conflict of goods argument,* extends the fundamental clash of human goods from exploitative societies to the first stage of communism. This objection pits a strong proponent of free speech, who agrees with a Marxian account of the facts, against an advocate of the dictatorship of the proletariat. Both acknowledge that in the immediate postrevolutionary era, capitalists would have important political advantages, for instance, the inherited influence of older, reactionary ideas and practices among the masses, or differential organizational skills, arising from the experience and coherence of a comparatively small number of exploiters who seek to *disorganize* the much larger number of workers and their allies. To counter these advantages, a dicatorship of the proletariat would have to curtail freedom of speech and association for its enemies. As Miller emphasizes, a Marxian would justify these restrictions "to reduce the level of violence and increase access to politics and culture," goods that a liberal would also endorse.

Nonetheless, depending on the severity and extent of such restrictions, a disagreement could arise between Marxians and liberals who affirm a common list of human goods and the same view of the facts. For instance, as part of the good of acquiring knowledge, both recognize the intrinsic value of being able to speak one's mind without restraint. Yet liberals might rank freedom of speech so highly that they would oppose the dictatorship of the proletariat. Thus, Miller contends, on quite reasonable assumptions, a clash of fundamental values in communism prevents any *determinate* moral judgment or course of political action to which every *eudaimonist,* let alone every rational person, must assent. But for Miller, any distinctively moral point of view requires universal rationality. On his account, it must be true that each rational person, capable of the normal range of emotions and fully informed of the facts, would reach the same ethical conclusion. This example suggests that Marxian "morality" fails such a test even when it makes judgments about the nearly ideal conditions of early communism.

Miller envisions a liberal and Marxian who agree about the facts. But this condition has a far more dramatic effect on the persuasiveness of the example, as a putative conflict over basic values, than Miller recognizes. In order to highlight this point, we need to examine the three ways in which a clash between a Marxian and a liberal might arise: First, those adhering to a roughly similar view about moral goods could clash over facts; second, eudaimonists who could even hold a similar ranking of goods could disagree given the novelty of and uncertainty about a future communism; third, proponents of a common view of the facts could clash about evaluation. Miller contends that the third kind of disagreement has great moral weight. But suppose that the basic dispute over the comparative goodness of liberal capitalism and early communism arises from factual clashes of the first kind. That debate contrasts a good society with a very bad one. If Miller did not recognize *how decisive* such factual disagreements are, he might conflate the two kinds of examples; he would then exaggerate the difference over ranking of goods. For instance, *if* Marxian theory is right, the dictatorship of the proletariat emerges as the only way to avoid increasingly destructive world wars and recurrent fascism; liberal objections would vanish. Similarly, suppose Sidney Hook's (1965) description of a barracks communism and the virtues of liberal capitalism were true. In that case, a formerly Marxian eudaimonist would be compelled to recognize the merits of liberalism. The sharp conflict between these two positions derives from *factual* disputes, not from clashing moral premises. This first kind of disagreement therefore casts no doubt on moral objectivity.

A dispute between a liberal and Marxian could arise in a second way. For a liberal might note that the future course of any Marxian experiment is unclear. Even if communism might secure some important goods, it might endanger others such as freedom of speech. But liberal objections on the grounds that communism is new, or that the first attempts to create a nonexploitative society have foundered, have nothing to do with a fundamental clash over the ranking of human goods. Instead, they are a species of factual disagreement, and might well, on further empirical examination or in the light of subsequent historical developments, turn out to be wrong.

For Miller, such disagreements challenge the notion of universal rationality, which he sees as basic to a moral point of view. Thus, even if the factual case for communism turned out to be substantial, the remaining disagreement of *some* liberal critics would rule out moral objectivity. But again in this case, Miller's argument is too *sweeping;* his criterion for a moral view would impugn scientific as well as moral rationality. For as a result of the complexities of scientific method, scientific rationality, especially during periods of discovery and dramatic theoretical change, does not require consensus. Thus, Priestley opposed the oxygen theory and Einstein quantum mechanics. No one considers their positions irrational for that time; yet their disagreement with what turned out to be the true theory does not throw scientific method or rationality into doubt. Similarly, the complexity or multidimensionality of human goods, given uncertain results, can lead – rationally – to different moral choices. Yet given further experience and further theoretical argument, there would turn out to be a fact of the matter as to which alternative is better. (Reverting to my earlier hypothetical examples: Even if Archimedes and Aristotle, lacking a full modern theory, had persisted in their original views, fool's gold would still be iron pyrites and slavery still a cruel and inhuman institution.) Contrary to Miller, the absence of moral consensus no more undermines ethical objectivity than lack of agreement on novel scientific achievements undermines scientific rationality.

Yet surely, one might insist, there must be some circumstances in which examples of the sort Miller stresses can arise. Such cases, however, would have to emerge from a *far less acute* conflict between the two societies than the one opponents envision who engage in the first kind of factual dispute. To arrive at the factual agreement that Miller requires, we would have to split the difference between liberal and Marxian social theory. Thus, imagine a nonbarracks communism that facilitates substantial worker participation, including the activity of specially oppressed groups in capitalist society such as women and the victims of racism. Nonetheless, in opposing counterrevolution, some intimidation of speech occurs for intellectuals; that intimidation harms the progress of knowledge. Imagine, further, a capitalist democracy that allows more erosion of racism and sexism than Marxian theory suggests; yet it still prevents working-class political participation and promotes ideas sanctioning "apathy" and the like. Finally, suppose that the two societies are roughly alike on other major moral dimensions; for instance, neither is prone to dominate others or to wage war. The disagreement between a Marxian and a liberal would then result from a difference over values. Would this dilemma then require the denial of moral objectivity?

The *indeterminacy* of this case arises precisely because it rules out so many of the things we commonly object to. Both the liberal and Marxian would condemn slavery, the servitude of women, colonialism, Nazism, aggressive war, and the like on grounds of their effect on life, the realization of individual potentials, and happiness. Indeterminacy in this particular choice coexists with and indeed presupposes moral discoveries about the nature of human goods and who counts as human. Thus, both of these societies, as described, would be *comparatively good societies*. But this example then proves to be an unusual, large-scale example of a common moral phenomenon. Individuals often confront choices between goods in which no moral extreme exists. A moral theory that leaves wide scope for individuality need offer no specific advice in such cases. Those choices are properly described as matters of individual preference. They are differences of *preference* precisely because they do not involve severe moral conflicts.

This argument against the *clash-of-goods objection* appeals to a distinctively Aristotelian conception of practical deliberation. Aristotle recognized a diversity of goods and suggested that individual choices among them, even when there is a limited conflict or sacrifice of one, do not involve important wrongs. Such cases fall short of the *excessive* pursuit of one good at the expense of another. Thus, the eudaimonism outlined earlier reveals the limited significance of the disagreement described by Miller. To be objective, a moral theory need not rule out ties or near-ties between such alternatives, including those between broadly morally similar types of society.

In order to construct a case that makes for a central conflict about values between a liberal and a Marxian, Miller has unintentionally conflated examples of the third kind (ones of value) with examples of the first kind (ones of fact). But the participants in this debate are no longer, say, Lenin and Sidney Hook; this disagreement is far more benign.

In his objections to characterizing Marxism as a moral point of view, Miller stresses the role of facts, including social theory, in Marxian normative judgments; he rightly opposes overrating the role of moral injunction in Marxian strategy and of ethical considerations in Marxian historical explanation. Yet a conception of the good society inevitably plays an important role in revolutionary movements, and Marx's vision provides an impressive example. Miller's argument that Marx's theory is decent but nonmoral is mistaken. His criticisms do not discredit the objectivity of Marxian moral judgments or of a eudaimonism of an Aristotelian or Marxian kind.

REFERENCES

Aristotle (1975). *The Nicomachean Ethics.* Loeb Classical Library. Cambridge, Mass.: Harvard University Press.

(1977). *Politics*. Loeb Classical Library. Cambridge, Mass.: Harvard University Press.

Avineri, Shlomo (1970). *The Social and Political Thought of Karl Marx*. Cambridge: Cambridge University Press.

Boyd, Richard N. (1979). "Metaphor and Theory Change." In Andrew Ortony (ed.), *Metaphor and Thought*. Cambridge: Cambridge University Press.

Cohen, G.A. (1978). *Marx's Theory of History: A Defence*. Princeton, N.J.: Princeton University Press.

Fisk, Milton (1975). "History and Reason in Rawls' Moral Theory." In Norman Daniels (ed.), *Reading Rawls*. New York: Basic Books.

Gilbert, Alan (1978). "Marx on Internationalism and War." *Philosophy and Public Affairs* 7: 346–69.

(1981a). *Marx's Politics: Communists and Citizens*. New Brunswick, N.J.: Rutgers University Press and Oxford: Martin Robertson.

(1981b). "Historical Theory and the Structure of Moral Argument in Marx." *Political Theory* 9: 173–205.

(1982). "An Ambiguity in Marx's and Engels's Account of Justice and Equality." *The American Political Science Review* 76: 328–46.

(in press). "The Storming of Heaven: *Capital* and Marx's Politics." In J. Roland Pennock (ed.), *Marxism Today, Nomos* 26. New York: New York University Press.

(1983). "Moral Realism, Individuality and Justice in War." Delivered at the annual meeting of the American Political Science Association; available from Graduate School of International Studies, University of Denver.

Hegel, G. W. F. (1975). *Lectures on the Philosophy of World History: Introduction*. Translated by H. B. Nisbet. Cambridge: Cambridge University Press.

Hook, Sidney (1965). *Political Power and Personal Freedom*. New York: Collier Books.

Kolakowski, Leszek (1978). *Main Currents of Marxism*. 3 vols. Oxford: Oxford University Press (Clarendon Press).

Kripke, Saul (1980). *Naming and Necessity*. Cambridge, Mass: Harvard University Press.

Mansfield, Harvey C., Jr. (1980). "Marx on Aristotle: Freedom, Politics and Money." *Review of Metaphysics* 34: 351–67.

Marx, Karl (1961). *Capital*. 3 vols. Translated by Samuel Moore and Edward Aveling. Moscow: Foreign Languages Publishing House.

(1967). *Writings of the Young Marx on Philosophy and Society*. Edited by Loyd D. Easton and Kurt H. Guddat. New York: Doubleday (Anchor Books).

(1970). *Ökonomisch-Philosophische Manuskripte*. In Herwig Förder, (ed.), *Der Bund der Kommunisten*. Berlin: Dietz.

(1972). *On America and the Civil War*. Edited by Saul K. Padover. New York: McGraw-Hill.

(1973). *Grundrisse*. Translated by Martin Nicolaus. New York: Random House (Vintage Books).

(1977). *Capital*, vol. 1. Translated by Ben Fowkes. New York: Random House (Vintage Books).

Marx, Karl, and Friedrich Engels (1956–68). *Werke.* 39 vols. Berlin: Dietz.
   (1962). *Selected Works.* 2 vols. Moscow: Foreign Languages Publishing House.
   (1964). *The German Ideology.* Edited by S. Ryazanskaya. Moscow: Progress Publishers.
   (1971). *Writings on the Paris Commune.* Edited by Hal Draper. New York: Monthly Review Press.
   (1974). *Selected Works.* New York: International Publishers.
Miller, Richard W. (1981). "Marx and Aristotle: A Kind of Consequentialism." *Canadian Journal of Philosophy* supp. vol. 7: 323–52.
   (in press). "Marx and Morality." In J. Roland Pennock (ed.), *Marxism Today, Nomos* 26. New York: New York University Press.
Ollman, Bertell (1971). *Alienation: Marx's Conception of Man in Capitalist Society.* Cambridge: Cambridge University Press.
Putnam, Hilary (1975). "The 'Meaning' of Meaning." *Minnesota Studies in Philosophy of Science* 7: 131–93.
   (1981). *Reason, Truth and History.* Cambridge: Cambridge University Press.
Rawls, John (1971). *A Theory of Justice.* Cambridge, Mass.: Harvard University Press.
Wood, Allen W. (1972). "The Marxian Critique of Justice." *Philosophy and Public Affairs* 1: 241–82.

CHAPTER 9

Exploitation, class, and property relations

JOHN E. ROEMER

Among the problems confronting contemporary Marxian theoretical work are these: explaining the political and economic developments of modern socialist societies, and providing a clear conception of why workers should be considered to be exploited in modern capitalism. That the second problem is not trivial is evidenced by the lack of communication between Marxist and neoclassical or pluralist social scientists on the question: Whereas Marxists insist that a certain share of the workers' labor is "unpaid," and workers are thereby exploited, non-Marxists respond by observing that everyone gains from the trade of labor power, and so how can exploitation be an appropriate description of that phenomenon? The myriad discussions of Marxian value theory do not, for the most part, get to the root of the matter by stating the problem in a sufficiently fundamental way that the antagonists can disagree in a constructive manner. Concerning the first problem (of modern socialism), no explanation should be needed to demonstrate the incompleteness of the Marxian (or any other) approach to the subject.

In this discussion, I propose a general theory of exploitation that can, it is hoped, clarify our approach to these questions. The theory is *general* in the sense that the Marxian conception of exploitation is

This chapter surveys parts of a book entitled *A General Theory of Exploitation and Class* (Harvard University Press, 1982), reprinted here by permission of the publisher. An article similar to this one appeared in *Politics and Society* 2, 1982. A full list of acknowledgments cannot be reproduced here; among those whose comments have been valuable are G. A. Cohen, Jon Elster, R. E. Howe, S. C. Kolm, Amartya Sen, and E. O. Wright. I also thank the National Science Foundation and the Guggenheim Foundation for fellowship support while engaged in this work.

one special case of it. Other special cases are feudal exploitation, socialist exploitation, status exploitation, and what might be called neoclassical exploitation (the type of inequality neoclassical economists consider exploitative). By embedding both the Marxian and neoclassical conceptions of exploitation in a more general setting, one is able to compare in a precise way the contrasting ethical principles that lie behind the two ideologies. By embedding socialist exploitation in the same general model, one gains some understanding of the types of inequality and perhaps class formation that exist in modern socialism. Hence, the justification for proposing such a general theory.

To see more precisely why I choose to construct a general theory of exploitation to study these problems, one must look back to the problem Marx faced in his study of capitalism. The economic problem for Marx, in examining capitalism, was to explain the persistent accumulation of wealth by one class and the persistent impoverishment of another, in an economic system characterized by voluntary trade. Regarding feudalism, it was perfectly clear where the locus of expropriation (or appropriation) of surplus was, since the ties of bondage of the serf to the lord required the former to perform corvée and demesne labor. To state the point in a slightly more relevant way, it was no surprise that the lords became rich from serf labor, since the institution of labor exchange was a coercive one, characterized by bondage. Obviously, the same is true of societies where the institution of labor exchange was slavery. The institutional innovation of capitalism, however, was to render labor exchange noncoercive: Wage workers voluntarily trade labor power on the labor market. Perhaps the bargaining power of the two sides is not in balance, but that does not obviate the fact that the institution itself is noncoercive. The riddle for Marx was: How can one explain the systematic expropriation of the surplus product (beyond subsistence requirements of workers) by one class, by one side of the market, when the institution for labor exchange is not coercive? To answer this query, Marx constructed his theories of value and exploitation. The purpose of the value theory was to make the point that exchanges under capitalism are not coercive but competitive, an idea that takes the form of insisting that all commodities exchange "at their values." (Coercive exchange would, on the contrary, involve one side being forced to exchange its service for less than its value.) Despite these competitive exchanges in the labor market (and elsewhere), Marx maintains that a systematic expropriation of surplus value emerges, which provides the theory of exploitation. The details of the classical theory need not be rehearsed here.

The institutional culprit in the emergence of Marxian exploitation was the private ownership of means of production, or more accurately, the concentration of such ownership in the hands of a small class. The prediction was that if the means of production were socialized and put in the control of the working class, then capitalist exploitation would cease. This recipe was not unique to Marxism but was shared by many socialists of the period. The contribution of Marx and Engels was to claim that such a development was possible, perhaps inevitable, and to display the mechanism by which the transformation would occur, a series of claims that were corollary to their theory of historical materialism.

Let us now draw the parallel we face in studying modern socialism. We understand the locus of surplus expropriation under capitalism, as Marx did of feudalism. In the transition to socialist society, the institutional culprit responsible for capitalist exploitation has been eliminated, namely, the private ownership of the means of production. Nevertheless, we observe certain systematic types of inequality, and certain political behavior, which are less than ideal — one might wish to think of them as an indication of exploitation (which, of course, is an undefined term in this context). The institutional dimension we are now required to vary is the one labeled "ownership locus of the means of production," not the one with which Marx was concerned, labeled "coerciveness of the institution of labor exchange." The formal problem, however, has the same abstract structure for us as for Marx. He required a theory of exploitation that was robust even when one relaxed the institutional specification of an economy concerning the coerciveness of its institution of labor exchange; we require a theory of exploitation that is robust even when one relaxes the institutional specification concerning the private locus of ownership of the means of production.

To put the matter still more generally, we would like to ask: Which institutions and characteristics of an economy are essential for some conception of exploitation to make sense, and which are incidental? Can we conceive of a theory of exploitation sufficiently general that it permits of definition even under conditions of considerable institutional variation? Such a theory should include as one special case the Marxian concept of exploitation, when the institutions are capitalist. Another special case would be the neoclassical concept of exploitation, the situation prevailing, roughly speaking, when labor is not paid its marginal product. As another special case, the theory would suggest a notion of socialist exploitation, when the institutions of the economy are socialist.

Although this introduction began by citing reasons for formulating a general theory of exploitation, I arrived at such a theory only after experimenting with many models whose purpose was to study the Marxian concept of exploitation. Since Marxian exploitation is the kind of exploitation we best understand, a natural approach to conceiving of a general theory is to perturb the institutional environment in which Marxian exploitation resides and to ask if a phenomenon of exploitation continues to exist. How robust is the exploitation phenomenon with respect to changes in its usual institutional habitat? I therefore report my work on the subject in the following way. Models are constructed showing that Marxian exploitation can exist even when the institutional structure is radically different from capitalism. The first set of models are ones of pre-capitalist, subsistence exchange economies. Indeed, in the first model (Section I), an instance of Marxian exploitation is shown to exist even when there is no institution of labor exchange, or any accumulation.

The models that discuss the variants of Marxian exploitation are presented in Sections I, II, and III. By performing these institutional experiments with Marxian exploitation, several important results emerge: An endogenous theory of class formation is developed, and the relationship between exploitation and class is demonstrated.

Many corollaries of the approach for classical issues in the Marxian theory of value and exploitation cannot be developed here. Instead the general theory of exploitation is outlined in Section V. It is not surprising, however, that in seeking to generalize a particular theory, one learns more about that theory. To use a mathematical simile, by embedding a theory in its natural general setting, one learns something about it from studying its local properties in its general environment. That is why perturbing the institutional habitat of Marxian exploitation teaches us something about the classical Marxian theory of value. Section VI summarizes some of the advantages of the new definition of exploitation proposed here.

I shall not deal with the application of the theory to the understanding of socialist society in any detail. This is partly for reasons of space and partly because this question is discussed more thoroughly elsewhere (Roemer 1982b, c). I will concentrate on what the theory has to say concerning *Marxian* exploitation, and the comparisons of that concept to the prevailing neoclassical notion of exploitation.[1]

I. EXPLOITATION WITHOUT A LABOR MARKET

What economic institutions appear to be necessary to generate the phenomenon of the appropriation of one producer's labor by another? Marx's task was to construct a theory of exploitation that was operative even when a coercive institution of labor exchange was absent. Eventually, the task will be to propose a theory of exploitation that is operative even when private ownership of the means of production is absent. Our first step, however, is not to abstract from private property, but to investigate models of pre-capitalist, subsistence, private ownership, exchange economies. In the first of these models there is: (1) no accumulation, and (2) no labor market or institution for labor exchange. Yet, surprisingly perhaps, there does emerge something like a Marxian form of exploitation. This suggests that there is a theory of exploitation considerably more general, in terms of the institutional variation permitted, than the Marxian theory of capitalist exploitation.

The pre-capitalist economy without a labor market is defined as follows. There are N producers, each holding an initial endowment of produced goods and his own labor power. Producers all have one unit of labor power to dispose of, but they possess, in general, different vectors of produced goods. Each producer will engage in production with the sole purpose of producing goods with sufficient exchange value, net of replacing what he used up in production, to be tradable for the producer's subsistence needs, at going prices. Subject to producing goods that can be traded for his subsistence, a producer *minimizes the labor he expends* on production.

All producers have the same subsistence needs and face the same technology. Where, then, do they differ? Only in their initial endowments of produced goods, and those enter into the problem in this way. Production takes time, and a producer must lay out the costs of production today, although not receiving revenues until sales are realized next period. The current costs of production must be fi-

[1] The models used employ two techniques of modern mathematical economics: general equilibrium theory and cooperative game theory. I have, however, presented the material in a nontechnical fashion. A more thorough and rigorous treatment of this material is in my book, *A General Theory of Exploitation and Class*, and in Roemer (1982a).

nanced out of current holdings: That is, given prices, a producer's endowment becomes finance capital, valued by the given prices, and this finance capital limits the production activities he can choose to engage in. A wealthy producer will therefore have more production options than a poor one, and hence, will be able to produce goods embodying the market value of his subsistence package by working less time than the poorer producer. (He can, essentially, choose capital-intensive activities to operate.)

The equilibrium in this model is a vector of commodity prices p that allows all markets to clear while every producer optimizes. There are two sets of markets: At the beginning of the period, producers come to the market for production inputs and trade their particular endowments of producer goods for the inputs they require to operate their chosen production plan; then, at the end of the period, they return to the market to trade their output for their subsistence needs. An equilibrium price vector must clear both markets, while allowing all stocks used up in production to be replaced as well. Since all stocks are replaced at equilibrium and each producer subsists, I call the equilibrium a *reproducible solution*.

It is important to reiterate that no producer works for any other producer in this economy. Producers each operate their own shops (fields, plots, etc.); that they choose to operate different processes, and hence work different amounts of time, is a consequence of their different financial constraints, which determine the scope of production possibilities open to each.

It is not surprising that one can prove that at a reproducible solution in the pre-capitalist subsistence economy, average time worked is precisely *socially necessary labor time* (SNLT) in the Marxian sense. This is because there is no accumulation. Socially necessary labor time is defined as the amount of labor time embodied in the subsistence bundle each producer consumes. It consists of the direct and indirect labor required to produce these goods. Thus, if t is SNLT for an individual, then society works Nt in total time at a reproducible solution.

The following dichotomous description of reproducible solutions results: Either such a solution is *egalitarian,* when each producer works exactly SNLT at the equilibrium, or the solution is *inegalitarian,* when some work less than SNLT and others must therefore work longer than SNLT.

Consider an inegalitarian solution in an economy with two producers. At the solution, Mr. i works more than SNLT, and Ms. j.

works less than SNLT. Then j is exploiting i, in the sense that she is able to work less than socially necessary labor time because i is working more; somehow, i is working "for" j, and i's surplus labor time is transferred to j through the market. Suppose j killed i and took i's endowment, and then tried to reproduce herself in the economy where only she existed: She would then have to work SNLT to reproduce herself. Thus, j is able to work less than socially necessary labor time (when i is present) because i is there: She is somehow expropriating labor from i. Yet, this exploitation can exist even though there is *no accumulation,* or *any* institution for labor exchange, or any surplus product being produced. The institutions of the model that drive exploitation are competitive markets and differential private ownership of the means of production, which is to say, differential financial capital. Not only could Marx produce a theory of exploitation when the institution of labor exchange was noncoercive, but we can produce such a theory, of exploitation as the expropriation of labor, *even vhen there is no institution for labor exchange.* Exploitation can be mediited entirely through the market for produced commodities.

This forces us to reconsider the claims of classical Marxism that the labor market and the extraction of surplus labor at the point of production are the *central* loci of exploitation. Indeed, competitive markets and private property in the means of production are implicated as the chief culprits. The advent of a labor market does enrich our understanding of exploitation, however, as it brings about a decomposition of society into *classes,* which do not exist in the model described thus far.

II. THE LABOR MARKET AND THE EMERGENCE OF CLASS

The foregoing model does not, of course, describe actual pre-capitalist history; it is a thought experiment performed to inquire into the logical prerequisites for a general theory of exploitation. I continue these experiments by introducing next a labor market. On Labor Market Island, producers are still operating a subsistence economy, availing themselves of a common technology and working only long enough to provide the funds to purchase their common subsistence requirement, after replacing materials used up. They have, however, one more option than the inhabitants of the economy in Section I: They can hire or sell labor power. Another market has opened, which increases the opportunities of the producers. Now a producer must decide what vector of activities to operate himself

Exploitation, class, and property relations

using his capital, what vector of activities to hire others to operate on his capital, and what amount of labor power to sell on the labor market.

Let:

$\mathbf{x}^v$ be the n-vector of activities that the owner v of the means of production operates himself (there are n processes in the Leontief technology)
$\mathbf{y}^v$ be the n-vector of activities v hires others to operate
$\mathbf{z}^v$ be the amount of labor time v sells.

The producer's optimization problem is now this: to choose a production plan that will minimize the total labor he expends (in his own shop and on the labor market), subject to the financial constraint, as before, that the production inputs he requires – to operate activities himself and to equip those whom he hires to operate his shop – can be financed out of his current financial holdings. The structure of the problem is the same as in the first economy (without labor market) except now there is a labor market.

The definition of a *reproducible solution,* an equilibrium, for this model is analogous to the previous one. A price-and-wage vector equilibrates the system if, when all producers optimize, aggregate production is feasible, global reproducibility is achieved, and the labor market clears. That is, the markets for inputs and consumption goods all clear.

At a reproducible solution, society works, as before, precisely aggregate SNLT. Thus, at an inegalitarian solution, society is divided into two groups of agents: the exploited, who work longer than SNLT, and the exploiters who work less then SNLT. (There may also be some agents who are neither exploiters nor exploited, but work precisely SNLT.)

But there is a second decomposition of producers in this economy of great interest, a decomposition into *classes.* Note that in the model of Section I, all producers are of the same class; that is, they all relate to the means of production in the same way. In this model, however, producers can relate to the means of production in different ways: they can work their own shop, hire labor, sell labor, or do some combination of these. Indeed, how he relates to the buying and selling of labor power defines an agent's class position. Schematically, this is represented as follows. To optimize, a producer chooses a long vector of the form $<\mathbf{x}^v, \mathbf{y}^v, \mathbf{z}^v>$ (where $\mathbf{x}^v, \mathbf{y}^v, \mathbf{z}^v$ are as defined previously.) We may represent a producer's optimal solution as a sequence of plus and zero symbols, such as $<0,+,0>$. If a producer has an optimal solution of the form $<0,+,0>$, that means

Table 1. *Class structure on Labor Market Island*

		$<\mathbf{x}^v$	$\mathbf{y}^v$	$\mathbf{z}^v>$	
Landlord	1.	<0	$+$	$0>$	Pure capitalist
Kulak	2.	$<+$	$+$	$0>$	Small capitalist
Middle peasant	3.	$<+$	0	$0>$	Petty bourgeois
Poor peasant	4.	$<+$	0	$+>$	Mixed proletarian
Landless laborer	5.	<0	0	$+>$	Proletarian

he optimizes by setting $\mathbf{x}^v = 0$ and $\mathbf{z}^v = 0$, but $\mathbf{y}^v > 0$: That is, he optimizes by only hiring labor power, but not working for himself or selling labor power on the market. The particular sequence of pluses and zeroes defines the producer's *class position*. Thus, we might call a producer possessing an optimal solution of the form $<0,+,0>$ a pure capitalist, as he optimizes by only hiring others.

There are, altogether, eight possible class positions as there are eight ways of arranging pluses and zeroes in the three places $<\,,\,>$. It can be proved, however, that every producer, at an equilibrium, is a member of precisely one of five classes, which I name as follows, (Table 1). The reader should check back against the definitions of $\mathbf{x}^v$, $\mathbf{y}^v$, and $\mathbf{z}^v$ to see the reasons for the names. The agricultural labeling is provided as well, as it coincides with the analysis Mao Tse-tung gave in his 1925 pamphlet, *Analysis of Classes in the Chinese Countryside*.

Recall that each producer has placed himself in one of these classes, by optimizing facing a wealth constraint. *Class position is endogenous to the model;* we are not told before the action begins who is a capitalist and who is a proletarian. That emerges as a consequence of the individual's behavior facing competitive markets.

The first theorem relates a producer's class position to his wealth. It asserts that if we list all agents from richest to poorest, then they will fall into classes in precisely the order indicated in Table 1. The richest bunch are pure capitalists, then will come a bunch of small capitalists, then the petty bourgeoisie, then the mixed proletarians, with the proletariat occupying the bottom of the wealth hierarchy. In fact, the proletarians are precisely those with no produced assets (zero wealth), those having nothing to trade but their labor power (and nothing to lose but their chains). Thus, the classical ordering of classes by wealth is a *theorem* of this analysis, not a postulate or a definition.

Exploitation, class, and property relations

The second theorem, which I call the Class Exploitation Correspondence Principle (CECP), relates the two decompositions of society: the decomposition of society into exploiters and exploited, and the decomposition into classes. The CECP states that *every agent who is in a labor-hiring class* (classes 1 and 2) *is an exploiter, and every agent who is in a labor-selling class* (classes 4 and 5) *is exploited.* (The exploitation status of members of the petty bourgeoisie is ambiguous. This turns out to be equivalent to the transformation problem, but that topic is beyond the scope of this survey.) Thus, we *prove* another classical Marxian idea, namely that the selling of labor power is associated with being exploited, and the hiring of labor power with being an exploiter.

The CECP may strike some as obvious or trivial, but I must insist this is not the case. We are used to *defining* exploiters as those who hire labor power and the exploited as those who sell it. But in this analysis, both exploitation status and class status emerge endogenously from agents' optimizing behavior, given their differential wealths. An individual is exploited, recall, if at the equilibrium he works more time than is socially necessary, SNLT, and he is an exploiter if he works less than SNLT. On the other hand, an individual's class position is defined by the relation to the labor market he has chosen in his labor-minimizing optimization. It is not trivial to demonstrate a relationship between two endogenously determined classifications. In this sense, the present analysis provides foundations for the Marxian theory of exploitation and class, as it produces our intuitive conclusions about those concepts from prior institutional and behavioral specifications of the agents.

It is important to note that producers choose their own class position. Their problem is to optimize, in this case a labor-minimizing program of production choices, subject to a capital constraint. All that is specified a priori is the optimizing behavior of agents and their differential initial endowments of capital stock. Given this, some producers must hire labor power to optimize (the two top classes) and some must sell labor power to optimize (the two bottom classes). Compulsory labor hirers necessarily emerge as exploiters and compulsory labor sellers as exploited. This result is driven entirely by the differential distribution of endowments and therefore wealths. (In particular, if all producers had the same wealth at a reproducible solution, then there would be no exploitation, and they would all be members of the petty bourgeoisie. In such a case, we might better think of the class [+,o,o] as self-employed artisans.) Optimization on competitive markets and differential ownership of the means of production result in producers sorting themselves into classes, with the classical association between exploitation and class.

In the economy with labor market of Section I, I showed that exploitation emerges logically prior to accumulation and any institution for labor exchange. When a labor market is introduced, we generate not only exploitation but also a class structure that relates to exploitation and wealth in the way it should, still without any accumulation. Although an institution for labor exchange was not necessary to produce exploitation, it does appear necessary to generate classes. In this sense, perhaps, the labor market *is* central to Marxian analysis. I next extend the heresy of Section I by showing that even the Marxian class structure can be produced *without any institution for labor exchange*.

III. THE FUNCTIONAL EQUIVALENCE OF LABOR AND CREDIT MARKETS

Imagine that instead of opening a labor market as a way of broadening choices in the original subsistence economy of Section I, a credit market is opened. On Credit Market Island, we have the subsistence economy, with markets in all produced goods, plus one more market, whose price is an interest rate, and on which agents can borrow or lend finance capital. On Credit Market Island, there is, however, no labor market. Thus, a poor producer, to whom few production options are open because of his limited finance capital, can borrow more capital at the going interest rate, allowing him to expand his production possibilities. As before, the goal of our typical agent is to minimize the labor he performs, subject to the constraint that he produce net exchange value sufficient to purchase his subsistence needs, and that he finance production out of his capital plus loans. The poor agent who borrows capital will have to pay back interest too, of course.

An equilibrium price vector now consists of commodity prices and an interest rate that clear all markets: the market for production inputs, the market for trades in final output against subsistence needs, and the credit market. As before, it can be proved that at an equilibrium, a reproducible solution, total labor time expended is just aggregate SNLT. Thus, either a solution is egalitarian (when each works just socially necessary labor time) or it is inegalitarian, and society is decomposed into exploiters working less than SNLT and exploited working more than SNLT.

There is also a class structure in this model. On Credit Market Island, there are three ways a producer can relate to the means of production: He can work borrowed capital, work his own capital, or lend his capital to others, or he can do some combination of these three things. Let, at given prices:

$\mathbf{x}^v$ be the vector of production activities the producer v operates using his own capital

$\mathbf{y}^v$ be the amount of capital (a number) the producer v chooses to lend to others

$\mathbf{z}^v$ be the vector of activities the producer v operates on borrowed capital.

An optimal solution for the producer v is some long vector $<\mathbf{x}^v, \mathbf{y}^v, \mathbf{z}^v>$. We can schematically denote a solution as a sequence of pluses and zeroes: For example, a producer v may optimize by choosing a solution of the form $<$o,+,o$>$, which means he is a pure lender, since $\mathbf{x}^v = \mathbf{z}^v =$ o and $\mathbf{y}^v >$ o.

It is proved that each producer, at a reproducible solution, belongs to precisely one of the following five classes (Table 2). Compare Table 2 with Table 1 and observe that the class structure appears formally identical. As on Labor Market Island, one proves that the ordering of the five classes on Credit Market Island, as presented in Table 2, is faithful to the wealth ordering. Moreover, the Class Exploitation Correspondence Principle holds on Credit Market Island, in this form: *Any member of a lending class* (class 1 or 2) *is necessarily an exploiter, and any member of a borrowing class* (class 4 or 5) *is exploited.*

But a stronger statement can be made. The economies on the two islands are isomorphic, in this sense: Suppose the inhabitants of Credit Market Island and Labor Market Island are identical, and the technologies and subsistence needs are identical on the two islands.

Table 2. *Class structure on Credit Market Island*

	$\mathbf{x}^v$	$\mathbf{y}^v$	$\mathbf{z}^v$	
1.	$<$0	$+$	0$>$	Pure lender
2.	$<+$	$+$	0$>$	Mixed lender
3.	$<+$	0	0$>$	Neither borrower nor lender
4.	$<+$	0	$+>$	Mixed borrower
5.	$<$0	0	$+>$	Pure borrower

One island is a copy of the other, which is to say each agent on one island has a twin on the other with the same endowment. The only difference between the islands is that on one the labor market operates and on the other the credit market operates, in addition to the markets for produced goods. Let there be a reproducible solution on Labor Market Island, entailing a price–wage vector $(\mathbf{p}, \mathbf{w})$. Then there is a companion reproducible solution $(\mathbf{p}, \mathbf{r})$ on Credit Market Island such that every agent on one island works precisely as long as his twin on the other island, and is, therefore, exploited or exploiting to the same degree, and also each pair of twins occupies identical class positions on the two islands, according to the class definitions of Tables 1 and 2. The two solutions are *isomorphic* as concerns class and exploitation properties, or, the credit market and labor market are functionally equivalent as regards class and exploitation. In particular, we can produce the highly articulated class structure, usually associated with a labor market, *with no institution for labor exchange*, using just a credit market. The heresy is complete: Not only does exploitation emerge logically prior to accumulation and institutions for labor exchange, but so does the articulation of exploitation into class.

It is worth modifying a venerable neoclassical adage at this point. On Labor Market Island, capital hires labor. On Credit Market Island, labor hires capital. The adage in question states, "It doesn't matter whether labor hires capital or capital hires labor in a competitive model." Truly, this is so; the wealthy exploit and the poor are exploited in either case: That is our modification. The neoclassical adage is often interpreted as implying there is nothing nasty about capital hiring labor, since labor could just as well hire capital. Our conclusion, on the contrary, is that labor can be just as exploited if it hires capital as if it is hired by capital. The key question is the wealth position of the laborer and not which market is used.

These results force some reevaluation, I think, of the classical belief that the labor process is or must be at the center of the Marxian analysis of exploitation and class. I have demonstrated that the entire constellation of Marxian "welfare" concepts can be generated with no institution for the exchange of labor. Furthermore, this has been done at the level of abstraction at which Marxian value theory is customarily performed. This casts serious doubt on the project of elevating the labor process to center stage in the Marxian theory of exploitation, a tendency that has become more prominent since the pioneering work of Braverman (1974). Just as Marx wanted to explain as much as possible about exploitation and class with the assumption of competitive markets, so I have tried to explain as much as possible without invoking the necessary existence of labor exchange.

To put the matter more sharply, this analysis challenges those who believe that the process of labor exchange is *the* critical moment in the genesis of capitalist exploitation. What has been shown is that such a position cannot be maintained at the usual level of abstraction at which Marxian value theory is applied. Such a position, in particular, would have to invoke critical differences between labor and credit markets. Certainly there are such differences: Labor markets require supervision on the factory floor, and credit markets require collateral, and these two enforcement costs may differ. Economies of scale certainly enter differently in the two markets, for one capitalist can hire many workers, and expand production indefinitely, but one worker cannot expand production indefinitely by borrowing a lot of capital.[2]

Informational constraints certainly enter differently, also, in a less abstract picture of Credit Market Island and Labor Market Island. In short, there may well be reasons to focus on the labor market as a key moment in the genesis of capitalist exploitation and class, but they do not exist at the level of abstraction of classical Marxian value theory. A resurrection of a Marxian theory of class with an important position for the labor market will depend on the types of imperfections I have mentioned – transactions costs, economies of scale, information, risk. As contemporary neoclassical economics is learning that it cannot produce a consistent theory of capitalism without serious study of these modifications of classical models, it is interesting that Marxian economics should be led to a similar conclusion.

IV. SUMMARY: EXPLOITATION VERSUS ALIENATION

The models thus far show that if producers have differential ownership of the means of production, then a regime of competitive markets is sufficient to produce the exploitation and class characterization of capitalism predicted by classical Marxism. It is more enlightening, perhaps, to emphasize what is not necessary to produce this result: that there be an institution for the exchange of labor. Exploitation can

[2] However, many workers could get together and take out a loan to run a factory, thus availing themselves of economies of scale by using the credit market. Why are there not more worker-owned firms under capitalism?

be mediated entirely through the exchange of produced commodities, and classes can exist with respect to a credit market instead of a labor market, at least at this classical level of abstraction.

This is not to say that coercion is not necessary to produce Marxian exploitation and class: Rather, it suffices that coercion occur at the point of maintaining property relations, and not at the locus of extracting surplus labor directly from the worker. Surely the latter struggle in the workplace exists also in capitalism. But the argument here implies that such coercion is (as Marx himself understood) of secondary importance in understanding exploitation and class. It is a mistake to elevate the struggle in the process of production between worker and capitalist to a more privileged position in the theory than the differential ownership of productive assets. I must emphasize that I do not mean that the study of the process of labor exchange and extraction does not have an important place in the theory. Clearly, at a more concrete specification of the economy than the models here allow, other factors enter (such as enforcement of property relations and costs of supervision) that make the labor market an important locus. The struggle between worker and boss on the factory floor over the extraction of labor from labor power is a dispute over the terms of the labor contract. If we wish to explain capitalist exploitation under an assumption of frictionless markets with costlessly enforceable contracts, as Marx did, then this struggle must be secondary. At the pertinent level of abstraction not only should contracts between capitalists be assumed to be costlessly enforceable, but so should contracts between capitalists and workers in the labor market.

A misplaced emphasis on the labor process can lead to faulty, or at least to a nonmaterialist, analysis. If, for instance, one observes that the labor process appears much the same in existing socialism as it does in capitalism, then one might conclude that existing socialist countries are not essentially different from capitalist countries, insofar as the exploitation of workers is concerned. This is, indeed, the inference of many Marxists who emphasize the labor process and industrial democracy as the defining characteristic of the mode of production, rather than property relations. There is, I think, a distinction between *alienation* and *exploitation*. Workers may always feel alienated, to some extent, in a labor process that employs the detailed division of labor, one-person management, and so on, but whether exploitation exists (or whether, more precisely, it is capitalist exploitation) is another matter. There is not a one-to-one correspondence between regimes of property relations and organizational forms of work, and when two different regimes give rise to similar organizational work forms, it is the former that defines the nature of exploitation and surplus extraction, not the latter, which defines the nature of alienation (in at least one of Marx's several senses). The labor process approach, on the other hand, takes the organization of work as the touchstone for passing judgment on a form of economic organization. Thereby alienation in work is elevated to a higher analytical plane than the relations of exploitation.

Capitalist exploitation is the appropriation of the labor of one class by another class because of their differential ownership or access to the (nonhuman) means of production. This can be accomplished, in principle, with or without a direct relationship between the exploiters and exploited in the process of work. One might even argue that there is exploitation without alienation in the economy of Section I, since each producer works for himself in his own shop. Conversely, capitalist exploitation can be eliminated, with or without eliminating relations of authority (and thereby alienation?) in the process of work. Given this muddy relationship between the organization of work (and thus alienation) and property relations (and thus exploitation), must one give priority to one of these two criteria as the more relevant one for understanding the laws of motion of society?[3] Historical materialism directs us to emphasize property relations (exploitation) as being of key importance. Historical materialism may be incorrect in so doing, but at least the implications of taking the other approach should be understood.

V. A GENERAL THEORY OF EXPLOITATION

In this section I characterize Marxian exploitation in another way that makes clear what the *ethical imperative* of the theory is. That is, why do we choose, pejoratively, to call workers *exploited?* Why should the inability to command labor value in goods in an amount equal to the labor a producer expends be considered an exploitative transfer? The bourgeois thinker argues that proletarians are gaining from trade, and their trade of labor power is voluntary, and so the trans-

---

[3] For a fuller discussion of Marx's conception of scientific "laws," see the chapters by Farr and Ball in the present volume (chaps. 10 and 11, respectively).

fer of "surplus" labor time should not be considered exploitative. The quid pro quo is: surplus labor in exchange for access to the means of production. This is a serious objection, and it is useful to clarify what one means by exploitation in general terms to understand the difference between Marxist and neoclassical views of exploitation. I shall outline a general theory of exploitation, which has various special cases of interest: feudal exploitation, neoclassical exploitation, Marxian exploitation, socialist exploitation, and status exploitation.

In virtually every society or economic mechanism, there is inequality. Yet not all inequality is viewed by a society as exploitative, or unjust. Certainly, however, the notion of exploitation involves inequality in some way. What forms of inequality does a particular society view as exploitative, and what forms does it not? The inequality of master and slave was viewed as nonexploitative in ancient society, as was the inequality of lord and serf in feudal society, although most inhabitants of the twentieth century consider both of these relationships exploitative. Similarly, Marxists view the inequality in the capitalist–worker relationship as exploitative, although this inequality is conceived of as nonexploitative by many people in capitalist society today. What device can be proposed that distinguishes accurately exploitative from nonexploitative inequality, according to the norms of a particular society?

To capture what is meant when it is said that a particular person or group is exploited, I propose this: A group is conceived of as exploited if it has some *conditionally feasible alternative* under which its members would be better off. Precisely what the alternative is, is left unspecified for the moment. The general claim is that this device can be applied whenever people use the word "exploitation" to refer to the human condition. If two people disagree on whether a particular group is exploited in some situation, then our device leads us to ask: Are they specifying the alternative for the group differently? I wish to propose different *specifications of the alternative* that will generate different definitions of exploitation.

Formally, this amounts to specifying a *game* played by coalitions of agents in the economy. To define the game, I specify what any particular coalition can achieve on its own, if it withdraws from the economy. The alternative to participating in the economy is for a coalition to withdraw and achieve what it can on its own, under the specified definition of the game. If a coalition can do better for its members under the alternative of "withdrawing,"

Exploitation, class, and property relations

then it is *exploited* under that particular specification of the rules for withdrawal.[4]

To make this less abstract, consider the usual notion of the core of a private-ownership exchange economy. The private-ownership core is the set of allocations (say, of goods or income) that no coalition can improve on by withdrawing under these rules: that it can take with it the original, private endowments of its members. Under these particular withdrawal rules, a certain class of distributions of goods is available to any coalition, and I say a coalition is exploited if it is receiving goods that can be dominated by some distribution achievable by the coalition on its own, given those withdrawal rules. More generally, if we adopt a different rule of withdrawal, which is to say a different way of specifying the achievable rewards of the various coalitions on their own, we will have a different game and a different core. (The *core* of a game is the set of allocations no coalition can improve on, by refusing to participate in society as a whole and organizing its own affairs internally, taking with it the dowry assigned under the specification of the game.) Our definition is simply this: Exploitation occurs, at a given allocation, if that allocation is not in the core of the game defined by the particular withdrawal specification under consideration. That is, a coalition is exploited if it can *block* an allocation, under the rules of the game.

[4] More precisely, a coalition S is said to be exploited at an allocation if two conditions hold:

1. S does better than at the current allocation by taking its payoff specified by the characteristic function of the game;
2. The complement of S (called S') does worse than at the current allocation by taking its payoff under the game.

If the game is superadditive and the allocation under investigation is Pareto optimal, then condition (2) can be shown to follow from (1); hence, in the text I have mentioned only condition (1). What condition (2) assures us is that if a coalition is exploited, then it is exploited by some other coalition; that is, S' is *gaining* (in the present allocation) at the expense of S. Without (2), this statement could not be made, and we would not have the exploitation of people by other people, but (for example) by nature.

There are some situations where conditions (1) and (2) hold for a coalition S, but we do not wish to view S as exploited or S' as exploiting. For instance, let S' be a set of invalids, supported by S, or the aged, or children. According to the definition, one would consider the coalition of socially supported invalids to be exploiting the rest of society, under most rules of withdrawal. I will not pursue this problem here, but simply note that the game-theoretical definition should be thought of as applicable in situations of arms-length economic transactions.

This device captures the idea that we conceive of exploitation as the possibility of a better alternative. Our proposal for what constitutes feudal exploitation and capitalist exploitation (and socialist exploitation) amounts to naming different specifications of withdrawal rules. One can then compare different concepts of exploitation by comparing the different rule specifications that define their respective games. We exhibit a particular concept of exploitation in explicit form, as it were, as the rules of a game.

A. Feudal exploitation

I shall not be precise concerning the underlying model of feudal economy. Think of agents with various endowments, who are engaged in production and consumption under feudal relations. We say a coalition is *feudally exploited* if it can improve its lot by withdrawing under these rules: The coalition can take with it its own endowments. Thus, feudally nonexploitative allocations are, in fact, precisely the private-ownership core of the exchange game, as conventionally defined, and discussed earlier here. The claim is that this withdrawal specification is the correct one for capturing feudal exploitation, as it gives the result that serfs are exploited and lords are exploiters, which is the notion we wish to capture. Moreover, non-serf proletarians, for instance, will not be a feudally exploited coalition, under these rules, and so the definition captures *only* feudal exploitation.

To see the first claim, I will assume that feudal serfs owned their own land. Feudal law required them to work the corvée and demesne, not in order to have access to the family plot, but in spite of this access. Thus, were a group of serfs to be allowed to withdraw from feudal society with their endowments, in which we shall include the family plots, they would have been better off, having the same consumption, but providing no labor for the lord. Withdrawal, under these rules, amounts to withdrawal from feudal bondage. In fact, it has been argued that many serfs would have been better off if they could have withdrawn from bondage, even *without* their land; surveillance of serfs was necessary to prevent them from running away to the towns, to which they could presumably carry only their non-land endowments. Indeed, an efficient improvement in capitalism as an economic mechanism contrasted with feudalism was the absence of such surveillance costs: Proletarians could not survive simply on their own endowments, and so were forced to participate in a voluntary labor market.

Exploitation, class, and property relations

There is, however, a possible counterargument, which could have been put forth by a feudal ideologue: Serfs would not be better off, he might say, by withdrawing with their own endowments, because they receive various benefits from the lord that they cannot produce on their own, the most obvious being military protection. Also, one might believe the lord possessed certain skills or abilities of organization of manor life, for example, military protection, without which the serfs would be worse off. (Indeed, the story has a familiar ring.) I will not attempt here to rebut this argument.[5] Let me simply observe that, concerning military protection, even were it necessary, the serfs' corvée labor produced a good deal more than that; witness the castles and extravaganzas of the lords. (One aspect of extravaganza was military adventure.) I think it can be maintained that large groups of serfs possessed the requisite skills to organize military protection and to take advantage of other externalities and economies of scale accompanying manor life.

The second claim, that non-serf proletarians are not feudally exploited, should become clear next.

B. Capitalist exploitation

To test whether a coalition of agents is capitalistically exploited, I specify a different set of withdrawal rules to define a different game. When a coalition "withdraws," it is allowed to take with it its *per capita* share of society's alienable productive assets, *not its own private assets*, as in the previous game. That is, a coalition can block a particular allocation if that allocation can be improved upon by the coalition, when the initial endowment of alienable assets is an equal-division, egalitarian endowment. Although the test for feudal exploitation amounts to eliminating feudal bonds in constructing the alternative against which a current allocation is judged, the test for capitalist exploitation amounts to equalizing every agent's access to society's alienable property (means of production) in constructing the hypothetical alternative. Under feudalism, we ask how well agents do if relations of feudal bondage are abolished; under capitalism, we ask how they fare if relations of alienable property are abolished. Given this phrasing of the alternative, it is not surprising that capitalist exploitation, as here defined, is equivalent to the usual Marxian definition of exploitation in terms of socially necessary labor time and surplus value.

[5] See North and Thomas (1973), who maintain that serfs were not feudally exploited, in my sense, and Brenner (1976) for a rebuttal.

That, indeed, is the main theorem. Any producer or group of producers who is Marxian exploited, according to the usual definition of surplus-value transfer, is capitalistically exploited, in the sense that the producer or group in question could improve its income by withdrawing with its per capita share of society's alienable productive assets; conversely, any group or individual who is capitalistically exploited is Marxian exploited. The game-theoretic characterization of capitalist exploitation, in terms of an alternative egalitarian distribution of private property in the means of production, captures precisely what Marxists mean by exploitation in terms of surplus-value transfer.[6]

I would argue that the characterization of Marxian exploitation in terms of property rights is superior to the classical definition in terms of surplus value because it makes clear the ethical imperative when one speaks of exploitation: Namely, one conceives of an alternative where the proletariat (or exploited coalition) has access to its per capita share of society's alienable productive assets. We shall see shortly, in contrast, what the ethical imperative for neoclassical economists is when they speak of exploitation.

Just as the feudal ideologue argued that, in fact, serfs would not have been better off had they withdrawn with their own endowments, so a bourgeois ideologue might argue that those who are Marxian exploited (i.e., whose surplus value is appropriated by others) would not, in fact, be better off were they to withdraw with their *per capita* share of society's produced goods. That is, he argues, the proletariat is not capitalistically exploited. The surplus value that workers contribute to the capitalists is, in fact, a return to a scarce skill possessed by them necessary for organizing production (for instance). In the models of Marxian exploitation discussed here, this is not an issue, as capitalists are pictured as simply owning resources, and not as the vessels of entrepreneurial talent. Nevertheless, the bourgeois argument is in principle a correct one: If, in fact, equalization of produced assets would not be sufficient to make Marxian-exploited workers better off on their own, then they are not capitalistically exploited. This is a nontrivial bone of contention between Marxist and bourgeois thinkers. I will call this the

---

[6] In the usual models, the game-theoretic and surplus-value characterizations of Marxian exploitation are equivalent. However, there are some important cases where the two definitions render different judgments on whether some groups are exploited. In these cases, I defend the property relations approach as superior. See Roemer (1982d).

subtle disagreement on the existence of capitalist exploitation under capitalism.

There is, however, a much less subtle disagreement also. A common neoclassical position, I believe, is that exploitation cannot be said to exist at a competitive equilibrium, because everyone has gained from trade as much as possible. How can one say A is exploiting B if B has voluntarily entered into trade with A? The aforementioned models of Marxian exploitation show that *gains from trade and Marxian exploitation are not mutually exclusive.* Proletarians gain from trading their labor power, since otherwise they starve, but their surplus labor is nevertheless expropriated. What is at issue here is precisely the difference between feudal and capitalist exploitation. The statement that no coalition can gain further from trade amounts to saying the allocation is in the (feudal) core of the economy: No group of agents, withdrawing with its private endowments, can trade to a superior allocation for its members. Hence, this variant of the neoclassical position says, "There is no feudal exploitation under capitalism," which is true by the well-known fact that competitive equilibria lie in the core of the private ownership game.[7]

It is not always obvious whether objections to the Marxian notion of exploitation are of the subtle form (in which case there is a substantial disagreement about the contribution of agents' *inalienable* assets to production), or of the nonsubtle form (in which case there are two different varieties of exploitation under discussion). In the nonsubtle case, the antagonists can agree to disagree: They are simply adopting different specifications of the hypothetical alternative that they respectively view as normatively cogent for testing "exploitation." I would argue that the nonsubtle disagreement is quite prevalent. In particular, if both parties to the discussion agree to model agents as differing only in their ownership rights of produced goods, then the disagreement *must* be of the nonsubtle variety. When the neoclassical party says that the proletarian is not exploited by the capitalist because the latter requires a return to this capital (being, we insist, produced goods, not skills) for whatever reason, what is in fact being said that ownership rights of produced means of production must be respected, and therefore, the test for capitalist exploitation is not appropriate.

To force more precision in discussions of this nature, it is conve-

---

[7] This is a well-known theorem of neoclassical economics. See, e.g., Varian (1978:180).

nient to differentiate between *entrepreneurs* and *coupon clippers* among the class of capitalists. Entrepreneurs presumably earn a high return to their inalienable endowments, whereas coupon clippers earn a return only to their alienable endowments. If we conceive of the capitalist class as predominantly composed of the former, then the statement that "exploitation does not exist under capitalism" can be consistently interpreted as referring to *capitalist* exploitation; if the latter, then the statement can only refer to feudal exploitation.

I will, therefore, tentatively conclude that a fair summary of prevailing liberal opinion, which argues against applying the term "exploitation" to the idealized equilibria of a private ownership market economy, is, in the terms of this taxonomy: "There is no (feudal) exploitation under capitalism." This is a true statement. Marxists would argue, however, that there is (capitalist) exploitation under capitalism, although—and this is critical—not all inequality would be eliminated by abolishing private ownership of the means of production.

Thus, the ethical imperative of feudal (or neoclassical) exploitation is to eliminate barriers to free trade (bondage, slavery, tariffs, etc.), while still respecting private property in the means of production. This is what is implied by the private ownership game. The ethical imperative of capitalist or Marxian exploitation is to eliminate barriers to production and income-generating activity that producers face as a consequence of their differential access to the alienable means of production.[8]

This section has presented a reason for choosing the *labor* theory of exploitation: The characterization of exploitation that thereby ensues is equivalent to the property-rights characterization of capitalist exploitation, calling for socialization of alienable productive assets.[9] This is so in the precise sense that Marxian surplus value theory of exploitation is equivalent to capitalist exploitation, in which the ethical imperative is the pooling of alienable productive assets. A

---

[8] There is an important exception to the claim that neoclassical notions of exploitation can be characterized as feudal exploitation: monopolistic exploitation. If the monopolist "exploits" the consumers of his services, the consumers will not be better off to withdraw with their own assets. Monopoly is a thin market, which is fundamentally different from a nonexistent market. Neoclassical exploitation, as I have characterized it, comes about from market failures; but a thin market may work "perfectly."

[9] For further elaboration of why Marxists choose to define exploitation using a labor numeraire, instead of a land or corn numeraire, see Roemer (1983b).

separate question now arises: Why do Marxists argue that the historical imperative of the capitalist epoch is to eliminate capitalist exploitation? That is, historical materialism's contention is that the equalization of producers' access to society's means of production is not simply (or some would say not at all) an ethical imperative of the capitalist period, but rather its historical task. Discussion of this question cannot be pursued here.

In this section I have briefly explained how both Marxist and neoclassical notions of exploitation are special cases of a general taxonomy of exploitation. A group is considered exploited with respect to some specific conception of alternate property relations. The conception of the alternative can be formally modeled using game-theoretic definitions; nonexploitative allocations are in the core of the game, and we vary the notion of exploitation by varying the rules of the game.

c. Socialist exploitation and status exploitation

A coalition is considered capitalistically exploited if it would be better off with access to its per capita share of society's alienable assets (means of production, resources). Note, however, that *inalienable* assets (skills) are not pooled in testing for capitalist exploitation. If capitalist exploitation were annihilated, inequalities would continue to exist, due to differential inalienable assets possessed by individuals. This inequality I call socialist exploitation. A coalition is socialistically exploited if it could improve its lot by withdrawing with its per capita share of society's inalienable assets, once alienable assets are distributed equally. Although carrying out such a redistribution of skills might be impossible, or at the least would involve formidable incentive problems, as a thought experiment the calculations can be made.

Socialist exploitation is supposed to exist in socialism, where people are to be paid "according to their work" and thus not in an egalitarian manner. The bourgeois argument is that what Marxists call capitalist exploitation is in reality socialist exploitation, that inequalities under capitalism are a consequence of competitive returns to differential skills.

If all individual endowments are of either the alienable or inalienable type, then a distribution of income is free of socialist exploitation when it is egalitarian. One should note how a certain classical conception of historical materialism is reflected in these definitions.

The task of the bourgeois revolution is to eliminate only feudal exploitation, leaving capitalist and socialist exploitation. The task of the socialist revolution is to eliminate only capitalist exploitation. Each revolution eliminates the inequalities associated with its characteristic form of property (the feudal bond, alienable means of production, and finally, inalienable assets); the scope of assets that are allowed to be private becomes progressively narrower as history proceeds. Historical materialism asserts that forms of exploitation are eliminated in a certain order.

Yet much inequality in existing socialism is not of the "socialist" variety. In addition, remuneration is made according to status, where the status is not representative of a special skill. It is difficult to separate status from skill, but to the extent that special incomes attach themselves to certain positions, entirely independently of the skills necessary to occupy those positions, I call the phenomenon status exploitation. Some people maintain that most inequality in existing socialist societies is of the status variety. Some maintain that it is of the capitalist variety, since bureaucratic status often gives its possessor some control of social capital.

D. Socially necessary exploitation

The withdrawal criteria proposed for testing the existence of the various forms of exploitation assume that incentives are unaffected by the new distribution of "property," whether it be alienable or inalienable property or property in position. If proletarians in early capitalism had withdrawn with their per capita share of capital, perhaps they would have been worse off than under capitalism, because of the alteration in incentives that would have accompanied socialization of the means of production. (Note that this is an entirely different argument from that of the bourgeois ideologue discussed earlier.) The test for exploitation should therefore be: If the coalition were to work just as hard after its "withdrawal," would it be better off (have more income)? If so, it is exploited, according to the particular exploitation concept in question. If, however, withdrawal altered incentives to the point that the coalition was worse off in terms of income (if not immediately, then soon), I refer to the exploitation as socially necessary. In general, Marxists believe early capitalist exploitation was socially necessary in this sense, and socialist exploitation is socially necessary in present-day socialism. Most bourgeois opinion maintains that capitalist exploitation is still socially necessary, that is, the abolition of private ownership in the means of production would render workers worse off due to failure of incentives of both capitalists and workers.

VI. SUPERIORITY OF THE PROPERTY RELATIONS APPROACH

I believe the property relations approach to exploitation is superior to the surplus-labor approach for at least four reasons:

1. It makes clear what the ethical imperative of the Marxian theory is, as the surplus-value theory does not. Surplus value may also be produced under socialism and under feudalism, but the classical Marxian theory does not adequately distinguish among the different natures of surplus production in the three modes of production. For instance, there has been a debate about whether socialism must entail zero growth, a confusion that comes about because the classical theory of exploitation does not adequately distinguish the different property relations under capitalism and socialism. With the property relations–game-theoretic approach, it is completely clear that the production of a surplus under socialist relations of property cannot be construed as capitalist exploitation.

2. The game-theoretic definition of capitalist exploitation generalizes immediately to the case of heterogenous labor, and even many primary factors. The test for capitalist exploitation remains identical: Evaluate how well an agent or coalition can do if it withdraws with its per capita share of the nonhuman alienable assets. However, I argue that the surplus-labor theory of exploitation fails with heterogenous labor, contrary to various attempts to save it. (But even if one disagrees with my diagnosis, it is incontestable that the game-theoretic approach has the merit of much greater simplicity.) With many primary factors, the labor theory of exploitation completely dissipates, but the property relations approach emerges unscathed. Thus, the surplus-labor characterization is good for one special and important case and only that case: when capitalism is modeled as a system with one primary factor, namely, labor, which is homogeneous and equally endowed to all. The property relations characterization liberates Marxists from the necessity to claim that capitalism *actually looks* like this special case, for it applies in a completely general environment.

Thus, not only must it be admitted that the labor theory of value is irrelevant as a theory of price, but it is also superseded in its role in the theory of exploitation.

3. The property relations approach clarifies the link between the Marxian concept of exploitation and the idea of "unequal exchange" between countries. In particular, unequal exchange can be viewed as an instance of capitalist exploitation where the agents are viewed as nations, not individuals. Elucidation of the connection between the property relations approach and unequal exchange is developed in Roemer (1983a)

4. Most generally, the property relations approach focuses on the differential ownership of the means of production as the culprit in capitalist exploitation, whereas the surplus-value approach focuses on the relationship between agents (capitalist and worker) in a particular market and process (the labor market and process). I think it is the *ownership relations* that are primary: the particular markets and processes through which exploitation is mediated are somewhat incidental, as I have attempted to show with the models of Sections I, II and III. Different regimes (capitalism, feudalism, socialism) are characterized by different property relations, and the kinds of exploitation characteristic of those regimes are best understood by taking the property relations rather than the surplus extraction approach.

REFERENCES

Braverman, Harry (1974). *Labor and Monopoly Capital.* New York: Monthly Review Press.
Brenner, Robert (1976). "Agrarian Class Structure and Economic Development in Pre-industrial Europe." *Past and Present* 70:30–71.
North, Douglass, and Robert Thomas (1973). *The Rise of Western Civilization.* Cambridge: Cambridge University Press.
Roemer, John E. (1982a). "Origins of Exploitation and Class: Value Theory and Pre-capitalist Economy. *Econometrica* 50:163–92.
  (1982b). "Exploitation, Alternatives and Socialism." *Economic Journal* 92: 87–107.
  (1982c). *A General Theory of Exploitation and Class.* Cambridge, Mass.: Harvard University Press.
  (1982d). "Property Relations vs. Surplus Value in Marxian Exploitation." *Philosophy and Public Affairs* 11: 281–313.
  (1983a). "Unequal Exchange, Labor Migration and International Capital Flows: A Theoretical Synthesis." In Padma Desai (ed.), *Marxism, the Soviet Economy and Central Planning: Economic Essays in Honor of Alexander Erlich.* Cambridge, Mass.: MIT Press.

(1983b). "Why Labor Classes?" Dept. of Economics, University of California Davis, Working Paper No. 195.

Tse-tung, Mao (1925). "Analysis of Classes in the Chinese Countryside." In *Selected Readings of Mao Tse-tung*, Peking.

Varian, Hal (1978). *Microeconomic Theory*. New York: Norton.

Methodology and criticism

Some forty years after Marx's death Georg Lukács observed that "orthodoxy" ought to refer not to this or that particular tenet of Marxian theory but should instead refer "exclusively to method" (1971: 1). But never has orthodoxy been so disputable, so open to different readings, so unsure about its articles of faith. If Marx meant to bequeath any sort of set orthodoxy, he was singularly unsuccessful. For even in his lifetime his complaints that his method had often been misunderstood even by would-be Marxists fell on deaf ears. These many misconceptions led Marx to deny that he was a Marxist (McLellan 1973: 443). And in 1873 he complained that "the method employed in *Das Kapital* has been little understood." This had been shown, he went on, "by the various conceptions, contradictory one to another, that have been formed of it" (1967: 17).

Marx's complaint has proved prophetic. Despite Lukács's assurances about orthodoxy, there are still "various conceptions, contradictory one to another" of Marx's method. Dialectical materialist, positivist, humanist, structuralist, realist – these are incompatible, even perhaps incommensurable, interpretations of Marxian method and theory. If blame need be laid somewhere, then it must in large part be laid at Marx's own door. For despite his oft-voiced complaint of having been badly misunderstood and his ready acknowledgment of the importance of matters methodological, he nevertheless wrote no sustained treatise on scientific method: no *Rules of Sociological Method*, no *Methodology of the Social Sciences*, no *Dialectics of Nature*. With the exception of two unpublished and unpolished drafts (1975), Marx's methodological self-reflections come down to us by way of scattered paragraphs and a few pregnant metaphors – like his having found Hegel's dialectic "standing on its head" and needing Marx to set it aright and thus to discover "the rational kernel within the mystical shell" (1967: 20).

Of all the concepts of figuring in what we might call the Marxist *Methodenstreit,* the dialectic is surely the most important and controversial. Marx failed to keep his promise to deliver a critique of Hegel's dialectic, complemented by a constructive account of his own. It was only much later, after Marx's death, that Engels took upon himself the task of elucidating a dialectical methodology and a synoptic view of the sciences. Unfortunately, Engels' *Dialectics of Nature* (and the earlier *Anti-Dühring*) only succeeded in setting an agenda for subsequent dispute. Was the dialectic a method of inquiry, a form of presentation, or a tool for prediction and control? Was it as genuinely applicable to nature as it was to history and society? Could it be assimilated into the prevailing views of scientific method, or was it a method of an entirely novel kind? Dialectical materialism subsequently turned Engels's ideas into an ossified orthodoxy, which was in turn challenged by humanist and critical Marxists, who were in their turn criticized and condemned by avowedly antihumanist "structural" Marxists.

Cutting across this Marxist *Methodenstreit* is the question of Marx's own beliefs and intentions. What did he mean by calling his theory and its methods dialectical and scientific? What precisely was his understanding of science, of method, of contradiction and critique? Did these understandings change over his lifetime? Just as Marx periodized history in various and sometimes contradictory ways, so Marxists and Marxologists have, in attempting to answer these questions, periodized Marx's own intellectual career in ways no less contradictory and confusing. Some have distinguished the young/humanist/left-Hegelian ideology critic from the old/antihumanist/positivist/post-Hegelian/protostructuralist social scientist. These commentators can, in their turn, be divided into two groups. Some contend that the former represents the "real" Marx, whereas others insist that the latter is the genuine article. Others, perhaps more sensibly, suggest that there was, after all, only one Marx, but that he was the ambivalent father of two mutually incompatible if not contradictory offspring. Thus Gouldner writes of *The Two Marxisms* (1980), the first being Marxism as critical method, the second a positivistically conceived science of society. Habermas likewise sees Marxian theory as having fallen somewhere between these two stools (1971: chaps. 2, 3; 1973: chap. 6). And whereas Albrecht Wellmer detects traces of "latent positivism" in Marx's theory of history (1971: chap. 2), G. A. Cohen finds evidence of blatant positivism (which, in his view, is not necessarily to be regretted). Marx, Cohen claims, "did not deviate" from "nineteenth century conceptions of science," that is, from one or another version of positivism. Hence, he concludes, "the fashionable effort to enlist him in the ranks of anti-positivist . . . philosophy of science is entirely misguided" (Cohen 1978: 46).

Misguided or no, the essays by Farr, Ball, and Carver argue otherwise. In quite different ways each maintains that Marx's conceptions of science, method, explanation, prediction, and political practice do not fit the standard positivist mold; on the contrary, there is reason to believe that Marx breaks that mold. James Farr argues that neither the young nor the old Marx ever subscribed to any characteristically positivistic theses. The most characteristic of these is the unity-of-science thesis, which holds that all sciences – natural and social – are either ultimately reducible to one unified science or, failing that, are at any rate united by a common method. Farr maintains that Marx, far from being a proponent of positivism, was an outspoken opponent and critic of one of its central theses.

Shifting the argument from methodology to politics, Terence Ball contends that Marx's critical and decidedly nonpositivist conception of science was largely supplanted by Engels's more patently positivist conception, and that the latter's positivism has precisely the sorts of political implications traced out in the writings of earlier positivists, particularly Saint-Simon and Comte. These implications are unabashedly elitist, inegalitarian, and undemocratic. According to Engels, all processes, including human thought, are the result of matter in motion. The natural and social sciences are accordingly reducible to a single science, namely, "dialectics." The upshot is that human reason and rational argument are reducible to a rather inefficient species of efficient causation. "Scientific" political practice thus becomes a matter of expert manipulation by other, more efficient means – coercive, "therapeutic," or otherwise. Thus, Ball argues, it is Engels – not Marx – who is the true progenitor of repressive Soviet-style "scientific" socialism.

"Scientific" Marxism, says Terrell Carver, was itself almost entirely Engels's own invention. For it is replete with epistemological and methodological pretensions that Marx viewed with suspicion if not utter hostility, and was moreover pervaded by Engels's own idiosyncratic interpretation of Hegelian concepts and categories, not the least of which is The Dialectic. In effect, Engels's contribution to Marxism consisted of recasting the dialectic as a method of inquiry, a cosmology of science, and a *Weltanschauung* – none of which it had been in Marx's own hands. Indeed, if Marx can be said to have left behind any "method" at all, it was surely the pluralistic and eclectic one that emerged in the course of his critical work on capitalist society. It was not some sort of fixed logic of scientific method, much less a philosophy of dialectical materialism. Carver concludes his essay, and this volume, with a salutary warning about the dangers of reducing Marxism to a method. Indeed, perhaps Marxian theorizing would proceed more promisingly if we paid closer heed to the sorts of problems that so angered Marx and animated his search for solutions to the riddle that modern man has become to himself.

REFERENCES

Cohen, G. A. (1978). *Karl Marx's Theory of History: A Defence*. Princeton, N.J.: Princeton University Press.

Gouldner, Alvin G. (1980). *The Two Marxisms*. New York: Seabury Press.

Habermas, Jürgen (1971). *Knowledge and Human Interests*. Translated by Jeremy J. Shapiro. Boston: Beacon Press.

(1973). *Theory and Practice*. Translated by John Viertel. Boston: Beacon Press.

Lukács, Georg (1971). *History and Class Consciousness*. Translated by Rodney Livingstone. Cambridge, Mass.: MIT Press.

McLellan, David (1973). *Karl Marx: His Life and Work*. London: Macmillan Press.

Marx, Karl (1967). *Capital*, vol. I. New York: International Publishers.

(1975). *Karl Marx: Texts on Method*. Translated and edited by Terrell Carver. Oxford: Blackwell Publisher.

Wellmer, Albrecht (1971). *Critical Theory of Society*. New York: Herder & Herder.

CHAPTER 10

Marx and positivism

JAMES FARR

At Marx's graveside Engels bade a final farewell to his lifelong
friend with this tribute: "This was the man of science." And so he
was. But unlike the other great sociological theorists of the nineteenth century – Mill, Weber, or Durkheim – Marx never composed a
systematic treatise on scientific method by which we might readily
identify the *kind* of science he was a man *of*. Others, however, not the
least of whom was Engels himself, soon stepped in to speak for
Marx. One especially influential interpretation finds in Marx's conception of scientific method a variant of positivism. Among those
who read Marx as a positivist, however, there is some quibbling as to
whether Marx's positivism is explicitly "acknowledged" or simply "latent," or whether there are only "traces" of it in his works (Wolin
1960: 358; Wellmer 1971: 67; McLellan 1975: 38; respectively).[1] Yet
this interpretation, I wish to argue, is pure myth. Marx's positivism,
far from being either acknowledged or latent, is largely an invention
of later interpreters.

If Marx's positivism is pure myth, it is nevertheless far from
simple. Marx's works are surely pervaded by the scientific spirit of
the nineteenth century, including its boasts, and there is no lack of
talk about facts, laws, and theory. Moreover, in 1844 Marx even
anticipated a time when "there will be *one* science" (1964: 143). Since
positivism in its many forms has held one or another version of the

I would like to thank Terence Ball, Paul Quirk, and James Noble for their
suggestions and criticisms on an earlier version of this chapter.
[1] Similar interpretations of Marx as a positivist can be found in Acton
(1955: 109), Jordan (1967: ch. IV), McMurtry (1978: 53), Cohen (1978:
46), and Hudelson (1982). Against this last, see Farr (1983).

unity of science, Marx's speculation looks like prima facie evidence of positivism. But, as I shall argue, Marx's version of the unity of science (which he tendered only briefly) is in no sense a *positivist* version. His is an ontological claim about the practical unity of human beings and nature in industry, the fulfillment of which is part of the movement toward communism. Only incidentally is it about the internal practices or methods of science. Moreover, what Marx says in other contexts about the methodology of the social and natural sciences negates positivism and its versions of the unity of science. Thus, upon closer inspection, what appeared to be prima facie evidence for Marx's positivism turns into decisive proof against it. There is a hermeneutic moral in this: Because of the unabashedly scientific intentions of Marx's works, voiced in an atmosphere thick with the rhetoric of science, we need to pay even closer attention to Marx's intentions and texts and not simply assume that his and all other nineteenth-century conceptions of science were identical, much less homogenize them all under a catchall category like positivism. In short, there is more to science than positivism, and there is no positivism at all in Marx's science.

Given the pervasiveness of the myth of Marx's positivism, a full-scale treatise would be required to do justice to the complex issues involved. To write such a treatise is not my aim here, however, and I can only hope that a critical analysis of this single issue will shed some light on the general interpretation of Marx's method and kick a prop from underneath the myth of his positivism. My argument and critique proceed as follows. I begin by canvassing three versions of the positivist unity of science and attend to some related theses of positivist philosophy of science. I then go on to reconstruct Marx's implied criticism of all three; what emerges are the outlines of Marx's own historical and critical conception of scientific method. And finally I present Marx's ontological, and decidedly nonpositivist, version of the unity of science, and conclude with some critical and historical remarks.

I. POSITIVISM AND THE UNITY OF SCIENCE

The unity of science occupies a hallowed place among the high principles of positivist philosophy of science. Positivists assume that genuine knowledge is of a single piece and that science alone supplies such knowledge. Yet the unity of science is a principle fired by positivist faith, not by the practice of science. For positivists have reluctantly recognized that the actual practice of the several sciences – natural and social – has been marked more by disunity than by unity. In particular, the social sciences have lagged far behind the natural sciences. The social sciences are, at best, infant sciences whose persistent immaturity and notable lack of explanatory success are a matter of some embarrassment. Faced with this lamentable situation, positivists have turned a matter of faith into a programmatic recommendation to bring scientific practice into line with positivist principle. The recommended program for unified science has assumed different forms at different times. But all are about practices internal to science, and all have gambled on the success of one or another version of reductionism. In a word, reduction is the key to the positivist unity of science.

The unity of science has characteristically assumed one of three forms, made most explicit by latter-day positivists: the unity of language, the unity of laws, and the unity of method (following Hempel 1969). Together these three entail or invoke a number of other important theses in positivist philosophy of science, including physicalism, methodological individualism, and universal covering-law explanations. As we shall see, Marx would have no truck with any of them.

The unity of language holds out the prospect of unifying science by reducing all scientific terms to a single universal language. The language of physics (or, of physical observation) seems especially promising in this regard. All are agreed that physics is the most successful science and, moreover, that observation terms are public and intersubjective in the way required by science.[2] So the unity of language prescribes reducing all scientific terms to physical terms, or more properly, to "observable thing terms" (Carnap 1938: 53). This essentially empiricist thesis boldly proclaims further that all scientific theories, including social and political theories, are reducible without loss of content to observations of "physical facts and spatio-temporal events" (Carnap 1934: 97). In short, physicalism is here deemed to be the route to unified science: "Physical language is the universal language and can therefore serve as the basic language of science" (Carnap 1934: 95).

The unity-of-laws thesis claims, in addition to the unity of lan-

---

[2] Among the early logical positivists, physicalism replaced phemonenalism largely because of the issue of intersubjectivity. Talk of impressions and sense data could hardly ground the language of science.

guage, that the laws of physics explain all phenomena without re-mainder. So the substantive laws of the social sciences can be re-duced, in principle, to the laws of physics. This reduction need not, and probably cannot, proceed directly. Rather, there will be a series of intertheoretical reductions that move from the social sciences through intervening theoretical sciences – psychology, biology, physi-ology, and chemistry – ultimately to physics. On this view, each sci-ence is microreduced to a more basic science in the way that wholes are reduced to their parts. Laws of social wholes are to form a link in the chain of scientific laws to the extent that they can be microre-duced to their parts, namely, to laws of individuals, and usually to laws of individual psychology. Thus, " 'The Principle of Methodological Individualism' . . . is nothing more than the special form [that the] working hypothesis [of unified science] takes in ap-plication to human social groups" (Oppenheim and Putnam 1958: 17).[3] Should methodological individualism prove successful, then the social sciences will have secured their place in a unified science. Of course, for the whole program of the unity of science to succeed on this basis, all other microreductions must go through, from psychol-ogy to physics. In sum, the unity-of-laws thesis holds that there is (in principle) an encyclopedic hierarchy of the sciences and that physics is the fundamental explanatory science to which all others can be reduced. In this way "the whole of science becomes physics" (Carnap 1934: 97).

Finally, the unity-of-method version of reductionism makes the weaker but more general claim that there is only one scientific method or methodology. Unlike the aforementioned versions of the unity of science, the unity of method admits that the languages and substantive laws of particular sciences will not only vary considera-bly, but may even differ irreducibly. Nonetheless, science is still uni-fied (in principle) because all particular sciences test and support their explanations in the same manner, and all explanations con-form to the covering-law model. Accordingly, all explanations of particular events must be deduced from statements of initial condi-tions and from universal laws that purport to hold at all times and in all places (Hempel 1965: chaps. 9, 10). Therefore, according to this last thesis, neither the language nor the laws, but only the methodo-

---

[3] Compare the arguments of Fodor (1974), whose examples could apply directly to Marx. Also, not all versions of methodological individualism are committed to psychological reductionism. See, for example, Popper (1966: 91–99).

logical or explanatory *form,* of the social sciences must be reduced to physics and the natural sciences.

These three versions of the unity of science were clarified and popularized by the logical positivists in our century. Their manifesto, the *International Encyclopedia of Unified Science,* documents their commitment to what was agreed to be a working hypothesis about the future state of science. There were, however, many anticipations of these developments in the eighteenth and nineteenth centuries, many of which were acknowledged by the logical positivists. These included the French Encyclopedists and David Hume, "the real father of positivism" (Kolakowski 1968: 30). Hume, it will be remembered, earmarked his *Treatise* as "an attempt to introduce the experimental method of reasoning into moral subjects," and in a renowned essay promised "to reduce politics to a science" (Hume 1978).[4] Among Marx's positivist contemporaries were John Stuart Mill and August Comte (who popularized the term "positivism"). In the *Cours de Philosophie Positive,* Comte anticipated some of the later versions of unified science. Principally he thought that "the only indispensable unity is unity of method." "All that we have to do," he told his would-be fellow scientists in 1832, "is to complete positive philosophy by including in it the study of social phenomena, and then reduce it to a single body of doctrine." This reduction would complete "the encyclopedic ladder of the fundamental sciences," which culminated in physics. So all that was required to redeem the promise of a unified science was a "social physics." This would at last fill "the great lacuna left in the system of positive philosophy by the deplorable state of prolonged infantilism in which social science still languishes" (Andreski 1974: 38, 41, 51, 124, 125).

With less zeal perhaps, but animated by essentially the same vision of a unified science, John Stuart Mill echoed most of Comte's programmatic proclamations. Indeed Mill's "Logic of the Moral Sciences" (Book VI of *A System of Logic*) quoted Comte profusely, at least until later, expurgated editions reflected Mill's disenchantment with Comte's authoritarian political developments. "Astronomy furnishes the most perfect example" of scientific method, Mill said, suggesting that the social sciences needed only to copy this method. He also speculated (unlike Comte) on the microreduction of sociology to psychology, averring that the "laws of the phenomena of

---

[4] There is more to Hume's conception of method than positivism, however. See Farr (1978, 1982).

society are derived from, and may be resolvable into, the laws of individual man." Mill's methodological individualism, however, was only a partial step toward a unified science, for "the laws of mind may be derivative laws resulting from animal life, and . . . their truth therefore may ultimately depend on physical conditions" (Mill 1965: 27, 59).

Marx came to his own methodological self-understanding in this historical context. He had before him the works of Mill and Comte and their followers. It would be a gross understatement to say that he found precious little in them that accorded with his own vision of a critical and "historical social science" (1973: 106). Marx never explicitly criticized Mill or Comte on unified science as such; but his criticism of their work was otherwise thoroughgoing and his differences with them, both methodological and political, virtually complete. His own version of unified science shared nothing in common with theirs, nor with the more developed versions of later logical positivists. Indeed, Marx's overall conception of scientific method precluded these versions altogether. Let us see how.

II. MARX AND POSITIVISM

In the nominalist climate of nineteenth-century positivist philosophy of science, Marx held the contrary realist view that social-scientific categories "express the forms of being" of the specific society they describe (1973: 106). Since society is the sum of social relations, Marx further held that social "categories are only abstract expressions of actual relations and only remain true while these relations exist" (1963: 186). As we might put it today, social relations provide the irreducible context of meaning for understanding actions and social events. If you change the social relations—for example, by investigating a different era—then you change the social and economic categories needed to describe them. Thus, "economic categories bear the stamp of history" (1967, vol. I: 169). If, further, you take away the context of social relations, then you cease using social and economic categories altogether. For example, if you take away the relations of exchange, then a unit of exchange, like gold or silver, ceases to be money: "Only its metallic existence would be left over, while its economic existence would be destroyed" (1973: 106). Herein lies the source of Marx's wholesale rejection of positivism and its versions of unified science.

In Marx's terms, the unity of language is a self-denying ordinance for a science of social relations. No distinctly *social* science would remain if the reduction of social terms to physical terms were successful. Social relations (and the terms that express them) identify actions and events. Therefore, social relation terms cannot be reduced to physical thing terms (or even to the terms expressing the material relations between physical things) without loss of content and social identity.

Marx is emphatic in pointing this out, especially with such terms as "commodities" and "money." Contrasting commodities with the act of seeing, Marx writes:

> In the act of seeing, there is at all events, an actual passage of light from one thing to another, from the external object to the eye. There is a physical relation between physical things. But it is different with commodities. There, the existence of things, *qua* commodities, and the value-relation between the products of labor which stamps them as commodities, have absolutely no connection with their physical properties and with the material relations arising therefrom. There it is a definite social relation between men, that assumes, in their eyes, the fantastic form of a relation between things. (1967, vol. I: 72)

Value is not, as perhaps it appears on the surface of economic exchange, describable in terms of – or reducible to – relations among things (or, contrary to certain strains of Marxist orthodoxy, to "matter in motion"). Rather, it is a product of the irreducibly social relations of the labor process. The realm of economic exchange may well be fantastic, but the critical social scientist must see through the fantasy. Consider money:

> The special difficulty in grasping money . . . is that a social relation, a definite relation between individuals, here appears as a metal, a stone, as a purely physical, external thing which can be found, as such, in nature, and which is indistinguishable in form from its natural existence . . . Nature does not produce money, any more than it produces a rate of exchange or a banker . . . To be money is not a natural attribute of gold and silver, and is therefore quite unknown to the physicist, chemist, etc., as such. (1973: 239)

Physical reductionists marching under the banner of unified science fail to understand this elementary but quite crucial point. They mistake the "language of commodities" for the language of physical things (1967, vol. I: 52). In so doing they are not only bad scientists, but fetishists as well. Physicalism, in short, is a version of fetishism. Physical thing terms cannot provide the bedrock of a unified scientific vocabulary because they misdescribe the very reality a social science attempts to capture. As thing terms, they 'fall through the language of *social* relations that make the social sciences possible.

JAMES FARR

The unity-of-laws thesis fares no better in Marx's method because it founders on similar defects. Without doubt Marx thought the search for a set of fundamental laws to which all others could be reduced to be utterly misguided. No science, on his view, could serve as the reducing science for the social sciences. For reasons already noted, physics and chemistry could not be candidates for this dubious honor. Nor, for that matter, could physiology – and certainly not the "anatomico-physiological method" defended by Wilhelm Roscher (whom Max Weber was later to criticize along lines Marx would almost certainly have approved) (Marx 1967, vol. I: 92; Weber 1975). Nor, despite another myth – the myth of "Socialist Darwinism" fostered by Engels, Kautsky, and others (Ball 1979) – did Marx believe that the laws of the social sciences could be reduced to laws of biology. In the hands of vulgar social evolutionists the law of natural selection became a trite *"phrase . . .* 'the struggle of life' " (Marx and Engels 1975: 225). This was "sham-scientific" at worst; at best it was a purely promissory interpretative framework whose main work remained to be done; namely, "analyzing the struggle of life as represented historically in various forms of society" (Marx and Engels 1975: 225). However, it was by no means a basis for inter-theoretic reduction in the way required by positivism. Moreover, Marx noted something of an irony in the vulgarized theory of evolution, much less in the whole program of biological reduction. The feasibility of reduction was appropriate to nineteenth-century biology, he observed, precisely because biological species were observed through nineteenth-century bourgeois lenses in the first place. It was as if the bourgeois social sciences provided the hidden basis for biology, not vice versa as required by the program for biological reduction. Even Darwin was guilty of this, Marx thought. After an initial fascination with Darwin, Marx viewed his achievements in a more skeptical light. Indeed, he finally found Darwin's theory downright "amusing" because it smuggled a social interpretation of capitalist society into biological law:

It is remarkable how Darwin recognizes among beasts and plants his English society with its division of labor, competition, opening up of new markets, inventions, and the Malthusian "struggle for existence." His is Hobbes' *bellum omnium contra omnes,* and one is reminded of Hegel's *Phenomenology* where civil society is described as a "spiritual animal kingdom," while in Darwin the animal kingdom figures as civil society. (Marx and Engels 1975: 120)

So much, then, for the biological foundations of a distinctively historical social science.

Marx and positivism

Marx was no methodological individualist, either, and certainly no psychological reductionist. Surprisingly, however, some have claimed otherwise:

> In the case of Marx the assumptions of classical political economy are openly made . . . From this assumption . . . Marx derives his major laws and predictions. Thus Marxist sociology is micro-reductionist in the same sense as classical economy, and shares the same basic weakness (the assumptions of "economic man"). (Oppenheim and Putnam 1958: 17)

But Marx repeatedly denied this, and his critique of political economy was directed in large part against the individualistic and psychologistic assumptions of so-called economic man. In his last theoretical work, *Notes on Adolph Wagner,* Marx declared himself against "the methodology of '*man*' " and once again repeated that "my analytic method does not start out from *man,* but from the economically given social period" (1975: 193, 201).[5] Marx begins his investigations, and ends them, with social relations. In the *Grundrisse* Marx attacks methodological individualism directly: "Society does not consist of individuals, but expresses the sum total of interrelations, the relations within which these individuals stand" (1973: 265). As against those, like Proudhon or John Stuart Mill, who would reduce social relations to attributes of individuals, Marx goes on to say that individuals as such are individuals only "outside society." However, "to be a slave, to be a citizen are social characteristics, relations between human beings A and B. Human being A, as such, is not a slave. He is a slave in and through society" (1973: 265).

The emphasis on relations, it bears mentioning, also prevents Marx from embracing holism, that is, the abstract antithesis of methodological individualism.[6] He chastises those who "regard society as one single subject . . . wrongly, speculatively" (1973: 94). He sneers at those who resort to "the fiction of the person, Society" (1963: 96). I daresay that Marx toed a difficult, though quite coher-

---

[5] This is not to deny that Marx embraced some philosophy of human nature, for he does. See, for example, Marx (1967, vol. I: 609). But his philosophy of human nature has as part of its core our sociality, and is not predicated on the kinds of claims made by classical political economy, as suggested by Oppenheim and Putnam (1958).

[6] This is Popper's charge against Marx, after applauding Marx's denial of psychological reductionism. But this is inadequate for reasons given and texts cited. Moreover, Popper's own recommendation to study "the relations of individuals acting in certain situations" sounds rather like Marx's real view, and is misleadingly called "methodological individualism." See Popper (1966: 88, 324).

ent, line betwen holism and individualism. Marx's view might best be dubbed *methodological relationism*. By taking as his unit of analysis the individual acting in social relations, Marx refuses to reify society as a suprahistorical person, on the one hand, while, on the other, he refuses to reduce the laws of social relations to the laws of individual psychology.

In sum, the positivists' purported unity of laws comes a cropper. In Marx's view there was no First Science, be it psychology, biology, or physics. On this score Marx was a methodological pluralist, not a monist.

Engels, it bears mentioning, was at times more monistic than Marx when it came to the unity of laws. Echoing the French Encycloped- ists – and anticipating later dialectical materialism – Engels held that "the unity . . . of the world consists in its materiality," and therefore he sought, like Holbach a century earlier, "a 'System of Nature' sufficient for our time" (Engels 1940: 51; Marx and Engels 1968: 622). This system was none other than the dialectical system of *Anti- Dühring* and the *Dialectics of Nature*. "The dialectic," Engels tells us, "is the science of the general laws of motion and development of nature, human society, and thought" (1939: 155). Moreover, "just as one form of motion develops out of another, so too must their reflections, the different sciences, necessarily proceed from one to the other" (1940: 179). Here then, cast not in a physical, but a dialectical-materialist mold, is Engels's own version of the unity of laws. Thus the mantle of positivism sits more snugly on Engels's shoulders than on Marx's (for discussion see Carver 1980, 1981; Thomas 1976; and Ball, ch. 11, this volume).

Finally, even on the weakest version of the unity of science – the unity of method – Marx cannot be properly termed a positivist. He recognized, of course, that the social and natural sciences shared many things in common, and he never hesitated to make compari- sons between the sciences either in strictly methodological contexts, or, better yet, when it might bolster a political argument. Moreover, Marx repeatedly spoke of laws and explanations in the social sci- ences. Hence, he would have had little sympathy with later nine- teenth-century philosophers who argued that laws were wholly out of place in social explanations. In this regard he would have sided with Comte and Mill and the later positivists against idealists and historicists, like Dilthey, Windelband, or Rickert. This, however, was only one side of the argument. For positivists misunderstood the nature of laws and explanations in the historical social sciences.

Against positivism, Marx thought that the program to reduce historical social explanations to the universalistic and ahistorical model of physics was ill conceived. It fell victim to "the weak points in the abstract materialism of natural science, a materialism that excludes history and its processes" (1967, vol. I: 373). Marx's own version of materialism was intended to remedy this defect, and thus to synthesize the competing methodologies of idealism and positivism (or abstract materialism). This is the upshot of the *Theses on Feuerbach* in particular. Against positivism, Marx thought that laws (like the categories in which they were framed) were abstracted from historically situated social relations. As social relations change, so do the laws that explain them. Marx repeatedly states that laws in the social sciences are "historical laws," that is, "laws only for a particular historical development" (Marx and Engels 1975: 34; 1973: 606). Even about the laws of population, supposedly the most natural laws of social phenomena, Marx argued that "in fact every special mode of production has its own special laws of population, historically valid within its limits alone" (1967, vol. I: 632). In short, such laws as are available to the social sciences are temporally restricted, not universal and transhistorical.[7] On this point Marx quite clearly anticipates the more recent defenses of restricted or limited generalizations in social and historical explanation (Ball 1972; Joynt and Rescher 1961).

This was not only a methodological issue for Marx, but a political one as well. In capitalism social-scientific laws express alienated social relations in general, and "the laws of political economy express the estrangement of the worker in his objects" in particular (1964: 109). Moreover, historical laws "appear to [ordinary agents] as overwhelming natural laws that irresistibly enforce their will over them, and confront them as blind necessity" (1967, vol. III: 831). But in reality, laws in the social sciences are neither natural, nor irresistible, nor blindly necessary. Rather, they are that only in appearance because the processes they explain operate "behind the backs" of those who are their real subjects (1967, vol. I: 44; 1973: 244, 255). Marx cites

[7] Marx makes a distinction between historical laws proper, and those transhistorical abstractions that figure in any interpretation of history. These abstractions identify those things that can be said to sustain changes through history, like labor, relations of production, forces of production, and the like. These are "without historical character, human if you like" (1973: 320). Marx usually calls these, not laws, but "premises," "principles even "tautologies" (1973: 489). The relationship between these near-tautological abstractions and historical laws proper requires more extensive elaboration than can be offered here, and I shall take it up at a later date.

Engels to the effect that these purported natural laws are really "founded on the want of knowledge of those whose action is the subject of it" (1967, vol. I: 75). Therefore, the political task of a critical, historical social science is to expose these alienated laws of appearances for what they really are and to help supply the knowledge and self-understanding required for agents to change the historical laws of their own behavior.

Positivists, on the other hand, dwelt at too great a length on a methodology appropriate to physics and the natural sciences and consequently denied, or ignored altogether, the political task of criticism. In Marx's eyes, the purportedly eternal or transhistorical laws of bourgeois economics were politically apologetic, as well as methodologically abstract. On this score, Marx indicted "August Comte and his school" for portraying "the lords of capital" as an "eternal necessity" (1967, vol. I: 332). Thus Marx confessed that "as a partisan I take up an entirely hostile attitude towards Comtism, while as a scholar I have a very poor opinion of it" (Marx and Engels 1975: 250). Indeed he went further: "Comte is known to the Parisian workmen as the prophet in politics of Imperialism (of personal dictatorship), of capitalist rule in political economy, of hierarchy in all spheres of human action, even in the sphere of science, and as the author of a new catechism with a new pope and new saints in place of old ones" (1974: 260). Similarly John Stuart Mill, whom Marx undoubtedly took to be one of the English to "make such a fuss" over Comte, cast the laws of bourgeois production as "physical truths" that never change. Marx thought this "highly absurd" (Marx and Engels 1975: 169; 1973: 832). So in Mill, "bourgeois relations are quietly smuggled in as the inviolable natural laws. This is the more or less conscious purpose of the whole proceeding" (1973: 87).

Marx recognized that some positivists had socialist tendencies. But this only intensified his ire, for their socialism was purely accidental and completely disconnected from their methodology or their economic theories. In the 1870s he belittled the "socialist sectarianism" of Comtism in general, and of the so-called Society of Positivist Proletarians, in particular (1974: 260).[8] Likewise, when John Stuart

[8] The General Council of the International Workingmen's Association allowed the Society of Positivist Proletarians to affiliate with the International providing the Society strike its defining principles, since "the positivist principles enshrined in the rules of the Society that dealt with capital are in flagrant contradiction with the preamble to the General Rules" of the International (Marx 1974: 288).

Mill made some socialist overtures later, though without fundamentally altering his positivism or his political economy, Marx accused him of a "shallow syncretism" (1967, vol. I: 15). So it was that whatever the posturing of its leading lights, Marx thought that the positivist political economist, whether in the person of Mill or Comte or Adam Smith, was the "ideological representative" of the capitalist class (1967, vol. I: 573).

The distance between Marx and the positivists on matters of method or politics could hardly be greater. Classical positivism no more recognized its science in Marx than Marx recognized his in positivism. The *Revue Positiviste* found *Capital* to be a mere catalogue of facts and to be merely "metaphysical," the greatest sin of positivism (1967, vol. I: 17). Not to be outdone, Marx hurled a final thunderbolt at *Dieser Scheisspositivismus* (Marx and Engels 1964–8, vol. 31· 234).

III. MARX AND THE UNITY OF SCIENCE

The critique of political economy provided Marx with a platform from which to reject positivism and its various versions of the unity of science. But paradoxical though it might at first seem, Marx *did* hold a version of the unity of science in *The Economic and Philosophic Manuscripts* of 1844, those sketchy fragments in which even the arch-idealist Hegel is found guilty of "uncritical positivism" (1964: 176). In the manuscript entitled "Private Property and Communism," Marx suggests that

industry is the *actual,* historical relationship of nature, and therefore of natural science to man. If, therefore, industry is conceived as the *exoteric* revelation of man's *essential powers,* we also gain an understanding of the *human* essence of nature or the *natural* essence of man. In consequence, natural science will lose its abstractly material–or rather, its idealistic–tendency, and will become the basis of human science.

History itself is a *real* part of *natural history*–of nature developing into man. Natural science will in time incorporate into itself the science of man, just as the science of man will incorporate into itself natural science: there will be *one* science. (1964: 143)

The unity of science is here conceived as a consequence of an ontological claim about the unity of human beings and nature. Yet, unlike some recent proponents of unified science, Marx does not conceive of this unity as one of a mere subsumption of people under nature, and therefore of social science under natural science.[9] Rather, Marx's ontology encompasses the social and dialectical interchange of human beings and nature, as exemplified in the history and development of human industry. It is in industry that we objectify ourselves and change nature. We confront nature qua objects, and in transforming these objects into articles of human use we transform ourselves. Indeed, "the *entire so-called history of the world* is nothing but the creation of man through human labor, nothing but the emergence of nature for man" (1964: 145). In short, we continually remake ourselves as we remake the world out of nature's material.

In this historical process science figures both as a precondition and as a product. It is a precondition in that industry applies science in practice. But industry supplies science with its "aim, as with its material," and so science is a product of industry and human objectification. Even "the science of man is itself a product of man's establishment of himself by practical activity" (1964: 165). Science, in short, is part and parcel of human practice, and since it reflects the society in which it develops, it has grave historical consequences. As Marx argues, "Natural science has invaded and transformed human life all the more *practically* through the medium of industry; and has prepared human emancipation, although its immediate effect had to be the furthering of the dehumanization of man" (1964: 142). In capitalism, science expresses human alienation because individuals are separated from each other, the objects of industry do not express our human nature, and nature is therefore estranged from us; just as we are from nature. But in communist society, as Marx envisions it, nature will be "humanized" because it will exist for people only as a bond with other people. Humanity will be "naturalized" because communism returns us to ourselves as social beings (1964: 135). So in communist society, "the *social* reality of nature, and human natural science, or the *natural science about man,* are identical terms" (1964: 143).

The unity of science Marx envisions here is a peculiar one, and quite unlike anything to be found in positivism. This unity is not to be a result of the internal unification of scientific language, laws, or method. Rather, science becomes more and more unified as the objects of science (both human beings and nature) become more and

9 Braithwaite's view is typical: " 'Science' is synonymous with 'natural science' if man is included in nature" (1959: 1).

more unified.[10] A humanized nature and a naturalized humanity make possible the unity of science in the peculiarly nonpositivistic Marxist sense. Therefore, the unity of science is not about reducing contemporary social science to contemporary natural science, no matter how we conceive of that reduction. On the contrary, Marx's view of the unity of science is *not reductive* at all, but is one of mutual incorporation: "Natural science will in time incorporate into itself the science of man, just as the science of man will incorporate into itself natural science" (1964: 143). Unity of science, when once effected, will be a two-way street. Finally, Marx's is a purely promissory, even prophetic, unity. The unity of science is part of the movement of history and it will uniquely characterize a future communist society because only that "society is the unity of being of man with nature – the naturalism of man and the humanism of nature brought forth to fulfillment" (1964: 137). A purely methodological, pre-communist unity of science is inconceivable.

In Marx's own terms, his ontological and future-communist version of the unity of science avoids the pitfalls of positivism and its abstract unity of science. Moreover, his version is appropriate to a science of social relations whose intentions are not only explanatory but also critical – critical of the practice of positivist science, and critical of the practice of capitalist industry as well. Yet, even if Marx was right in criticizing positivism, his own thesis suffers from abstract speculation and is perhaps inconsistent with his own considered methodology of the historical social sciences. The thesis of the (future) *identity* of human beings and nature is stronger than is required by his ontology of human objectification. Marx later adopted a much weaker thesis, preferring to speak mostly of "mediations" (1973: 93). Indeed, for Marx to make the kinds of claims he wants to about the historical social sciences, and thus to block the positivist unity of method, he must make and preserve some categorical distinctions within the mediated unity of human beings and nature. This he frequently does. "We presuppose labor in a form that stamps it as exclusively human," as opposed to the "labor" of spiders or bees (1967, vol. I: 178). There are those things in Marx's ontology that are "not *natural,* as opposed to *historical,*" and still others that, to the contrary, are "natural (not historical)" (1973: 222, 460). Citing

[10] Even before the full unification foreseen in communism, Marx sees the effect of the mutual conditioning of human beings and nature. Thus, "an abstract law of population exists for plants and animals only, and only in so far as man has not interfered with them" (1967, vol. I: 632).

Vico, Marx avers that "human history differs from natural history in . . . that we have made the former but not the latter" (1967, vol. I: 372). Moreover, inasmuch as Marx's thesis looks to the future, communism is as much to be the historical liberation of human beings from nature as it is to be their identity with nature. The object of science, therefore, will not be strictly identical for all particular sciences, and this precludes the possibility of there being a strict unity of science, even in Marx's peculiar sense. Indeed, even to the extent that some measure of unification will be attained, Marx admonishes scientists to pay attention to the "essential differences . . . within unity" (1973: 85). Special languages, laws, and methods will, accordingly, still need to be preserved by particular sciences. Finally, it is conceivable that Marx anticipates in communism not that science will be unified, but that like the state, it will wither away (see appendix to Cohen 1978).

The unity of science, whether in positivist or in Marxist clothing, has serious defects indeed. But I shall not pursue such criticisms here, for that is a work in itself. I hope to have shown, however, that Marx's conception of science is not positivist, and this includes the unity of science. I hope, in other words, to have dealt a blow to the myth of Marx's positivism.

Our tale remains to be concluded. By 1845, a year or so after he put aside his *Manuscripts,* Marx apparently abandoned his own (nonpositivist) unity-of-science thesis, perhaps because of his having reflected on the kinds of problems I have briefly sketched. In drafting *The German Ideology* Marx declared again, though now for the last time, that

we know a single science, the science of history. History can be contemplated from two sides, it can be divided into the history of nature and the history of mankind. However, the two sides are not to be divided off; as long as men exist the history of nature and the history of men are mutually conditioned. (Marx and Engels 1964–8, vol. 3: 18; quoted in Schmidt 1971: 49)

Significantly, Marx struck this passage from the final version of *The German Ideology* before submitting it, not to a willing publisher and a literate public, but to "the gnawing criticism of the mice." Marx retains the ontology of human objectification and the dialectical symbiosis of human beings and nature, but he never again ties this to the unity of science. Nor did he need do so. The much-vaunted unity of science had but short tenure in the development of Marx's method. Like a fetter, it was burst asunder.

Marx and positivism

The theme of unified science would appear, therefore, to provide less continuity in Marx's works than the concept of alienated labor, the method of critique, or the influence of Hegel. For those who find a tidy demarcation between the young and the old Marx, this should prove to be an embarrassing irony. The young "humanist" Marx uses the language of unified science, which on its face suggests positivist conclusions, whereas the old "determinist" Marx eschews talk of unified science altogether! But this demarcation into two periods is yet another myth foisted on Marx, and the judicious reader will rightly refuse to swap one myth for another. Young or old, humanist or determinist, Marx is no positivist.

REFERENCES

Acton, H. B. (1955). *The Illusion of the Epoch*. London: Cohen & West.
Andreski, Stanislav, ed. (1974). *The Essential Comte*. New York: Barnes & Noble Books.
Ball, Terence (1972). "On 'Historical' Explanation." *Philosophy of the Social Sciences* 2: 181–92.
 (1979). "Marx and Darwin: A Reconsideration." *Political Theory* 7: 469–83.
Braithwaite, Richard (1959). *Scientific Explanation*. Cambridge: Cambridge University Press.
Carnap, Rudolph (1934). *The Unity of Science*. London: Kegan Paul.
 (1938). "Logical Foundations of the Unity of Science." In O. Neurath, R. Carnap, and C. W. Morris (eds.), *International Encyclopedia of Unified Science*. Chicago: Chicago University Press.
Carver, Terrell (1980). "Marx, Engels, and the Dialectic." *Political Studies* 28: 353–63.
 (1981). *Engels*. New York: Hill & Wang.
Cohen, G. A. (1978). *Karl Marx's Theory of History: A Defence*. Princeton, N.J.: Princeton University Press.
Engels, Friedrich (1939). *Anti-Dühring*. New York: International Publishers.
 (1940). *Dialectics of Nature*. New York: International Publishers.
Farr, James (1978). "Hume, Hermeneutics, and History: A 'Sympathetic' Account." *History and Theory* 17: 285–310.
 (1982). "Humean Explanations in the Moral Sciences." *Inquiry* 25: 57–80.
 (1983). "Marx No Empiricist." *Philosophy of the Social Sciences* 13: 465–72.
Fodor, Jerry (1974). "Special Sciences (Or: The Disunity of Science as a Working Hypothesis)." *Synthese* 28: 97–115.
Hempel, Carl (1965). *Aspects of Scientific Explanation*. New York: Free Press.
 (1969). "Logical Positivism and the Social Sciences." In Peter Achinstein and Stephen F. Barker (eds.), *The Legacy of Logical Positivism*. Baltimore: Johns Hopkins University Press.
Hudelson, Richard (1982). "Marx's Empiricism." *Philosophy of the Social Sciences* 12: 241–53.

Hume, David (1978). *A Treatise Concerning Human Nature.* Oxford: Oxford University Press.

Jordan, Z. A. (1967) *The Evolution of Dialectical Materialism.* London: Macmillan Press.

Joynt, C. B., and Nicholas Rescher (1961). "The Problem of Uniqueness in History." *History and Theory* 1: 150–62.

Kolakowski, Leszek (1968). *The Alienation of Reason: A History of Positivist Thought.* Garden City, N.Y.: Doubleday.

Marx, Karl (1963). *The Poverty of Philosophy.* New York: International Publishers.

(1964). *The Economic and Philosophic Manuscripts.* Edited by Dirk J. Struik. New York: International Publishers.

(1967). *Capital,* vols. I–III. Edited by Friedrich Engels. Translated by Samuel Moore and Edward Aveling. New York: International Publishers.

(1973). *Grundrisse.* Translated by Martin Nicolaus. New York: Random House (Vintage Books).

(1974). *The First International and After.* Edited by David Fernbach. New York: Random House (Vintage Books).

(1975). *Karl Marx: Texts on Method.* Translated and introduced by Terrell Carver. New York: Barnes and Noble Books.

Marx, Karl, and Friedrich Engels (1964–8). *Marx-Engels Werke.* vols. 1–39. Berlin: Dietz.

(1968). *Selected Works.* New York: International Publishers.

(1975). *Selected Correspondence.* Edited by S. W. Ryazanskaya. Translated by I. Lasker. Moscow: Progress Publishers.

McLellan, David (1975). *Karl Marx.* Harmondsworth: Penguin Books.

McMurtry, John (1978). *The Structure of Marx's World View.* Princeton, N.J.: Princeton University Press.

Mill, John Stuart (1965). *On the Logic of the Moral Sciences.* New York: Bobbs-Merrill.

Oppenheim, Paul, and Hilary Putnam (1958). "Unity of Science as a Working Hypothesis." *Minnesota Studies in the Philosophy of Science* 2: 3–36.

Popper, Karl (1966). *The Open Society and Its Enemies.* Princeton, N.J.: Princeton University Press.

Schmidt, Alfred (1971). *The Concept of Nature in Marx.* London: New Left Books.

Thomas, Paul (1976). "Marx and Science." *Political Studies* 24: 1–23.

Weber, Max (1975). *Roscher and Knies: The Logical Problem of Historical Economics.* New York: Free Press.

Wellmer, Albrecht (1971). *Critical Theory of Society.* New York: Herder & Herder.

Wolin, Sheldon (1960). *Politics and Vision.* Boston: Little, Brown.

CHAPTER 11

Marxian science and positivist politics

TERENCE BALL

To what extent, if any, do the more repressive features of Soviet political practice follow from Marx's own ostensibly scientific premises? "On the answer to this question," says Peter Singer, "our attitude to Marx must in large part rest. If the state created by Stalin can without distortion be traced back through Lenin to Marx's ideas, Marx stands condemned by his own offspring. If, however, these same offspring can be shown to be bastards fathered onto Marx's writings in violation of their letter and spirit, Marx can be cleared of the heaviest charge against his name" (1980: 62). My aim here is to at least partially exonerate Marx and to bring a bill of indictment against Engels. I shall argue that the missing link in the transition from classical Marxian theory to contemporary Soviet practice is to be found in Engels's philosophical labors. For it is from Engels's metascientific premises – his positivism, his materialist metaphysics, and his instrumentalist view of scientific theory's relation to political practice – that some of the more repressive features of Soviet practice follow as a conclusion. The moral of my argument, if correct, is that Hume was surely wrong in suggesting that the mistakes made by philosophers are merely foolish and not dangerous.

I shall begin by briefly delineating several features common to classical and contemporary positivism. Focusing particularly on its conception of causation and explanation via general laws, I argue that positivist metascience logically entails an instrumentalist conception of political practice; a cursory examination of the schemes of Saint-Simon and Comte will, I hope, make the connection clear. I

I am grateful to Robert Pippin and my coeditor for criticizing an earlier version of this essay.

then go on to consider Marx's conception of causation and explanation, arguing that his metascientific principles and presuppositions entail a decidedly nonpositivist vision of human emancipation and self-transformation. My third move is to argue that Engels's metascience is markedly more positivistic than Marx's, and resembles rather closely that of Saint-Simon and Comte. Engels's several substantive affinities with positivism – the stress on "scientific" socialism, the disinterested rule of scientific experts, the displacement of politics by rational administration, and even perhaps the sociolatrous "religion of humanity" – are, I believe, traceable to their shared metascientific premises. All are agreed that explanation in all sciences, natural or social, is causal explanation via universal laws. A knowledge of these laws permits one to produce or prevent certain outcomes simply by manipulating the relevant variables. And since it is the task of theory to supply such nomological knowledge, the relation of theory to practice is necessarily instrumental. Thus there is a logical link between positivist metascience and the view that social relations are best managed by technical experts and administrators. Saint-Simon, Comte, and Engels – and their Soviet successors – subscribed to this instrumentalist view of the relation of scientific theory to social and political practice; Marx, I argue, did not. I shall conclude by suggesting that it is Engels's positivist metascience, not Marx's, that undergirds and legitimizes social control of the modern Soviet sort.

I. POSITIVIST METASCIENCE AND THE IDEA OF SOCIAL CONTROL

What, if anything, connects modern logical positivism (or logical empiricism) with classical nineteenth-century positivism? All that they initially appear to share is the label "positivist." For what connection can there possibly be between the sober philosophers of science of our day and the fanciful utopians of an earlier time? Modern positivists confine their attention to epistemological and methodological questions; theirs are metalevel labors having no necessary connection with matters partisan or political. Just as metaethics is concerned with clarifying the conceptual foundations of ethical theory, saying nothing about actual moral conduct, so likewise is metascience concerned with clarifying the conceptual foundations of the natural and social sciences, saying nothing about their practical application. Against this compartmentalizing view I shall argue that such metalevel inquiries do in fact entail substantive social and political conclusions.

Positivists, both old and new, are alike in sharing at least three metascientific principles and presuppositions. The first of these, says Von Wright, "is methodological *monism,* or the idea of the unity of scientific method amidst the diversity of subject matter of scientific investigation." A second feature is "the view that the exact natural sciences, in particular mathematical physics, set a methodological ideal or standard which measures the degree of development and perfection of all the other sciences," including the social sciences. The third (and for our purposes most important) feature of positivism is its deductive-nomological or "covering-law" model, which views scientific explanation as broadly causal. Explanation "consists, more specifically, of the subsumption of individual cases under hypothetically assumed general laws of nature, including 'human nature' " (Von Wright 1971: 4).

It might be objected that no political conclusions could possibly follow from such abstract, metascientific principles. After all, a Hempel or a Nagel, unlike their nineteenth-century forebears, does not concoct "scientific" schemes for social reform and reorganization. Indeed they do not. But this does not mean that there is no connection. The connection between metascientific principles and political practice is concealed by the compartmentalizing curricular divisions of our day. The current division of philosophical and practical labor obscures an otherwise obvious fact: The political implications of positivist metascience are followed out, not by the philosophers of science themselves, but by their practical counterparts, viz., the social managers, planners, and policy scientists claiming to possess the requisite nomological knowledge of human behavior and social organization (Fay 1975: chaps. 1–3; MacIntyre 1981: chaps. 7–8). There are, as we shall see, good reasons, both logical and historical, for using the shorthand phrase, "positivist politics."

Before elaborating these reasons, however, one word of warning is perhaps in order. Although highly critical of positivism, I do not use the term as a swearword. Nor do I believe positivism in its various versions to be an unalloyed evil. Quite the contrary. Positivism was at one time a liberating doctrine. Critical of the ideologies of its day, it has become the dominant ideology of our own time. "The history of thought and culture," writes Isaiah Berlin, is "a changing pattern of great liberating ideas which inevitably turn into suffocating straightjackets" (1979: 159). The history of positivism surely bears this out.

The story begins with the promise of human power over nature; it ends with the peril of human power over other human beings. We could begin our story with Bacon's equating of knowledge and power, or with Hobbes's new science of politics, or perhaps with Hume's naturalist conception of the moral sciences. But I shall, for the sake of brevity, begin by considering the positivism of Saint-Simon and Comte.

Sounding remarkably like Hobbes and Hume, Saint-Simon holds that historically mutable "conjectural ideas" and imprecise, non-nomological political theories must now give way to a methodologically unified "positive" science modeled on the more mature natural sciences. The previously "interminable discussions" of political philosophers can at last be ended by the "certain proof" afforded by the method of the positive sciences. The strength of this method resides in its utter indifference toward its subject matter. The method applicable to any of the positive sciences, says Saint-Simon,

should be applicable to all . . . ; for this method is an instrument entirely independent of the objects to which it applies and changes nothing in their nature. Moreover, it is from the application of this method that every science derives its certainty: by this it becomes positive, and ceases to be a conjectural science; and this only happens after centuries of vagueness, error, and uncertainties.

Hitherto, the method of the sciences of observation has not been introduced into political questions; every man has imported his point of view, method of reasoning and judging, and hence there is not yet any precision in the answers or universality in the results. (1964: 39–40)

"The time has come," Saint-Simon proclaims, "when the infancy of the science [of man] should cease, and certainly it is desirable it should cease, for the troubles of the social order arise from obscurities in political theory" (1964: 40).

Unlike the obscure, contentious, and prescientific political theories of yesteryear, Saint-Simon's *science de l'homme* discloses "a form of government good in itself, founded on certain, absolute, universal principles, independent of time and place" – founded, in other words, on unvarying and universal laws of human behavior and social organization (1964: 39). Just as physical objects are subject to natural laws, so too are human beings, duly reconceptualized as material objects, subject to timeless laws. After all, he avers, "We are organic bodies; and it is by conceiving our social relations as physiological phenomena that I have arrived at the plan which I put forward." Believing that "domination should be proportionate to enlightenment," Saint-Simon calls for the management and coordi-

238

nation of social and economic relations by twenty-one enlightened experts (1964: 8–9, 77). The authority of this vanguard party of social technologists, *les industriels,* derives solely from their scientific expertise. Conversant with the heretofore hidden "general laws governing the organization of man," they are thus equipped to organize, coordinate, and manage the affairs of the nation (Iggers 1972: 27). Rightly applied, science will at last make society safe, secure, productive, and prosperous. Only science can save us from superstition and, ultimately, from ourselves.

The details of Saint-Simon's scheme for social reorganization do not concern me here. My aim is simply to underscore the conceptual connection between positivist metascience and positivist programs for social reorganization. As a philosophy of science, positivism proclaims the unity of scientific method amid a welter of different subject matters and advances the nomological or covering-law model of explanation as the only scientifically defensible one. As we have seen, this model maintains that explanation and prediction are symmetrical in that every explanation can in principle function as a prediction, and vice versa. To explain a phenomenon is to cite the causal antecedents required to produce or prevent it. "To grasp the cause of the order of events which has preceded us in the past is of great value," says Saint-Simon, "since it enables us to predict what will happen in the future" (1964: 22).

The ability to predict is, in principle, the ability to control. As Auguste Comte, the most ambitious and astute of the Saint-Simonians, pithily put it, *savoir pour prévoir, prévoir pour pouvoir* – "From science comes prevision; from prevision comes control." Knowledge, understood as the nomological knowledge of causes and effects, is indeed power. "There can be no doubt," Comte continues, "that man's study of nature must furnish the only basis of his action upon nature; for it is only by knowing the laws of phenomena, and thus being able to foresee them, that we can . . . set them to modify one another for our advantage. Our direct natural power over everything about us is extremely weak, and altogether disproportionate to our needs. Whenever we effect anything great it is through a knowledge of natural laws, by which we can set one agent to work upon another" (Comte 1975: 88). And, as with nature, so too with human society: "Social phenomena are subject to natural laws, admitting of rational prevision," and, hence, of purposive human intervention, manipulation, and control (1975: 223).

This is not, however, to be the control by the citizenry of their own affairs. Rather, "the elite of the human race," having "raise[d] politics to the rank of the positive sciences," must now be trusted to manage the affairs of the whole society (Comte 1975: 57). Not surprisingly, Comte denigrates the possibilities of political action by well-meaning but scientifically naive laymen or legislators. For "political action," he writes, "is limited by determinate laws, since, if social events were always exposed to disturbance by the accidental intervention of the legislator, human or divine, no scientific prevision of them would be possible" (1975: 223). But since such prevision is indeed possible, the Comtean conclusion is clear: Government is properly the business of scientific experts.

To this technology of social life nothing is more dangerous than critical reflection or, as Comte calls it, "the critical spirit." In the positivist polity the citizenry must be manipulated and made to believe that theirs is the best of all possible worlds; otherwise they might, in their misguided hubris, take it upon themselves to change the world in which they live, with disastrous results. To prevent such self-inflicted disaster, criticism must be discouraged; for "the critical spirit . . . is directly contrary to that which ought to reign in scientific politics" (Comte 1975: 54). In the positivist polity a little critical reflection is evidently a dangerous thing.

From this cursory account of classical positivism several conclusions can be derived. The first is that there is a logical link between positivist metascience and the political program of such prominent positivists as Saint-Simon and Comte. More specifically, the connection between metascientific ideals and political program can be traced to the obvious affinity between nomological explanation and expert manipulation: Those armed with the necessary nomological knowledge are presumably in a position (as others are not) to produce or prevent specific sorts of social and political outcomes. Politically speaking, then, positivism's second pertinent feature is its notion of "scientific politics," understood as rational administration by experts. Corresponding to this is, of course, a deep-seated distrust of democracy and even, indeed, of independent critical thinking by those whose behavior is presumably governed by natural laws. A third feature of positivism is its profoundly ahistorical character. Despite all their talk about the different "stages" of history, the early positivists – like their greater grandchildren, the logical positivists and logical empiricists of our day – are agreed that there are timeless, transhistorical "laws" of human behavior. Finally, positivist politics purports to be both nonpartisan and humane, its credo contained in the Saint-Simonian aphorism about the governance of men being replaced by the administration of things. The heretofore unnoticed irony in this ostensibly humane ideal is, of course, that it is predicated upon the supposition that men *are* "things." Conceived materialistically, as physical (or physiological) objects obeying natural laws, human beings are *ex hypothesi* capable of being controlled by nomologically knowledgeable experts. This, as we shall now see, is a far cry from Marx's critical vision of science as a subversive activity.

II. MARX'S METASCIENCE

Marx's contempt for positivism of the Comtean variety was both ill concealed and unqualified. Never one to mince words, he condemned the "shit positivism" (*Scheisspositivismus*) of Comte and vehemently denied ever "writing Comtist recipes for the kitchens of the future."[1] More tellingly, Marx insisted that the vaunted value neutrality and expertise of Comtean social engineers was a sham, inasmuch as they purport to stand above society, manipulating social variables and changing the circumstances of everyone except themselves. "The materialistic doctrine concerning the changing of circumstances and education," wrote Marx, "forgets that circumstances are changed by men and that the educator himself must be educated. This doctrine has therefore to divide society into two parts, one of which is superior to society" (Marx and Engel, 1968b: 28). This is, of course, impossible. For the social technician is also human, and is therefore "no abstract being squatting outside the world. Man is the world of man, the state, society" (Marx 1970: 131). Contra Comte, there can be no objective, asocial Archimedean point from which expert engineers may move people and manage societies.

In these respects Marx repudiated the central articles of the positivist faith. And yet, like the positivists, he makes much ado about "science," "laws," and the like. Does this not suggest that his metascience meshes rather closely with theirs? And if so, must not his politics, in the final analysis, also resemble theirs? These considerations have led some commentators to conclude that Marx was at the very least a "latent" or "special sort of positivist."[2] But if Farr and I are

---

[1] Marx to Engels, 7 July 1866, in Marx and Engels (1968a, vol. 31: 234), and gingerly mistranslated as "trashy positivism" in Marx and Engels (1975: 169). Contra Comtist "recipes," see Marx (1967: 17).

[2] See, respectively, Wellmer (1971: chap. 2) and Fay (1975: 25). This also appears to be G. A. Cohen's view (1978: 46).

correct in claiming that Marx was not a positivist – latent, special, or otherwise – how are we to understand all his talk about science and general laws?

Marx never spoke of a social physics or of "science" *simpliciter*, but of a *wirkliche Wissenschaft*. His English translators' renderings – "real science," or "true science" – are doubly misleading. First, to translate *Wissenschaft* as "science" is only partially satisfactory since by science we usually mean the stock of laws and theories of the natural sciences. *Wissenschaft*, by contrast, refers to any systematically organized body of knowledge, whether its object domain be nature (*Naturwissenschaften*), or human culture and society (*Geisteswissenschaften* or *Sozialwissenschaften*), or indeed any branch of human thought (vide Hegel's *Wissenschaft der Logik*). Still, this is a familiar and easily avoidable pitfall. Less familiar, and more difficult to comprehend, is the meaning of the adjective *wirklich*. In everday German it is not a particularly problematic term; it can, depending on context, mean real, true, genuine, or actual. But to translate *wirkliche Wissenschaft* as "real" or "true" science is to mistranslate it. Why?

The answer is that *wirklich*, as used by Marx, is a technical term with a very specific meaning and a distinctly Hegelian patrimony. In Hegel's philosophy, *wirklich* ("actual") is not synonymous with *reell* ("real" or "existent"). Something may be real without, however, being actual. As Walter Kaufmann explains, "It would prevent some confusion if Hegel's term *wirklich* were translated *actual*, seeing that he opposed it to *potential* rather than to *unreal* or *nonexistent*. An acorn, though certainly real enough in the usual sense of that word, is not, as Hegel used that term, *wirklich*. Only that is actual in Hegel's sense which fully realizes its own nature" (Kaufmann 1972: 37).[3]

---

[3] This goes some way toward dispelling the confusion surrounding Hegel's oft-quoted aphorism, "What is rational is actual and what is actual is rational" (*Was vernünftig ist, das ist wirklich; und was wirklich ist, das ist vernünftig*) (Hegel 1967: 10). In Hegel's day, as in ours, this remark was quoted by critics to prove that he was the rankest of reactionaries, a defender of and apologist for the Prussian police state. Was this state not, after all, real; and, since real, then rational? Engels's reaction was altogether typical. "Hegel's famous statement," he wrote, "was tangibly a sanctification of things that be, a philosophical benediction bestowed upon despotism, police government, Star Chamber proceedings and censorship" (Marx and Engels 1968b: 596–7). And in our own time Engels' interpretation is reiterated by Sir Karl Popper. (Marxology, like politics, evidently makes strange bedfellows.) "Hegel," writes Popper, "maintain[s] that everything that is reasonable must be real, and everything that is real

This sheds some light on Marx's idea of a *wirkliche Wissenschaft*. Briefly, Marx's "science" is distinguished from other sciences by having as its "object" the only self-actualizing *subject,* viz., human beings. It is through their labor that human beings transform themselves and their world, and in this way proceed to "actualize" their species' unique potential. Marx's conception of a "historical, social science" is more closely akin to Hegel's (and perhaps to Aristotle's) teleological conception than to Hobbes's and Hume's causalist conception (Gould 1978: chap. 3; Salkever 1981).

There is, however, an important contrast between Marx's and Hegel's conceptions of "actuality." For Hegel, as for Aristotle, a person, object, or process is actual (or fully actualized) when it reaches its immanent end or *telos.* Thus, the oak is the actuality (*Wirklichkeit*), end, or actualization (*Verwirklichung*) of the acorn. Every process of actualization (*Verwirklichungsprozess*) has its natural or innate end point. Once that point is reached, the story of its development – its history – comes to its natural end. For Marx, by contrast, there is no final terminus or *telos;* there is only the ongoing self-transformation of the human species through its members' "actual life process" (*wirklicher Lebensprozess*) of socially shared labor.[4]

Even communism is not, for Marx, the full actualization or final end point of human history. "Socialism," he writes in 1844, "is man's positive self-consciousness, no longer mediated through the annulment of religion, just as *actual life* (*wirkliches Leben*) is man's positive reality, no longer mediated through the annulment of private property, through communism." Indeed, communism, he continues, "is the position of the negation of the negation, and is hence the *actual* (*wirkliche*) phase necessary for the next stage of historical development in the process of human emancipation and rehabilitation. *Communism* is the necessary pattern and the dynamic principle of the immediate future, but communism as such is not the goal of human

---

must be reasonable." This boils down to the view that "everything that is now real or actual exists by necessity, and must be reasonable as well as good. (Particularly good is . . . the existing Prussian state.)" (Popper 1963, vol. II: 41). Had Engels and Popper bothered to consult Hegel's *Logic,* or the later editions of his *Encyclopaedia,* they would have seen firsthand Hegel's own repudiation of the views attributed to him. But they did not, and so the Hegel myth has not, even today, been laid to rest. See, further, Theunissen (1970) and Pippin (1979).

Marx and Engels (1968a, vol. 3: 26). In the English translation *wirklicher Lebensprozess* is misleadingly rendered as "real [sic] life-process" (Marx and Engels 1963a: 14).

development" (Marx 1964: 146). Two years later Marx put the point more succinctly: "Communism is for us not a stable state, an *ideal* to which reality will have to adjust itself. We call communism the *actual* movement (*wirkliche Bewegung*) which abolishes, preserves and transcends (*aufhebt*) the present state of things" (Marx and Engels 1963a: 26). Human history is the story of the species' self-actualizing activity. It is a story without end, without a terminal *Wirklichkeit*.

What Marx means by referring to his science as a *wirkliche Wissenschaft* can best be seen by briefly comparing and contrasting his view of scientific explanation with the standard covering-law account examined earlier. We should be careful not to allow superficial similarities of terminology to mislead us. For although Marx, like the positivists, speaks of causal generalizations or general laws (*allgemeine Gesetze*), his view of causal relations and explanatory laws differs radically from theirs.

The difference between Marx's conception of causation, law, and explanation and that of the positivists is ultimately an ontological one. Hume and the positivists are atomists; Marx subscribes to a "relational" social ontology (Ollman 1971: chaps. 2–3). And inasmuch as methodology recapitulates ontology, Marx's method of inquiry and explanation also differs radically from the standard positivist view. Consider, for example, Marx's non-Humean conception of causation. Marx averred that the agents or agencies whose activities are supposedly law governed cannot be separately identified in the way that Hume required causally related entities or events to be. It is impossible, on Marx's "relational" view, to identify one social entity without implicitly or explicitly referring to other, socially related entities; for it is their relations that make them what they are, that is, gives them the identities they have. Thus one cannot, for example, identify or describe the social role of husband without reference to the role of the wife, and to such social institutions as marriage and the family. Similarly, to identify A as a master is necessarily to imply that A has a slave, B, to do his bidding. These are socially defined roles, and this is a socially constituted relationship. "To be a slave or to be a citizen," says Marx, "are *social* determinations, the relationships of Man A and Man B. Man A is not [a master, nor B] a slave as such. He is a slave within society and because of it" (1973: 265). Similarly, to identify a as a capitalist is not only to identify the class A to which he belongs, but to imply the existence of another class B to which wage-laborers b_1, b_2, etc., belong, and to which a stands in a socially determinate relation (1973: 303).

Explanation presupposes description; that is, in order to explain a phenomenon by identifying its cause(s) you must first be able to describe it. Hume held that causes must be wholly identifiable and describable without any reference whatever to their effects, and vice versa. The entities figuring in any causal explanation must be onto-logically autonomous and capable of existing on their own. But this, Marx maintains, is precisely what socially constituted entities like masters and slaves cannot do; each lives and moves and has its being only in relation to the other, and both in relation to the "totality." Masters and master actions, and slaves and slave actions, simply cannot be individuated in the way that Hume required causes and effects to be.

Consider next the character of Marxian explanations and the sorts of "laws" that warrant them. Explanatory laws, as Marx understands them, are either artifacts or presuppositions of particular social formations and modes of production (1973: 450; 1967: 169, 574). The "laws" governing the behavior of capitalists vis-à-vis industrial wage laborers apply, not to any or all (possible) societies, but only to those having the historically specific social formation characteristic of the capitalist mode of production. Thus the laws of production described by Smith and Ricardo are indeed valid, and verified by the facts of capitalist production. But these laws are "universal" only within the historically restricted universe of capitalist production; outside that universe they are demonstrably false, or at any rate inapplicable (since the relevant social entities, concepts, categories, and relations exist only within that historically specific social formation). The laws of political economy are, in short, parasitic upon the particular social relations of production obtaining in capitalist society.

At least some of these laws amount to (and can be restated as) role-related requirements of rational action and identity maintenance within a particular social formation. Since this is rather a mouthful, an example might help to clarify the point. Consider the lawlike generalization that class A will tend to pay class B no more than is required to keep B working (Marx 1973: 90–94; 1967: 571–3). Under this generalization we can subsume the particular instances of a_1's relation to b_1, a_2's relation to b_2, etc. These instances can, in short, be "covered" by the generalization. Note, however, that this generalization does not describe a contingent causal relation of the Humean type. For not only are the entities not individualizable, but the generalization itself can be restated as a *rule* or *maxim of action* adopted by all rational members of class A. This maxim is not, however, freely or arbitrarily chosen; its adoption is, rather, *rationally required* of all *a*'s, so long as they remain members of *A*. In other words, maintaining their identity *as* members of *A* logically entails their treating members of *B* in the way described (and implicitly prescribed) by the "law." If *a* did not do so, he would no longer belong to *A;* for the kind of behavior prescribed by the maxim is itself partially definitive of membership in *A*. To speak of a capitalist who extracts no surplus value from labor would not be to speak of a *capitalist* at all, for the social relations constituting that role would be missing. In order to explain why *a* pays *b* a subsistence wage, we must first note that they belong to classes *A* and *B,* respectively; that one of the defining characteristics of *A*-type entities is their extraction of labor power from *B*-type entities; that the *point* of the relation is, from *A's* standpoint, to maximize surplus value; that maximizing surplus value requires that *A* minimize costs; and that one way of doing this is to reduce labor costs to a minimum. Hence the relative poverty of the proletariat.

In this cursory explanatory sketch we find at least some of the elements of Marx's account of exploitation (a fuller elaboration of which can be found in John Roemer's contribution to this volume; see chap. 9). I mention it only to underscore my point that Marxian explanations, far from conforming to the classic covering-law model, characteristically consist of showing what constraints are imposed by systems of social roles and relations ("structures," if you like) upon agents qua role bearers and rule followers in the course of maintaining their socially defined identities.[5] For Marx, any adequate explanation of social phenomena must begin with an understanding of the roles and relations, categories and concepts, that are constitutive of the social formation in which these phenomena are situated.

Marx's mode of explanation typically traces the "dialectic of concepts" that characterize and constitute historically specific social formations.[6] But since the conceptual relations constituting a social formation are not static but dynamic, the dialectic of concepts discloses internal contradictions, that is, logical lacunae within the social formation itself. Conceptual analysis of the Marxian variety leads logically to conceptual history, i.e., to an analysis of conceptual

---

[5] On the explanatory significance of social identity formation and maintenance, see Connolly (1981: chaps. 2, 3).

[6] Marx (1973: 109). Elster quite correctly characterizes *Capital I*, particularly its chapters on manufacture and machinery, as "*a conceptual analysis of the process of production*" (Elster 1980: 121; italics in original).

change. Such conceptual change is not without its causes; but these are not causes of the contingent Humean type, namely, causes linked to effects via transhistorical general laws. To speak of contradictions as causing social and conceptual and categorial change is, from the positivists' perspective, well-nigh nonsensical. For contradictions, they say, can exist only in our theoretical *account* of reality, not in that reality itself. But from the perspective of Marx's relational social ontology, there is nothing nonsensical in claiming contradictions to be real; for social reality is itself partially constituted by the concepts characteristic of a particular social formation (Ball 1983). Social life changes; concepts change; contradictions develop, are recognized, and are at least momentarily resolved, only to reveal new contradictions. The dialectic of concepts is itself the dialectic of social life.

Of course, explanations of social phenomena cannot be couched exclusively in terms of the participants' own reasons, intentions, purposes, and self-understandings. For one thing, people can, and often do, systematically misunderstand their own situation. For another, purposive actions often produce unintended consequences; hence, these consequences cannot be explained in terms of the agents' aims or intentions.[7] Yet, although the explanatory strategy of Marx's *wirkliche Wissenchaft* precludes reducing all explanations to particular human purposes, it nevertheless requires reference to that peculiarly human mode of purposive action, viz., labor. Indeed, it is the activity of laboring that provides the paradigm of causation central to his *wirkliche Wissenschaft*. By briefly examining this paradigm of the causal relation, and contrasting it with Hume's, we can detect crucial differences between Marx's critical-emancipatory conception of "science" and the positivists' nomological-manipulatory conception.

Hume took as his model of the causal connection the "external" relations of colliding billiard balls. Through all their repeated collisions the balls remain intact, their identity or "nature" unchanged. But human beings, in Marx's view, resemble Aristotle's acorns rather more than Hume's billiard balls; they change their identities as they actualize their species's unique potential. Unlike acorns, however,

---

7 Popper (1963, vol. II: 88) credits Marx for having criticized the "psychologistic" view that all social phenomena are ultimately explicable in terms of human motives and intentions. For an argument that some reference to intentions is required to explain unintended consequences, see Ball (1981) and the reply by Popper (1982).

human beings determine, by their own efforts (and not always intentionally), what they will become. Marx's model of the causal relation is the world-transforming activity of productive labor. In transforming an object into a humanly useful artifact or into a commodity having exchange value, the laborer not only transforms the object into a qualitatively different entity, but he transforms himself as well. The identity or nature of each is thereby transformed. "By acting on the external world and changing it," says Marx, "man changes his own nature," and, of course, the world-constituting objects upon which he acts and the fellow creatures with whom he interacts (1967: 177). And in so doing he transforms the social relations that constitute his very identity.

Timeless and universal "laws" of the positivist variety can, of course, apply only to entities whose identities are stable and unchanging. Yet this is precisely what, in Marx's view, human beings are *not*. The very essence of their species-being is their capacity for self-transformation through labor. Human beings are forever changing their own natures. It is just these subjects, whose very "nature" it is to transform nature itself and their own natures as well, who constitute themselves as the object of Marx's *wirkliche Wissenschaft*. On this score he is etymologically explicit. He connects the adjective *wirklich* and the verb *wirken* (to effect, do, work, produce, bring about, operate [on], transform). "The social formation and the State," wrote Marx, "are continually evolving out of the life-process of definite individuals, but of individuals, not as they may appear in their own or other people's imagination, but as they *actually* are; i.e., as they operate upon and transform reality [*wie sie wirklich sind, d.h. wie sie wirken*]."[8] Nor is this mere word-play; it constitutes a conceptual clue to an "actual connection." Socially organized labor is the medium of self-transformation, of human actualization. Labor is thus regarded by Marx as the "actual life-process" (*wirklicher Lebensprozess*) of the human species (1967: 14; 1973: 450). It is through his "actual practical activity" (*wirkliche praktische Tätigkeit*), carried on through the "actual relations" (*wirkliche Verhältnisse*) comprising spe-

---

[8] Marx (1967: 13; Marx and Engels 1968a, vol 3: 25). Avineri rightly notes the connection between *wirklich* and *wirken*, but he (a) mistranslates the former as "real," (b) overlooks its Hegelian origins and meaning, and (c) fails to connect it to Marx's idea of a *wirkliche Wissenschaft*. See Avineri (1970: 77).

cific social formations, that man comes to recognize himself as the active "actual subject" (*wirkliches Subjekt*), not the passive predicate, of the production process (Marx and Engels, 1968a, vol. 3: 20–45; vol. 13: 620–33). Speaking in the Sartrean idiom, we might say that man is his own project. "To be radical," Marx wrote in 1843, "is to grasp matters at the root. But for man the root is man himself" (1970: 137). We as a species live in a world of our own making and are indeed our own creation.

Creatures who specialize in changing their own natures can scarcely be subject to timeless universal laws. On this score Marx is again quite explicit. Such "laws" as are available to us, he emphasizes repeatedly, are *historical* laws of temporally restricted scope; they hold true only for situations, relations, and event-types of particular social formations and modes of production. Such historically restricted generalizations cannot qualify as general laws of a Humean or Hempelian sort (Ball 1972). Yet Marx insists that the "laws" of the "historical, social sciences," including his own *wirkliche Wissenschaft*, are of a definitely delimited historical character. Thus Marx's "laws," and indeed the very "science" they comprise, once again fail to fit the positivist mold.

For his ahistorical opponents Marx reserved his most pointed and exquisite barbs. Much of modern social science, he suggested, mistakes historically variable art or convention for nature, *nomos* for *physis*. Political economists, he thought, were peculiarly prone to such ahistorical assininity. "The economists," he wrote in a drolly mordant methodological aside,

have a singular manner of proceeding. There are for them only two kinds of institutions, those of art and those of nature. Feudal institutions are [in their view] artificial institutions. In this they resemble the theologians, who also establish two kinds of religion. Every religion but their own is an invention of men, while their own religion is an emanation from God. In saying that existing conditions – the conditions of bourgeois production – are natural, the economists give it to be understood that these are the relations in which wealth is created and the productive resources are developed conformably to the laws of nature. Thus these relations are themselves natural laws, independent of the influence of time. They are eternal laws which must always govern society. Thus there has been history, but there is no longer any. (1963: 120–1)

Marx's almost Heraclitean sense of historical mutability is especially evident in his discussion of the temporally delimited scope of all social-scientific laws, including his own. When he speaks of nat-

ural laws—of "the natural laws of capitalist production," for example—he refers, not to nature itself but to the "nature" of the
capitalist and of the mode of production over which he presumably
presides (Marx 1967: 8). But since, as we have already seen, his
nature or identity is itself constituted via a set of historically transitory social relations, there can be no transhistorical laws concerning
the behavior of capitalists. Capitalists have not always existed; nor
will they always exist. The roles and relations, concepts and categories (capitalist and proletarian, capital, wages, prices, and profits,
etc.) figuring in such laws are themselves part of an eminently mutable mode of production. Once this is recognized by the subjects
themselves, the historical and conventional character of these laws
will be brought up to the level of conscious awareness. "From the
moment that the bourgeois mode of production and the conditions
of production and distribution which correspond to it are recognized as *historical*," Marx insists, "the delusion of regarding them as
natural laws of production vanishes and the prospect opens up of a
new society, a new economic social formation, to which capitalism is
only the transition" (1968, vol. 3: 429). In short, unlike the laws of
the natural sciences, the laws of Marx's *wirkliche Wissenschaft* are quite
self-consciously framed as "historical laws" holding true "only for a
particular historical development" and whose "presuppositions . . .
by no means apply to all stages of society" (1963: 186; 1973: 606;
Marx and Engels 1975: 99).

The point of identifying such historical laws is less to *use* them
than to *change* and *overcome* them. The aim of Marx's critical "science" is to penetrate the veil of appearances and to reveal the conventional and therefore changeable social character of ostensibly
universal social-scientific laws; the purpose of political praxis is to
change the relations described by these laws, and in so doing to
invalidate those very laws. Far from being natural objects of the kind
analyzed and manipulated by the natural scientist, sentient human
subjects are potentially self-actualizing. And one of their potentials is
the ability to falsify or invalidate the very laws to which their actions
are supposedly subject. Hence the knowledge supplied by Marx's
wirkliche Wissenschaft is essentially subversive of, and antithetical to,
any notion of a nomologically based science of social control. This is
a far cry from the instrumentally useful nomological knowledge
prized by positivists. In this crucial respect Marx's science differs not
only from that of the positivists but also from that of his confidant
and collaborator, Friedrich Engels.

III. ENGELS'S POSITIVISM

Like his friend and sometime collaborator, Engels has often been called a positivist (see, e.g., Carver 1981: 51). If the label fails to fit Marx, it nevertheless fits Engels very well indeed. For Engels, in his later years at least, subscribed to all the tenets of positivism: the nomological or covering-law model of explanation; the methodological unity of all the sciences, natural *and* social; and, more radically still, the reductionist view that all sciences deal ultimately with the same object, viz., matter in motion. These metascientific presuppositions give rise in Engels's case, as in Saint-Simon's and Comte's, to an instrumentalist view of political practice. According to this positivist view, practice is essentially a matter of manipulating the relevant variables in order to obtain the desired results. These variables are ultimately reducible to (i.e., redescribable as) matter in motion; thus they are, in the final analysis, governed by the same set of immutable laws. Knowing these laws enables us to produce or prevent certain outcomes, thus making possible a technology of social life of the sort envisioned by Saint-Simon – and presumably practiced today in the Soviet Union.

A scientific theory, as Engels understands it, consists of an interconnected set of explanatory generalizations or laws. The adequacy of such a theory must, moreover, be assessed according to the amount of practical power it affords its possessor. An adequate theory in the natural sciences will provide laws giving us leverage and control over nature. "Our mastery of [nature]," Engels writes, "consists in the fact that we have the advantage over all other beings of being able to know and correctly apply its laws." And because "we are learning to understand these laws of nature more correctly, . . . we are more and more getting to know, and hence to control, even the more remote natural consequences of . . . our . . . productive activities" (Engels 1963: 292–3).

The same considerations apply in the social sphere. For social relations, no less than natural phenomena, are governed by general laws. To know these laws is, in principle, to be able to control the phenomena with which they deal. Consider, for example, the production of commodities in capitalist society. This, "like every other form of production, has its peculiar, inherent laws inseparable from it." As long as these laws remain unknown to producers, they lack control over production. These laws "work themselves out, therefore, independently of the producers, and in antagonism to them, as inexorable natural laws of their particular form of production. The product governs the producers" (Marx and Engels 1968b: 421). The results of such ignorance are ever more wrenching and destructive cycles of overproduction and underconsumption, boom and bust. A knowledge of the laws of production, rightly applied, would "become the most powerful lever of production itself." "Active social forces," wrote Engels, "work exactly like natural forces: blindly, forcibly, destructively so long as we do not understand, and reckon with them. But when once we understand them [and] grasp their action, their direction, their effects, it depends only upon ourselves to subject them more and more to our own will, and by means of them to reach our own ends." Once these underlying laws are understood, they can "be transformed from master demons into willing servants. The difference is as that between the destructive force of electricity in the lightning of the storm, and electricity under command in the telegraph and the voltaic arc; the difference between a conflagration, and fire working in the service of man" (Marx and Engels 1968b: 428–9). Engels's view of the relation between social theory and political practice is unreservedly and enthusiastically instrumentalist.

It might be objected that Engels, though clearly an instrumentalist, was no positivist. Consider, for example, his ostensibly nonpositivist emphasis on temporally restricted *historical* laws. Political economy (i.e., "the science of the laws governing the production and exchange of the material means of subsistence in human society") is "essentially a *historical* science. It deals with material that is constantly changing." And Engels, like Marx, writes of "laws which are valid for definite modes of production." Thus, for example, "anyone who attempted to bring Patagonia's political economy under the same laws which are operative in present-day England would produce only the most banal commonplaces" (Engels 1966: 163). On this much, at least, Marx and Engels were in full agreement.

But Engels then goes on to make a further reductionist move that Marx never made. Historical "laws," Engels avers, are ultimately reducible to more basic, transhistorical laws. Far from being irreducibly historical, "All knowledge of nature is knowledge of the eternal, the infinite, and hence, essentially absolute." Natural laws express timeless, transhistorical truths (1963: 326). Engels is not suggesting that "nature" is one thing, "society" another, or that there is an essential difference between the natural and the social sciences. On the contrary, he holds that "[human] history is only differentiated from natural history as the evolutionary process of *self-conscious* organisms" (1963: 164). As self-conscious organisms we are capable of discovering, and using for our own purposes, the timeless laws of natural and human existence: "We, with flesh, blood, and brain, belong to nature, and exist in its midst, and . . . all our mastery of it consists in the fact that we have the advantage over all other [non-self-conscious] beings of being able to know and correctly apply its laws" (1963: 292). The laws of nature are *pari passu* the laws of human history and society.

What then are these laws, and what is Engels's unified science? The laws are those governing matter in motion; the science is "dialectics." Dialectics, Engels wrote, is "the science of the most general laws of *all* motion. Therein is included that their laws must be equally valid for motion in nature and human history and for the motion of thought" (1963: 314). All "motion" – whether of physical movement, human action, or thought – is governed by the same set of laws. This is so, Engels emphasizes, because these laws deal ultimately with the same object, viz., matter in motion. This indeed is all that remains after all particular or accidental (i.e., historical) features are stripped from all phenomena, whether natural or social. Hence historical laws are merely "different phenomenal forms of the same universal motion." Penetrating beneath these historically transient forms we discover that "nothing remains as continually and universally valid except – *motion*" (1963: 242).[9]

It is through law-governed "motion" that matter is transformed. But this is not, contra Marx, the purposive-teleological motion of human labor. For in Engels's account, human thinking and purposes are themselves governed by "laws of thought," which are further reducible to the timeless laws of matter in motion. In the final analysis human purposes and projects count for nothing, for we inhabit an indifferent universe where "everything is equally transient, and wherein nothing is eternal but eternally changing, eternally moving matter, and the laws according to which it moves and changes." Amid this flux, says Engels, "we have the certainty that matter remains eternally the same in all its transformations, that none of its attributes can ever be lost, and therefore, also, that with the same iron necessity that will exterminate on the earth its highest crea-

---

9 Ironically, Engels's conception of "motion" parallels precisely that of Marx's *bête noire*, Proudhon. For Proudhon, "motion" (*le mouvement*) is "the basic fact" (*le fait primitif*) of natural and human existence," and "the laws of motion are alone eternal" (Proudhon 1946: 27, 30).

tion – the thinking mind – it must somewhere else and at another time again produce it" (1963: 24–5).

Human beings, their thoughts, and their actions are therefore, in the final analysis, physical objects whose "motion" is governed by the the same general laws governing the motion of all matter. In effect, Engels overcomes the subject–object dichotomy by conceiving of the human subject as a material object. In this respect he differs from Marx and agrees implicitly with the manipulative materialism of Saint-Simon. Engels even goes so far as to quote approvingly, though without acknowledgment, the Saint-Simonian slogan about the government of persons being replaced by the administration of things (Marx and Engels 1968b: 430). But of course the irony is that given Engel's presuppositions, this is a distinction without a difference. For in the end Engels, like Saint-Simon, cannot distinguish persons from things. Human beings *are* material things; the motions of both are governed by the same laws. Human thought and purposive activity, world-transforming labor and political praxis, are, for Engels, simply more complex forms of material motion.

Engels's ontological, metaphysical, and metascientific presuppositions – his materialism, his instrumentalism, his determinism ending in fatalism – are worlds away from Marx's own rather more "humanist" views.[10] But they are not, as we shall now see, so far from contemporary Soviet orthodoxy.

IV. SOVIET POSITIVISM AND POLITICS

I return, finally, to the question with which I began: To what extent does contemporary Soviet practice represent the application of Marxian theory? We are now in a better position to supply a sketchy

[10]   For further discussion of Marx's and Engels's differing views of nature and the natural and social sciences, see Schmidt (1971), Thomas (1976), and Ball (1979). Exactly why Engels departed from Marx's views must remain a matter of conjecture and speculation. David McLellan suggests that Engels's later positivist pronouncements were prompted primarily by considerations of political expediency (1977: 56–8). Was Marx aware of Engels's emergent positivism and, if so, did he concur? Engels claimed, though rather confusedly and contradictorily, that he did (see Carver, 1981: chap. 6). Yet we know that after Marx's death, his daughter Eleanor burned all of her father's notes and letters that might embarrass or offend Engels (Mayer 1934, vol. II: 356). Might these have contained criticism of his old friend's forays into the philosophy of science? We shall never know.

and provisional answer. That answer, briefly, is that "scientific" Soviet practice is in part predicated on and legitimated by metascientific principles and premises defended, not by Marx, but by Engels.[11]
This is not to say that Engels would necessarily agree with, or ap-
prove of, contemporary Soviet practice; it is entirely possible that he
would not. But mine is not a psychological claim belonging in some
sort of speculative or counterfactual biography. I wish instead to
defend a stronger, and essentially nonpsychological, claim, namely,
that there is a logical or conceptual connection between certain kinds
of metascientific principles and a particular conception of political
practice. If I am right, the former stands to the latter pretty much as
premises stand to conclusion. More specifically, a positivist and instrumentalist view of the social sciences is logically linked to a restricted range of possible political practices. Even though their specific form may vary, these practices, and the self-understandings of
their practitioners, characteristically partake of positivist views about
explanation and prediction, the aim of science, and the relation between scientific theory and social practice. So large and controversial
a claim cannot be fully defended here; so I shall, using the Soviet
Union as an illustration, sketch some of the arguments developed
more fully elsewhere.[12]

The harshness of Soviet repression has been explained in many
different ways. Some nonofficial explanations invoke the psycho-
pathic cruelty of Stalin himself, others the tsarist tradition to which
he and his successors were heir, whereas still others emphasize the
predominance of "oriental" over "occidental" values. The most common explanation offered by Soviet authorities is that the Soviet
Union is beset by external enemies and their willing or unwitting
internal allies and sympathizers. The former entails and legitimizes
an assertive, if not expansionist, foreign policy; the latter, an unre-
lenting suppression of all internal dissent, whatever the intentions
and affiliations of the dissidents.

However suspect or unsatisfactory, these explanations are not entirely without foundation. Doubtless they do help to explain (and not

---

[11]   And amplified and amended in certain respects by Lenin, whose part in
the story is omitted here for the sake of brevity.

[12]   In a study tentatively titled *Positivism, Politics, and Social Science*. Lest I be
suspected of harboring some visceral anti-Soviet bias, I should add that
this fuller version of my argument includes a similarly critical analysis of
the "science of politics" upon which the United States was founded in
1787.

infrequently to rationalize) certain Soviet practices, past and present. But they do not penetrate to the premises upon which Soviet society was first founded and is still today maintained and legitimated. Because that society purports to be built on "scientific" foundations, an understanding of its practices requires a prior understanding of its metascientific premises. (In a self-consciously "scientific" society, philosophy of science *is* political philosophy.)

These premises, far from being suppressed or hidden, are widely advertised and indeed form the basis of the self-understanding of Soviet officialdom. This self-understanding consists, at its simplest, of communist commonplaces in the form of a catechism. But, just as we would not take the Pledge of Allegiance to be a full and reasoned account of American self-understanding, neither should we take the ritual forms of other societies to provide an adequate account of theirs. Ideally, we should have at our disposal a reasonably complete, yet concise, catalogue or textbook in which fundamental philosophical premises are articulated and systematically linked to political conclusions. Fortunately, several such catalogues or textbooks are available. The most comprehensive of these is the standard Soviet "manual," *Fundamentals of Marxism-Leninism* (Kuusinen et al. 1963).

Billed in the preface to the second edition as "a useful educational aid, easy to understand while being at the same time a competent scientific exposition of the fundamentals of Marxism-Leninism as an integral science," the *Fundamentals* is not without its ambitions – or its pretensions. Not surprisingly, it dwells at considerable length on the "science" of dialectics and its immutable "laws." This science "devotes itself to the most general laws of all motion, change, and development. The universality of its laws lies in the fact that they operate in nature and society, and that thought itself is governed by them." Comtean to the core, the *Fundamentals* tells us that our knowledge of these "general laws of development makes it possible to analyze the past, to understand [the] present, and to foresee the future" (Kuusinen et al. 1963: 60). Genuine (i.e., scientific) knowledge is knowledge of what is necessary. "Necessity in nature and society is most completely revealed in its laws . . . [which] exist independently of man's will or desire." Then, continuing in a distinctly Humean vein, the *Fundamentals* defines a "law" as "a profound, essential, stable, and repeated connection or [regularity]" (1963: 66). Without such laws there can be no knowledge of causes. This is crucial, "since it is only by knowing the causes of phenomena that [they] can be scientifically explained, and only by knowing the laws governing phenomena that their further development can be predicted" (1963: 69). Under the heading of "Scientific Prevision," the Comtean connection becomes even more explicit. "In principle," the expert knowledge and application of sociohistorical laws do not differ from the aeronautical engineer's use of "the laws of aerodynamics" in designing and building aircraft capable of countering the law of gravity; it is merely a matter of rationally manipulating the relevant variables figuring in any causal relation. In this way, "people become masters of the relations between themselves and of the laws that control these relations" (1963: 69).

Such nomological knowledge is not, however, the property of the people per se but, in standard Saint-Simonian fashion, of a select band of experts: "Under socialism, this [nomological knowledge and prevision] finds expression primarily in the activity of the Marxist *party* in guiding economic life. The deeper *their* knowledge of the objective laws, . . . the more confidently the *party* and the *state* act." (Kuusinen 1963: 140; my italics). From this it follows that those who disagree with, or depart from, the party line are either pitifully ignorant or contemptibly counterrevolutionary. The former can in principle be rather readily enlightened; the latter require sterner measures.

It is just here that the manipulative materialism of the positivists, and of Engels in particular, is most directly transmitted into political practice. For if human beings are self-conscious organisms whose thoughts are subject to "laws of thought" that are in turn reducible to the "dialectical" laws of matter in motion, then dissident or deviant "thought" is *necessarily* symptomatic of deranged "matter." From this it follows that one can, if armed with a knowledge of the appropriate laws, rearrange such mental matter so as to obtain socially desirable "motions." For, after all, thought itself is ultimately explicable, in good Engelsian (and Saint-Simonian) fashion, in terms of matter in motion. Or, as Pavlov put it, "Mental activity is the result of the physiological activity of a definite brain mass." Thought, like behavior, "is a reflex action of . . . the whole organism, to one or another stimulus" (quoted in Kuusinen 1963: 37). It follows that deviant or dissident thoughts and actions, having physiochemical causes, can and indeed should be "corrected" through manipulative material means.

Given these assumptions, we should not be surprised that dissidents are regularly committed to asylums, where their "treatment" includes involuntary injections and electroshock "therapy." That Soviet psychiatrists (with some few notable – and noble – exceptions) speak in the medical idiom of the "illness," "treatment," and "recovery" of political "patients" is not so cynical or hypocritical as it might at first appear. For, given their Engelsian presuppositions, injections or shock treatments merely make instrumental use of the materially based "laws of thought." One might induce someone to change his belief by reasoning, remonstrating, or arguing with him. But this is inefficient and cumbersome, particularly if other, speedier means are available. Simple coercion, though effective in the short run, is rather crude and passé, and is in the long run likely to undermine the legitimacy of the entire enterprise. Hearts and minds must therefore be won by speedier and more surely "scientific" means.

For anyone armed with a materialist theory of the mind, as readers of the *Fundamentals* presumably are, there is no scientifically relevant difference between giving someone a reason and giving him an injection; both represent attempts to use the "laws of thought" to intervene in, and alter, the material "motions" of his mental processes. Reasons, on this view, are causes; but if by "reason" we refer to noninstrumental "reflection," we have fallen into the snare of philosophical idealism, which grants some degree of autonomy to critical human thought. If we are to avoid this snare we must conceive of reasons as efficient causes of a peculiarly inefficient sort. This is particularly evident in dealing with an obviously "deranged" dissident like Vladimir Bukovsky, who is himself armed with apparently well-reasoned criticisms of the Soviet regime. Anyone so reasonable *must* be insane, and therefore not to be reasoned with (see Bukovsky 1978).

With this we seem to have entered the world of Kafka, a world of non sequiturs in which conclusions have nothing to do with premises and contradiction is king. Upon closer inspection, however, we find a curious kind of consistency. If we look at the metascientific premises, we find that the political (and psychiatric) conclusions *do* follow from Engels's positivist premises. Mind is matter; thought is matter in motion; changing someone's mind, by whatever means – whether by reasoned argument or electroshock – is merely a question of altering the "motion" of such "matter." Given a choice between an inefficient and ineffective means and an efficient one, the rational instrumentalist will, of course, choose the latter; hence the practices described in Bloch and Reddaway's study of punitive psychiatry in the Soviet Union (Bloch and Reddaway 1977). These punitive practices, I have argued, follow from positivist premises. For dissidents are, after all, critics; and the "critical spirit," as Comte quite rightly remarked, "is directly contrary to that which ought to reign in scientific politics."

REFERENCES

Avineri, Shlomo (1970). *The Social and Political Thought of Karl Marx*. Cambridge: Cambridge University Press.
Ball, Terence (1972). "On 'Historical' Explanation." *Philosophy of the Social Sciences* 2: 181–92.
  (1979). "Marx and Darwin: A Reconsideration." *Political Theory* 7: 469–83.
  (1981). "Popper's Psychologism." *Philosophy of the Social Sciences* 11: 65–8.
  (1983). "Contradiction and Critique in Political Theory." In John S. Nelson (ed.), *What Should Political Theory Be Now?* Albany: State University of New York Press.
Berlin, Isaiah (1979). *Concepts and Categories*. New York: Viking Press.
Bloch, Sidney, and Peter Reddaway (1977). *Psychiatric Terror: How Soviet Psychiatry is Used to Suppress Dissent*. New York: Basic Books.
Bukovsky, Vladimir (1978). *To Build a Castle – My Life as a Dissenter*. Translated by M. Scammell. New York: Viking Press.
Carver, Terrell (1981). *Engels*. Oxford: Oxford University Press.
Cohen, G. A. (1978). *Karl Marx's Theory of History: A Defence*. Princeton, N.J.: Princeton University Press.
Comte, Auguste (1975). *Auguste Comte and Positivism: Selections From His Writings*. Edited by Gertrud Lenzer. New York: Harper & Row (Harper Torchbooks).
Connolly, William E. (1981). *Appearance and Reality in Politics*. Cambridge: Cambridge University Press.
Elster, Jon (1980). "Cohen on Marx's Theory of History." *Political Studies* 28: 121–8.
Engels, Friedrich (1963). *Dialectics of Nature*. New York: International Publishers.
  (1966). *Anti-Dühring*. New York: International Publishers.
Fay, Brian (1975). *Social Theory and Political Practice*. London: Allen & Unwin.
Gould, Carol C. (1978). *Marx's Social Ontology*. Cambridge, Mass.: MIT Press.
Hegel, G. W. F. (1967). *Philosophy of Right*. Translated by T. M. Knox. New York: Oxford University Press.
Iggers, Georg G., ed. and trans. (1972). *The Doctrine of Saint-Simon: An Exposition*. New York: Schocken Books.
Kaufmann, Walter (1972). "The Hegel Myth and its Method." In Alasdair MacIntyre (ed.), *Hegel: A Collection of Critical Essays*. Garden City, N.Y.: Doubleday (Anchor Books).
Kuusinen, O. V., chief author (1963). *Fundamentals of Marxism-Leninism*, 2d ed. Moscow: Foreign Languages Publishing House.
MacIntyre, Alasdair (1981). *After Virtue*. Notre Dame, Ind: University of Notre Dame Press.

Marx, Karl (1963). *The Poverty of Philosophy.* New York: International Publishers.

(1964). *Economic and Philosophic Manuscripts of 1844.* Translated by Martin Milligan. New York: International.

(1967). *Capital,* vol. I. New York: International.

(1968). *Theories of Surplus-Value.* 3 vols. Moscow: Progress Publishers.

(1970). *Critique of Hegel's "Philosophy of Right."* Translated by A. Jolin and J. O'Malley; edited and with an introduction and notes by J. O'Malley. Cambridge: Cambridge University Press.

(1973). *Grundrisse.* Translated by M. Nicolaus. Harmondsworth: Penguin Books.

Marx, Karl, and Friedrich Engels (1963). *The German Ideology.* New York: International Publishers.

(1968a). *Marx-Engels Werke.* 39 vols. Berlin: Dietz.

(1968b). *Selected Works.* New York: International Publishers.

(1975). *Selected Correspondence.* Moscow: Progress Publishers.

Mayer, Gustav (1934). *Friedrich Engels: Eine Biographie.* 2 vols. The Hague: Nijhoff.

McLellan, David (1977). *Engels.* London: Fontana.

Ollman, Bertell (1971). *Alienation: Marx's Conception of Man in Capitalist Society.* Cambridge: Cambridge University Press.

Pippin, Robert B. (1979). "The Rose and the Owl: Some Remarks on the Theory-Practice Problem in Hegel." *Independent Journal of Philosophy* 3: 7–16.

Popper, Karl R. (1963). *The Open Society and Its Enemies,* 4th rev. ed. 2 vols. New York: Harper & Row (Harper Torchbooks).

(1982). "Popper's Psychologism: A Reply to Ball." *Philosophy of the Social Sciences* 12: 69.

Proudhon, Pierre-Joseph (1946). *Philosophie du Progrès.* Paris: Marcel Rivière.

Saint-Simon, Henri Comte de (1964). *Social Organization, the Science of Man, and Other Writings.* Translated and edited by Felix Markham. New York: Harper Torchbooks.

Salkever, Stephen G. (1981). "Aristotle's Social Science." *Political Theory* 9: 479–508.

Schmidt, Alfred (1971). *The Concept of Nature in Marx.* Translated by B. Fowkes. London: New Left Books.

Singer, Peter (1980). "Dictator Marx?" *New York Review of Books* 25: 62–6.

Theunissen, Michael (1970). *Die Verwirklichung der Vernunft: Zur Theorie-Praxis Diskussion in Auschluss an Hegel. Philosophische Rundschau,* supp. 6. Tübingen: Mohr.

Thomas, Paul (1976). "Marx and Science." *Political Studies* 24: 1–23.

Von Wright, G. H. (1971). *Explanation and Understanding.* Ithaca, N.Y.: Cornell University Press.

Wellmer, Albrecht (1971). *Critical Theory of Society.* New York: Herder & Herder.

CHAPTER 12

Marxism as method

TERRELL CARVER

Karl Marx denied that he was a Marxist. Friedrich Engels repeated Marx's comment but failed to take his point. Indeed, it is now evident that Engels was the first Marxist, and it is increasingly accepted that he in some way invented Marxism (see, for example, Rubel 1981: 15–25). The way in which he did this is extraordinarily difficult to specify. This is because a great deal turns on Engels's use of certain categories to restate what, in his view, was said in the few works he wrote jointly with Marx and in works written by Marx alone. The effect of those categories was far from neutral with respect to the interpretation of Marx's intellectual and political activity.

Engels's categories affected the way in which Marx's purposes were presented to Marxists and to the world at large; they influenced the interpretation of the propositions Marx actually put forward in his writings, and even the apparent significance of his comments, asides, or particular words that have survived. That passages from Marx support Engels's views cannot merely be assumed. The burden of proof rests squarely on those who aim to establish the validity of Engels's interpretation of Marx's work.

In determining Marx's meaning, context is all-important. As early as 1859 Engels erected an interpretative context around Marx's work that we recognize today as characteristically Marxist rather than strictly true to his writings. Engels did this when he introduced the phrase "materialist conception of history" and the allegedly helpful consideration of the categories metaphysics, materialism, idealism, dialectic, interaction, contradiction, and reflection as a prolegomenon to Marx's achievements (see Carver 1981: 37–40, 45–78). With that context established the import of Marx's actual assertions in his own "guiding thread" of 1859 and elsewhere in his works was subtly changed (see Carver 1982: chaps. 1, 6).

Though Engels developed his interpretative approach in works published under his own name, it did not itself assume its final form, with all implications made clear, until the second preface to *Anti-Dühring* published in 1886 shortly after Marx's death. Once Engels got into his stride as chief interpreter and popularizer of Marx's works, the actual propositions from those works, whether dating from before or after 1859, took on an altered significance (see Carver 1983: passim). Indeed, in the new framework they sometimes became ambiguous or took on a different meaning altogether. Nothing sinister about Engels's intentions need be assumed – merely his dedication to an interpretative framework different from Marx's own presuppositions. Of course, Engels's view may have been a convenient one for political and personal reasons at the time (see McLellan 1977: 72–5), since his positivism (established in this volume by James Farr) put the certainty of science behind socialist politics. The consequences of this positivism, which no doubt were unintended consequences, have been traced in this volume by Terence Ball (chap. 11). But there is more to Engels's views than his positivism, and there is more in his intellectual relationship to Marx than mere divergence.

Within his interpretative framework Engels elevated method to a level of importance far higher than it assumed in any of Marx's very sparing comments on the subject. And within his account of Marx's allegedly "true" methodology, Engels placed particular emphasis on a debt to G. W. F. Hegel, which was but critically and very briefly acknowledged by Marx in private correspondence and contemporary political debate. Engels's emphasis on method over substance and his focus on Hegel's work as the sine qua non for coming to grips with Marx had important intellectual and political consequences. One of the effects of Engels's work has been to shift critical attention away from Marx's own propositions about capitalist society, which actually merit considerable scrutiny.

When Georg Lukács said that "orthodoxy" in Marxism refers exclusively to "*method*," he reinforced a tradition that began with the anonymous 1859 review by Engels of Marx's *A Contribution to the Critique of Political Economy* (Lukács 1971: 1). Despite the criticism (veiled and overt) of Engels's dialectics, Lukács's approach to Marx's work follows the path established in the 1859 review. Engels's text was reprinted in 1915 and 1920 in *Die Neue Zeit*, the socialist weekly founded by Karl Kautsky, and it was cited by Lukács in *History and*

Class Consciousness, though it is not identified in the English references (Lukács 1971: 14–15).

Engels's review contained assertions about history and political economy that cannot be supported; it misconstrued the opening sections of Marx's critique; and it offered an account of Marx's method that does not fit his work. Engels misrepresented Marx's enterprises as Hegelian in scope, and he initiated the now commonplace but profoundly unhelpful view that a study of Hegel is essential to an understanding of Marx.

I conclude that the traditional interpretation of Marx stemming from Engels is not merely incorrect. It is seriously misleading because it overrates the importance of Hegel, methodology, and dialectic in understanding Marx's work. Even if Engels's positivism were rejected, his framework might stand. That framework originated in his 1859 review, examined below. It bears extended examination because of what it says about how to read Marx, not merely because it puts forward certain views on what he said. These overall opinions on what Marx was doing and what we need to know in order to understand his project have become the commonplaces of Marx interpretation, whether pro- or anti-Marxist or conventionally academic. They need explication and require refutation, because they are untrue to Marx's project and to the substance of his work. For that reason, and that reason only, does what follows seem to lack charity for Engels. The charity he usually receives, which indeed he himself encouraged, is part of Engels's own view of the Marx-Engels relationship that accompanies and allegedly supports *his* version of Marx (see Carver 1983, passim).

I. ENGELS AND METHOD

In the 1859 review Engels introduced his readers to "scientific, independent *German economics*," which he described as new precisely because it "is grounded essentially upon the *materialist conception of history*," the first use of this phrase.[1] The "revolutionizing discovery" made by Marx in his 1859 *A Contribution to the Critique of Political Economy* was applicable, according to Engels, not merely to economics but to "all historical sciences," by which he presumably meant social

---

[1] All quotations, unless otherwise identified, are from Friedrich Engels, "Karl Marx: *A Contribution to the Critique of Political Economy*," in Marx and Engels (1962, vol. 1: 366–76).

sciences, since he claimed, somewhat mysteriously, that "all sciences which are not natural sciences are historical." (Physics and chemistry might count as nonhistorical natural sciences, unlike geology and natural history, which are historical, though not about society.)

Even more curiously Engels wrote that the basic proposition of this "materialist conception of history" is "so simple that it must be self-evident," though the intention of his remark was to ridicule those "bemused by idealist delusions." Idealism, of course, was Engels's target, though he did not explain precisely why he was attacking a philosophical doctrine as such. What he did claim is that the new outlook "runs directly counter to all idealism, even the most concealed." Evidently the "whole traditional mode of political reasoning," the "representatives of the bourgeoisie," the "French Socialists," and the "German vulgar-democratic vociferators," so Engels claimed, participated in idealist delusions and had, at the same time, "attempted to exploit [Marx's] new ideas in plagiaristic fashion." Idealism, it seems, had some of the same characteristics for Engels as the new outlook of "our party": Both made their marks, depending on circumstances, in the study and "on the political stage." Moreover, the new treatment of economics bore another important similarity to the great works of idealist philosophers. To develop this point Engels appealed explicitly to Hegel. The tradition that "you cannot understand Marx without reading Hegel" was first established in Engels's review.

Engels took Marx's mature critique of political economy (the first installment of which was the 1859 *Contribution*) to be "a systematic integration of the whole complex of economic science [and] . . . at the same time a criticism of the whole of economic literature." Then Engels implied that Hegel's work (without specifying any particular books at this stage) was the model for this kind of enterprise – the development of "a science in its own inner interconnection." Hegel's own approach to philosophy and logic might have served Engels in developing this alleged analogy with Marx, since Hegel's *Science of Logic,* for example, presents a systematic account of logic as a whole with Hegel's own critical improvements and philosophical gloss.

Instead of establishing his case with respect to Hegel and Marx, Engels rushed to ridicule the "official Hegelian school," which "had appropriated from the dialectic of the master only the manipulation of the simplest of all tricks." In Engels's view the achievements of Hegel were eclipsed by the "ludicrous clumsiness" of his followers, by the transformative criticism of Feuerbach (who "declared speculative conceptions untenable"), and by the development of the natural sciences in Germany, "which correspond to the powerful bourgeois development after 1848," not least in industry. Engels took the approach of natural scientists to be gratifyingly nonidealist but disappointingly un-Hegelian. Their "natural-scientific materialism" ("almost indistinguishable theoretically from that of the eighteenth century") unfortunately presupposed "fixed categories" rather than a "speculative tendency." A speculative tendency, as happily developed in idealist philosophy, was able to leap "the ditch which separates essence from appearance, cause from effect." Rather eccentrically Engels referred to the un-Hegelian belief in "fixed categories" (a view that concepts have fixed referents) as "the old metaphysics." This "metaphysics," according to Engels, was reflected in certain philosophical works of the last century or so, notably those by Christian Wolff, Ludwig Büchner, and Jakob Moleschott. It was also reflected in the works of "the bourgeois economists" (including, presumably, the English and French authorities who wrote long before 1848), as well as in contemporary works by Engels's fellow countrymen.

Engels dismissed this metaphysics of fixed categories as "annihilated theoretically by Kant and particularly by Hegel." Natural scientists, philosophers, and bourgeois economists had simply failed to grasp the philosophical (albeit idealist) critique of their "Wolffian-metaphysical method." Unsurprisingly, Engels's alternative to this alleged metaphysics of fixed categories was not Hegelianism itself, because it "was essentially idealistic," took "pure thinking as its start," and " 'came from nothing through nothing to nothing' " on its own admission (no reference was provided here by Engels). Yet logically Hegelianism was far superior to its rival, so Engels argued, though "absolutely unusable in its *available* form." One appropriate use for the logical content of Hegelianism was in solving this problem: "How was science to be treated?" Not, it should be noted, how was science to be *done?*

What Engels had in mind was the development of "a science in it own inner interconnection" on the model of Hegel's encyclopedic treatment of all the sciences of his time – philosophical, historical, and natural – using "the Hegelian method." Political economy was merely one of those sciences, and it had, indeed, been treated by Hegel himself in his *Philosophy of Right*. Thus Engels's notion of the project, for which a revised Hegelianism was the appropriate method, was an interpretative, recapitulatory, critical, systematic treatment of all knowledge (since, in his view and Hegel's, knowledge of any importance coincided with science conceived broadly, in the German manner, as *Wissenschaft*). Quite what the *point* of such an encyclopedic system would be was never demonstrated by Engels. He merely took it that this kind of exercise would in itself contribute to knowledge through its substantive criticism of work already done, through its systematic account of the interconnections between laws already formulated, and through the establishment of the principles that underlay the interconnections put forward in the work itself. Engels's view of the Marxian project was profoundly philosophical, even quasi-Hegelian.

The required revision of Hegelianism comprised, according to Engels, the development of "a world outlook more materialistic than *any* previous one [my italics]", including presumably previous materialisms! Quite how this was possible was not explained. Because of his concept of Marx's ultimate project (or at least the project allegedly implied by Marx's critical work on political economy), Engels assigned to Marx a method that was said to be of "hardly less importance" than the "revolutionizing discovery" that (in Marx's words) " 'the mode of production of material life conditions the social, political and intellectual life process in general.' " Engels referred to that proposition as part of "the basic, materialist outlook itself." Method, however, was his overriding concern.

II. ENGELS AND HISTORY

Once Engels had left aside (temporarily) the nature of Marx's "materialistic" revision of Hegel, he faced the daunting task of showing how Marx had extracted "from the Hegelian logic the kernel which comprises Hegel's real discoveries in this sphere, and to reconstruct the dialectical method." Once Marx had (in an unspecified way) "divested" Hegel's method "of its idealistic trappings" he had produced, so Engels claimed, not merely the method most suitable for developing "science in its own inner interconnection," he had revealed "the simple shape in which it [the dialectical method] becomes the only true form of development of thought." What this grand claim amounts to was not really specified, but I presume that it was the way in which all "science" was "to be treated."

However far Engels intended to push his claims concerning this revision of Hegelian method, it is clear that methodology for him was a substantial part of Marx's legacy, indeed the most substantial part, since its applicability was allegedly very wide or possibly even universal. The "basic materialist outlook itself" would hardly amount to much, on this view, were there no method that presupposes this "discovery" and actually leads to results.

Curiously, Engels fastened on the historical character of Hegel's thought as the methodological feature that distinguishes it "from that of all other philosophers," rather than Hegel's more obviously innovative method of developing a succession of concepts as in the *Phenomenology of Mind* (sense-certainty to absolute knowledge) and the *Science of Logic* (being to absolute idea). Those two Hegelian works were the ones used by Marx in his own methodological inquiries in the *Economic and Philosophical Manuscripts* of 1844 and the *Grundrisse* notebooks of 1857–8. Nonetheless, Engels was right in suggesting that Hegel's philosophy has a historical character in scope and method that set him apart from other philosophers:

Hegel – in contrast to his disciples – did not parade ignorance, but was one of the finest intellects of all time. He was the first who attempted to show a development, an inner coherence, in history; and while today much in his philosophy of history may seeem peculiar to us, yet the grandeur of his fundamental outlook is admirable even today, whether one makes comparison with his predecessors or, to be sure, with anyone who, since his time, has indulged in general reflections concerning history. Everywhere in his *Phenomenology, Esthetics, History of Philosophy,* this magnificent conception of history prevails, and everywhere the material is treated historically, in a definite, even if abstractly distorted, interconnection with history.

Engels commented further that for Hegel, world history was the "test" of his philosophical conception. "Test," however, implies a criterion by which a theory should be *adjusted,* and this was not Hegel's view. But Engels observed correctly that the "real content [of historical events] entered everywhere into the philosophy," though he added that "the real relation was inverted and stood on its head" – a mysterious reference by Engels to Hegels' idealism, I think, rather than to Hegel's alleged use of history as a test.

Actually, Hegel argued that his account of history relied on a purely philosophical proof that was *confirmed* by all actual events:

The only Thought which Philosophy brings with it to the contemplation of History, is the simple conception of *Reason;* that Reason is the Sovereign of the World; that the history of the world, therefore, presents us with a rational process. This conviction and intuition is a hypothesis in the domain of history as such. In that of Philosophy it is no hypothesis. It is there proved by speculative cognition, that Reason . . . is *Substance,* as well as *Infinite Power;* its own *Infinite Material* underlying all the natural and spiritual life which it originates, as also the *Infinite Form* – that which sets this Material in motion . . . While it is exclusively its own basis of existence, and absolute final aim, it is also the energizing power realizing this aim; developing it not only in the phenomena of the Natural, but also of the Spiritual Universe – the History of the World. That this "Idea" or "Reason" is the *True,* the *Eternal,* the absolutely *powerful* essence; that it reveals itself in the World, and that in that World nothing else is revealed but this and its honor and glory – is the thesis which, as we have said, has been proved in Philosophy, and is here regarded as demonstrated. (Hegel 1956: 9–10)

At the same time Hegel recognized the possible charge that he was merely applying a priori conceptions to history and thus forcing historical facts into a preconceived mold:

In this science it would seem as if Thought must be subordinate to what is given, to the realities of fact; that this is its basis and guide: while Philosophy dwells in the region of self-produced ideas, without reference to actuality. Approaching history thus prepossessed, Speculation might be expected to treat it as a mere passive material; and, so far from leaving it in its native truth, to force it into conformity with a tyrannous idea, and to construe it, as the phrase is "*a priori.*" But as it is the business of history simply to adopt into its records what is and has been, actual occurrences and transactions; and since it remains true to its character in proportion as it strictly adheres to its data, we seem to have in Philosophy, a process diametrically opposed to that of the historiographer. This contradiction, and the charge consequently brought against speculation, shall be explained and confuted. (Hegel 1956: 8–9)

Hegel offered this solution:

Universal history – as already demonstrated – shows the development of the consciousness of Freedom on the part of Spirit, and of the consequent realization of that Freedom. This development implies a gradation – a series of increasingly adequate expressions or manifestations of Freedom, which result from its Idea . . . To accomplish this, pre-supposes not only a disciplined faculty of abstraction, but an intimate acquaintance with the Idea. The investigator must be familiar *a priori* (if we like to call it so), with the whole circle of conceptions to which the principles in question belong – just as Keppler [sic] (to name the most illustrious example in this mode of philosophizing) must have been familiar *a priori* with ellipses, with cubes and squares, and with ideas of their relations, before he could discover, from the empirical data, those immortal "Laws" of his, which are none other than forms of thought pertaining to those classes of conceptions . . . It must be observed that in this very process of scientific *Understanding,* it is of importance that the essential should be distinguished and brought into relief in contrast with the so-called non-essential. But in order to render this possible, we must know what *is essential;* and that is – in view of the History of the World in general – the Consciousness of Freedom, and the phases which this consciousness assumes in developing itself. (Hegel 1956: 63–5)

Engels thus misinterpreted Hegel's use of history in relation to his philosophical conception because of his positivism (established in this volume by Ball and Farr). The philosophical conception was, in Hegel's eyes, proved already, and historical events merely confirmed this. But having introduced Hegel's conception of the relation between philosophy and history (albeit erroneously), Engels created two problems for himself: the substitution for Hegel's idealism of a "world outlook" that was "more materialistic," and the delineation of the correct relationship between historical events and their "reflection" in "abstract and theoretically consistent form" (as allegedly found in Marx's work). Once those problems were solved (to his satisfaction), Engels would then progress in his 1859 review to the method used by Marx. This was the method, so Engels claimed, of dealing scientifically, that is, materialistically, logically, and dialectically, with a given historical "relation."

III. ENGELS AND MATERIALISM

By remarking that in Hegel's idealist philosophy "the real relation was inverted and stood on its head," Engels the "materialist" made himself less than clear, since he failed to specify the terms of the "relation" and the way they were related so that we could know what was "inverted" and what was "stood on its head." Within the 1859 review Engels sometimes seems to have meant by "materialist conception" a view that social production is crucial when people (who are both conscious *and* material) make their own history. But he also referred in the same text to the new "materialist conception" as one in which "it is demonstrated in each particular case how every time the action originated from direct material impulses." Quite what "material" was intended to mean in the latter context is far from clear, but the juxtapositon of "material impulses" with "the phrases that accompanied the action" suggests something rather more like the matter–consciousness dichotomy generally accepted by natural scientists and in particular adopted by positivists than the thesis in *The German Ideology* that "consciousness can never be anything else than conscious being, and the being of men is their actual life-process." In *The German Ideology* the matter–consciousness dichotomy was itself presented as ideological, insofar as an "idealist" realm of consciousness (a "heaven") independent of men's real lives was postulated (Marx and Engels 1976, vol. 5: 36).

Although Engels certainly rejected idealism, his works after 1859 were *ambiguous* because of his failure to define precisely the "materialist" nature of the "materialist conception of history." He employed the matter–consciousness dichotomy as found in contemporary natural science (which hypothesized that consciousness was ultimately a material phenomenon) *and* the "new" materialism of *The German Ideology*, which related events to man's productive development in history. This is the inconsistency noted by Farr in this volume (chap. 10).

But in his new materialism Marx did not take up a position on the matter–consciousness dichotomy, since what was important for him was the *relationship* between social being and consciousness, not their ultimate constituents, material or otherwise. In any case social being and consciousness were never defined dichotomously by Marx, since social being did not exclude ideas (used in practice) and consciousness (i.e., mere ideas) did not exclude a possible connection sooner or later with practical activities (see Carver 1982: chaps. 4, 5).

Contrary to Marx's discretion Engels introduced an ontological issue into his account of the new outlook that was not a problem in *The German Ideology* or in Marx's other works, namely, the implications of the matter–consciousness debate in natural science for the study of history and contemporary society. In what way could social events be linked to "material impulses," which are, following the matter–consciousness dichotomy, exclusive of "phrases" or "consciousness" or "ideas"? Engels never resolved this problem in his successive accounts, begun in 1859, of "the basic materialist outlook."

Marx's "new" materialism (as he identified it in the *Theses on Feuerbach*) had in fact sidestepped the matter–consciousness dichotomy in natural science by making it irrelevant to his theories of society and social change. In opposition to "all previous materialism," which accepted a matter–consciousness dichotomy, Marx took as a first proposition "the mode of production of material life," that is, what *people* do in "social production" (Marx and Engels 1962, vol. 1: 362–3). By implying, contrarily, that the matter–consciousness dichotomy *was* relevant in interpreting Marx's work as materialist, Engels unnecessarily identified Marx's theories with a view in natural science that material and conscious phenomena are or merely appear to be ultimately distinct, and did nothing to clarify the ontological relationship between the two categories anyway, save to reject an idealist view that matter is in some sense an emanation of consciousness.

IV. ENGELS AND THE CRITIQUE OF POLITICAL ECONOMY

The "materialist outlook" itself was in any case subordinated by Engels to "the method which forms the foundation of Marx's criticism of political economy." This emerged, in Engels's account, as the "logical method," and it, like the "materialist outlook," also derived from Hegel's "magnificent conception of history": "[Hegel's] epoch-making conception of history was the direct theoretical premise for the new materialist outlook, and this alone provided a connecting point for the logical method, too." The logical method arose from Engels's consideration of the relationship between Hegel's "thoughts" and the "development of world history." Hegel had used history, so Engels claimed, as the "test" of his philosophy by showing "a development, an inner coherence, in history." Engels praised this method very highly in the 1859 text, while implying that the "inner coherence" identified by Hegel could not be the correct one, because his idealist view that history was the realization of an *idea*, namely, freedom, was in Engels's opinion quite erroneous. The logical method, however, was "simple" (Engels's word) and was (after some nugatory discussion) "nothing else but the historical method, only divested of its historical form and disturbing fortuities." That method was applied by Marx to the "criticism of economics," but was not by any means limited to such a project, in Engels's view, since it was, after all, "the only true form of development of thought."

How then were "disturbing fortuities" to be sorted out from the "historical course" of economic development in "theoretically consistent form"? According to the method, a reflection was "corrected according to laws furnished by the real course of history itself." Engels explained that the corrected reflection revealed "each factor" in historical succession at "the point of development of its full maturity, of its classic form." But that account linking mature "factors" together was to be obtained by using "laws" that were nowhere defined in the 1859 text. And no "laws" were mentioned by Marx in his 1859 Preface.

In support of his view Engels made two sweeping claims about history and political economy as follows:

1. "In history . . . development as a whole proceeds from the most simple to the more complex relations."
2. The "literary reflection" of history, including "the historical development of the literature of political economy", also develops "from the most simple to the more complex relations."

For neither of those claims was any evidence whatsoever offered by Engels. The alleged facts in (1) and (2), however, were the ones that were supposed to form the "test" (as in Engels's view of Hegel's method) that in a logical development of concepts (in this case the "economic categories"), it is "the *actual* development that is followed." In that way Engels thought he had justified the presentation of "the economic categories as a whole . . . in the same sequence as in the logical development."

It is possible that in formulating this argument Engels had in mind certain passages from the "general introduction," which Marx told his readers was scrapped in favor of the 1859 Preface to the *Contribution* (Marx and Engels 1962, vol. 1: 361). In his posthumously published "general introduction" of 1857 Marx commented:

The economists of the seventeenth century, for example, always begin with the living whole, the population, the nation, the state, more states etc.; they always end, however, in such a way that they discover a few determining, abstract, universal relationships, like division of labor, money, value etc., through analysis. As soon as those individual moments were more or less fixed and abstracted, the economic systems which ascend from the simple [moment], such as labor, division of labor, need [and] exchange-value, up to the state, exchange among nations and the world market, began [to be formulated]. The latter is obviously the scientifically correct method. (Carver 1975: 72)

Although we do not know whether Engels actually read this text, or had parts of it communicated to him verbally while Marx was at work, there is no reason to rule this out. But when Engels fastened on his "logical method" as scientifically correct because it embodied a historical sequence from simple categories to complex ones, he did so in defiance of Marx's conclusion to his discussion in the 1857 general introduction. In that text Marx queried his initial view on scientifc method thoroughly: "However, do these simple categories not have an independent historical or natural existence before the more concrete categories? That depends" (Carver 1975: 74). His crucial example was "labor," which "appears to be a quite simple category." Also, Marx continued, "the conception of it in that universality – as labor generally – is very old." Nevertheless, he concluded, labor is "a modern category in the same way as the relations which produce that simple abstraction" (Carver 1975: 76). From his investigation of labor Marx generalized as follows:

That example of labor shows strikingly how the most abstract categories themselves are, in the determinateness of that abstraction itself – in spite of their validity just on account of being abstractions – just as much the product of historical relations, and how they possess their full validity only for and within those relations. (Carver 1975: 78).

And about the implications for his own critical work on political economy Marx was unequivocal:

Therefore it would be impracticable and false to let the economic categories succeed one another in the sequence in which they were the determining categories historically. Rather, their order of succession is determined by the relationship which they have to one another in modern bourgeois society, and that relationship is exactly the reverse of that which appears as their succession in accordance with nature or that which corresponds to the order of their historical development. We are not dealing with the relation [to each other] which the economic relations take up in the sequence of different forms of society . . . Rather [we are dealing] with their arrangement within modern bourgeois society. (Carver 1975: 81)

Marx did not hold the view that the historical development of an economic category was necessarily a progression from simplicity to complexity, nor did he think that a historical progression of categories (whether according to their first appearance or their importance in successive economic systems) was the proper model for his theoretical presentation. Rather he proposed to examine the economic categories that "constitute the inner arrangement of bourgeois society" according to a plan that identified capital as "the economic power of bourgeois society, the power ruling over everything." For that reason, he argued, "it must form the starting point." And to explain capital, he began with the commodity and money (Carver 1975: 81–2, 134–6, 151–3).

Although Marx observed a certain necessary correspondence between logical and historical development, this was very much a subordinate point to the main argument rather than his organizing principle. In his view there was never any possibility that the sequence commodity–money–capital could have appeared historically in some other order, since another order would be logically impossible. How could capital *be* what it is in a society without money, or money *be* money in a society without commodity production? Marx's starting point in his critique of political economy was never identified with the presumed historical origin of capitalist society, and he only occasionally amplified his abstract "arrangement" of the elements of capitalist society with historical asides (see, e.g., Marx 1971: 50–1).

When Engels wrote that the "chain of thought must begin with the same thing with which this history begins," he ran directly counter to Marx. And he misconstrued Marx's abstract arrangement of the essential elements of "the economic conditions of life [in] . . . modern bourgeois society" because of his unwarranted assumption that historical development advances from the most simple to the more complex relations. In fact, Marx advised his readers in the 1859

Preface to "be resolved to ascend from the particular to the general" as he moved from the commodity to money to capital (Marx and Engels 1962, vol. 1: 361).

Proceeding then from what he took to be the "first and simplest" relation in history, Engels discerned a "dialectical method" in Marx's work: "In this method we proceed from the first and simplest relation that historically and in fact confronts us; here, therefore, from the first economic relation to be found. We analyse this relation."

The recommended method was extraordinarily abstract and wholly without justification:

> Being a *relation* of itself implies that it has two sides, *related to each other*. Each of these sides is considered by itself, which brings us to the way in which they behave to each other, their interaction. Contradictions will result which demand a solution. But as we are not considering here an abstract process of thought taking place solely in our heads, but a real process which actually took place at some particular time or is still taking place, these contradictions, too, will have developed in practice and will probably have found their solution. We shall trace the nature of this solution, and shall discover that it has been brought about by the establishment of a new relation whose two opposite sides we shall now have to develop, and so on.

Engels then praised Marx's presentation of the commodity, not merely as a successful result of the dialectical method he had just outlined, but as the correct solution to certain problems posed in political economy:

> If now we consider commodities from their various aspects, commodities, to be sure, in their complete development and not as they first laboriously developed in the primitive barter between two primitive communities, they present themselves to us from the two points of view of use value and exchange value, and here we at once enter the sphere of economic dispute.

Although we might go on to agree with Engels that Marx's treatment of the commodity was "as superior to the old, shallow, garrulous metaphysical method [of Adam Smith and others] as the railway is to the means of transport of the Middle Ages," it is difficult to see that Marx's procedure was successfully epitomized in Engels's schematic account, in which a commodity was said to be a *relation* that was then assumed to have two sides (use value and exchange value) that interact, producing contradiction and solution (the commodity as "immediate unity of both"). Marx's initial move in his 1859 *Contribution*, as in *Capital*, was to consider the "wealth of bourgeois society," a *particular* "unit" of which was the "commodity." He then clearly identified a commodity as a "thing" and an "object." For Marx commodities were, of course, objects to which people *have* a relation; a commodity is an object "of human wants, a means of existence" (Marx 1971: 27).

Engels severely confused the purposely abstract character of Marx's presentation by introducing an irrelevant distinction between producer and consumer of commodities at this early stage of explication. The distinction was not present at all in Marx's opening chapter, because any given person might be both or either with respect to the commodity as a value-in-exchange, though not of course to any particular commodity at any one time. Otherwise, on Marx's definition, the object in question would not *be* a commodity. Inaccurately, then, Engels described something as a commodity when "a *relation* between two persons or commodities attaches to the *thing*, the product, the relation between producer and consumer who are no longer united in the same person." But mere disjuncture between producer and consumer was never, for Marx, the sufficient condition for commodity exchange. Engels concluded, sweepingly, that "economics deals not with things but with relations between persons." Moreover, those "relations are . . . always *attached to things* and *appear as things*," though he did not explain how exactly a relation may be "attached" to a thing.

Marx's careful analysis, which began with things and the relations in which people stand to them, has a clarity that quite escaped Engels. This makes it difficult to conclude with Engels that it was the proposition about history, political economy, and commodities that he had outlined in the 1859 review that enabled Marx to make "the most difficult questions so simple and clear that now even the bourgeois economists will be able to grasp them." If Marx had in any sense accomplished that, it was not for the reasons given by Engels.

In his closing paragraph Engels returned to his theme that the theoretical and historical aspects of Marx's criticism of political economy proceeded in "constant contact," something that was not true of Marx's account of the commodity in the *Contribution*, even taken in conjunction with the "Historical Notes on the Analysis of Commodities," in which he gave an overt, critical treatment of the history of political economy later dropped from the main text and squeezed into the footnotes of *Capital*. Engels's apparatus of historical and literary development was simply an inaccurate reflection of the true state of affairs in history, the literature of political economy, and Marx's critique. His "dialectical" method – imputing an ontology of relations, and a specific methodology of "sides," "interaction," "contradiction," and "solution" to Marx – was erroneous in its presuppositions about the plan of Marx's presentation and unhelpful in its formulation of an overly abstract and allegedly universal procedure.

Engels's preoccupation with method corresponds almost perfectly to Sheldon Wolin's "methodism," insofar as Wolin defines the idea of method as "faithfully following a prescribed sequence of mental steps," finding a "short-cut," sifting and ordering all "inherited knowledge and experience," and promising not only the use but also the progression of knowledge (Wolin 1969: 1066–7). Marx's own methodological claims were profoundly modest, and the methods he employed, even when characterized by him (very rarely) as dialectical, were irreducible to propositions and procedures of the sort offered by Engels.

V. MARX AND METHOD

Marx's actual method in dealing with political economy was eclectic and very complex. Farr rightly refers to him as a methodological pluralist (chap. 10, this volume). Marx used classical and Hegelian logic, and the techniques of mathematical, sociological, economic, historical, and political analysis. These came into play when they were appropriate to the matter at hand. This eclectic method included a notion of dialectic as the specification of conflictual, developmental factors in analyzing social phenomena, and we know that Marx found this helpful in dealing, for example, with the concepts of money and profit (see Carver 1976: 60–8). But neither "dialectic" nor any other methodological formula represents a "master key" to Marx's work; he rightly denied that such master keys were of any use to anyone:

Thus events strikingly analogous but taking place in different historical surroundings led to totally different results. By studying each of these forms of evolution separately and then comparing them one can easily find the clue to this phenomenon, but one will never arrive there by using as one's master-key a general historico-philosophical theory, the supreme virtue of which consists in being super-historical. (Marx and Engels 1965: 313)

In particular, Engels's 1859 presentation of Marx's method failed to do justice to Marx's work, since Engels gave the reader the impression that Marx perceived idealism as "inverted" (without explaining what this means); that he ordered economic concepts from the simple to the complex as history (allegedly) dictates; and that he treated things and objects as relations in a ready-made "dialectical" fashion, that is, "sides," "interaction," "contradiction," "solution."

Marxism as method

When introducing Marx's critique of political economy Engels seemed to reminisce about the days of *The German Ideology* – the battles against idealism. But he adopted the Hegelian notion that science as *Wissenschaft,* including history, can be treated in its "inner interconnection," and he projected that encyclopedic preoccupation (erroneously) onto Marx. He further assumed (unnecessarily) that Marx's new materialism was predicated on the materialism of natural science; hence he attributed to Marx a social science that (ambiguously) did and did not presuppose the matter–consciousness dichotomy, Moreover, to Marx he assigned (fictitiously) a plan and "dialectical method" that he never employed.

But since Marx was eager for any publicity at all he need not have taken the import of Engels's remarks too seriously. He could hardly have imagined that Engels's all too inadequate views would establish a tradition that almost eclipsed his own results and even his project itself (see Carver 1981: 1–2, 67–8, 74–8). Significantly, Marx was far more concerned to get on with the substance of his work than to explain his methodology, a project briefly mentioned in a letter to Engels of 16 January 1858 and never carried out. Thus it was the 1859 review by Engels that set the pattern for substantive and methodological inquiry for much of the Marxist tradition and for non-Marxist accounts. Obviously I think this a pity. The sooner the tradition realigns itself with Marx, the better. Moreover, the substance and methodology of Marx's work have a great deal to offer social inquiry generally.

We should beware of claims that Marxism is ultimately or essentially a *method,* particularly if the method implied is the one that descends from Engels's review and directs us with leaden inevitability to Hegel. Although Marx was ready (in an afterword to *Capital* and very occasionally in correspondence) to acknowledge a debt to Hegel, the depth of his distaste for a prolix, idealist prolegomenon to his own works can hardly be imagined. A victory of the Hegelianizing Engels over the meticulously investigative Marx would be appalling.

It seems to me rather too early to retreat from the propositions of Marx's 1859 Preface and *Capital* – and indeed from the activity of making such propositions, if those seem inadequate – to an engagement with methodology as such, despite the brave words from Lukács about practical political results (Lukács 1971: 23). Marx's methodology emerged in the course of his critical work on capitalist society, and I think his example a good one.

Lukács suggested that even if "every one of Marx's individual theses" had been disproved, orthodox Marxism, because it is exclusively a *method,* would emerge unscathed. Every one of Marx's individual theses may indeed be false, but method provides a poor refuge. He did not really have one method (however broadly conceived) that is applicable to all problems in social analysis, never mind the grander schemes propounded in the philosophy of dialectical materialism. In fact, it is difficult to believe that he had a method that was wholly independent of the problems he wanted to solve; it does not seem unreasonable to believe that to some extent his methods were entailed by the problems he took on, and that new problems would, on this model, mean new methods. Why not? The contrary view, that Marx had *one* method to leave us and that it is more important than his substantive propositions and somehow guaranteed to work on problems he never attempted, originated with Engels. His strong suit was never Marx's lifework, the critique of political economy, in which Marx expected to find the "anatomy of bourgeois society," the society in which we live. The promised third section of Engels's 1859 review, on Marx's "economic" discoveries, was unsurprisingly never written.

In writing his 1859 review Engels did not merely invent the characteristic categories of Marxism in glossing the generalizations of the 1859 Preface; he deflected virtually everyone's view of Marx's work itself by presenting it as a Hegelian-style exercise, philosophical in character and peculiarly dedicated to philosophical issues for their own sake; he assumed that Marx had *a* methodology and elevated it in importance above his substantive propositions; and he specified a unitary, "dialectical" method that was miles away from Marx's painstaking eclecticism.

Engels's spurious science and factitious method are distractions from Marx's substantive analysis, which might be of help to us. Even if it were not, Marx's vision of what constitutes a *problem* in society and his eclectic approach to method would stand us in good stead. On both those points the influence of Engels has not merely been distracting; his Hegelian pretensions and methodological monism have for many years obscured Marx's achievements.

REFERENCES

Carver, Terrell, trans. and ed. (1975). *Karl Marx: Texts on Method.* Oxford: Blackwell Publisher.

(1976). "Marx–and Hegel's *Logic.*" *Political Studies* 24: 57–68.

(1981). *Engels.* Oxford: Oxford University Press.

(1982). *Marx's Social Theory.* Oxford: Oxford University Press.

(1983). *Marx and Engels: The Intellectual Relationship.* Brighton: Wheatsheaf (Harvester Press).

Hegel, G. W. F. (1956). *The Philosophy of History.* Translated by J. Sibree. New York: Dover.

Lukács, Georg (1971). *History and Class Consciousness.* Translated by Rodney Livingstone. London: Merlin.

McLellan, David (1977). *Engels.* Glasgow: Collins.

Marx, Karl (1971). *A Contribution to the Critique of Political Economy.* Translated by S. W. Ryazanskaya. London: Lawrence & Wishart.

Marx, Karl, and Frederick Engels (1962). *Selected Works in Two Volumes.* Moscow: Foreign Languages Publishing House.

(1965). *Selected Correspondence,* 2d ed. Translated by I. Lasker. Moscow: Progress.

(1976). *Collected Works,* vol. 5. London: Lawrence & Wishart.

Rubel, Maximilien (1981). *Rubel on Karl Marx: Five Essays.* Cambridge: Cambridge University Press.

Wolin, Sheldon (1969). "Political Theory as a Vocation." *American Political Science Review* 63: 1062–82.

Name index

Adorno, T., 2
Althusser, L., 2
Amott, T., 137–8
Anderson, P., 2
Annenkov, P. V., 79
Archimedes, 176–7, 180, 241
Aristotle, 115, 123, 155–77, 180–1, 243, 247

Babeuf, G., 163
Bacon, F., 238
Barry, B., 17
Bell, D., 143, 149
Bentham, J., 145, 150, 156, 163
Berlin, I., 237
Boyd, R., 176
Braverman, H., 196
Buchanan, A., 13, 15–17, 19, 21, 23, 26–8, 30–3
Büchner, L., 265
Bukharin, N., 2
Bukovsky, V., 258

Chernyshevsky, N., 40, 44
Cohen, G. A., 9–11, 42, 50, 62, 64, 66, 79, 88–109, 113, 117, 215
Comte, A., 7, 215, 221–2, 226, 228–9, 235–6, 238–41, 256–7, 259

Dahl, R., 145
Darwin, C., 66, 68, 224
Diderot, D., 7
Dilthey, W., 226
Durkheim, E., 36, 217

Einstein, A., 180
Elster, J., 26, 29n, 94n, 108, 246n, 247n
Engels, F., 2, 13, 78, 84, 122, 141–3, 151–2, 163, 166n, 186, 214–15, 217, 224, 226–7, 235–6, 242n, 243n, 250–5, 257–8, 261–78

Feuerbach, L., 130–1, 264
Fourier, C., 142

Galileo Galilei, 68
Gellner, E., 38
Gershenkron, A., 40
Gouldner, A., 214
Gramsci, A., 2

Habermas, J., 2, 143, 214
Hegel, G. W. F., 7, 31, 75, 84, 125, 131, 167, 171, 213–15, 224, 229, 233, 242–3, 248, 262–9, 271, 276–8
Hempel, C., 107n, 109, 114, 219, 237, 249
Herzen, A., 40
Hilferding, R., 86
Hill, C., 86
Hilton, R., 86
Hobbes, T., 32, 132, 224, 238, 243
Hobsbawm, E. J., 9
Holbach, P. H. T., Baron de, 226
Hook, S., 179, 181
Horkheimer, M., 2

Name index

Wallerstein, I., 90, 98
Weber, M., 47, 173, 217, 224
Wellmer, A., 214
Wesson, R. G., 1
White, L., 61
Windelband, W., 226
Winstanley, G., 145, 150

Wolff, C., 265
Wolff, W., 163
Wolin, S., 139, 276
Wright, E. O., 94n, 95

Zasulich, V., 44

Subject index

(All technical concepts in Marxism have their own separate entries, e.g., forces of production, labor theory of value, surplus value, etc.).

284